*Become the Squeaky Wheel, A Credit & Collections Guide for Everyone*

*First Edition*

*Never Dunn Publishing LLC • Plymouth, New Hampshire*

*By Michelle Dunn*
*© Michelle Dunn*

*Published by:*

*Never Dunn Publishing LLC*
*PO Box 40*
*Plymouth NH 03264*

*www.michelledunn.com*
*www.credit-and-collections.com*

*Cover design, book layout, and production by*
*WoW! Graphic Designs   www.wowgraphicdesigns.com • 800-962-4254*

*Author photos by Timothy Cameron, Achber Studio, Laconia, NH*

*Editing by Bert Sutcliff, Plymouth, NH*

*ISBN#:  0-970664516*
*Library of Congress control Number: 2005926611*

*This book is designed to provide accurate and authoritative information in regard to the subject matter covered. It is sold with the understanding that the author is not engaged in rendering legal advice or services. If legal advice is required, please see your attorney.*

*Printed in the United States of America.*

## Disclaimer

*This book is designed to provide information to help you successfully use collection letters and forms in your agency. It is sold with the understanding that the publisher and author are not giving legal, accounting or other professional services. If legal or other expert assistance is required, please consult an attorney or accountant.*

*Every effort has been made to make this book as accurate as possible. However, there may be mistakes. This book is sold as a guide with what information is current as of the date of this printing.*

*This book is sold to provide information, Never Dunn Publishing, LLC and Michelle Dunn shall have no liability or responsibility to any person or entity that any damage or alleged damage caused directly or indirectly by the information contained in this book.*

**Special thanks to:**

*Nathan & Jonathan, my awesome children who inspire me always.*

*Kevin Maass, my biggest supporter, advisor and friend.*
*I feel like I can do anything because I have him as my partner.*

*Deborah Berry & Cheryl Microutsicos of WoW! Graphic Designs*
*for their ideas, support, dedication and HARD WORK in publishing my books.*

*Rebecca Game, Brett Rabideau, Britta Puffer, Bert Sutcliff, Evan Zucker, Jessica Tiles,*
*Jae Demers, Carolyn See and John Payette.*

*The members of my Credit & Collections Group and <u>you</u> ...*
*without you I could not continue my success.*

*Thank You!*

# Table of Contents

## Letter and Forms

# APPENDIX: Acts & Laws

# Chapter 1

# Introduction

I have been in the credit and collections field since 1987. I never aspired to be a debt collector, I just kind of fell into it. I was living in RI and moved to NH and went out looking for an office job. I found a job at a company that makes cedar shoe trees, as an Accounts Receivable clerk. I then took over the Collections aspect of the job and found I liked it and did a great job at it. One of the things I like about collection work is that you can see your results. I also like making people happy and one of the things that makes people happy is receiving money. So I make my collection calls and send my letters and money comes in and everyone is happy, except maybe the person who had to send the money.

I have been a Credit Manager at quite a few different companies and written credit and collection policies for many companies.

I have tried to give you an example of some of those policies in this book. Some of the information may not work with your specific line of business but there is something for everyone in this book. This can be used as a guide for your own credit policy. You can use parts of this policy or adjust any parts of it to fit your business.

I have included a procedure on what to do when you get a new customer, how to extend credit to them, how to read a credit report if you pull reports on new customers. What to do once you have credit approved customers and they don't pay, putting them on hold and procedures you can follow as well as collection call procedures and examples of conversations you might have. Credit card procedures for automatic charge accounts, information on COD payments received from shippers, what to do with all the small balance accounts you may have, what to do when you get an NSF check, Dunning letters procedures and examples of many letters you might be able to use. Information on payment plans, placing accounts with a collection agency and how to place them. How to write off bad debt, what you need to have on your credit applications, and examples of credit applications.

A large portion of this book includes the laws you must be familiar with. Also included are Federal credit laws you must follow. Information on doing business online, electronic contracts and electronic signatures. I have also included information on state laws regarding adding interest and/or late fees.

Many businesses do not have a credit and collections policy. The reasons for this could be that the business owner is afraid that asking for the money that is owed to them will make their customer mad and he will go somewhere else with his business. If they are not paying you, is this a bad thing? Why waste your time chasing money when you can have good paying customers. There will always be a few customers who are payment problems but the fewer the better and you have some control over that.

Also, many business owners do not know how to get the customer to pay or don't know what they can legally do to obtain payment. This book will help you get paid on time and therefore save you money and help you to make more money.

The longer you don't do anything about getting paid, the chances you will get paid are much less. This book is to help you, the business owner to keep your customers, and get paid. Having a credit and collections policy sets a positive credit tone for your business. It also lets potential customers know that you mean business!

Don't let your slow paying customers control you, it's up to you to take the wheel and drive.

# Chapter 2

# Objective

Some business owners ask why do I need a credit policy? I don't have much bad debt. The following will help you understand and decide if you want or need to implement a credit policy. It is my belief that every business should have a credit policy.

The objective of a Credit Policy should be:

- To provide timely notification to customers regarding past due amounts, and therefore eliminating old balances from being carried on the receivables.
- To outline a procedure that will provide customers with options when they cannot pay in full and on time.
- To provide a procedure on when and what to do with small balances on customers accounts.
- To provide a procedure that will enable a company to adequately provide reasonable credit limits for customers with revolving credit.
- To provide guidelines to legally collect money due your company that was lost due to bad checks.
- To have a system that will maintain timely contact with customers when they are past due.
- To provide a procedure that will enable your company to keep credit card numbers on file for customers and automatically charge them when they place an order.
- To have a procedure that will enable your company to be aware of when an account should be placed for collection and to avoid carrying bad debts on the receivables.
- To provide a procedure that will enable your business to legally charge customers credit cards at the time they place an order.
- To provide a procedure that will eliminate orders being held, and to better serve customers in a timely manner.
- To provide a procedure on how to post a UPS payment when you do not have account information.
- To have a procedure that will enable your business to be aware of when to write a balance off to bad debt.

# Chapter 3
## Improving Your Collection Procedures

It is important that your customers know your credit policy and/or terms of payment before they start doing business with you. Reiteration of your credit policy, when payment is overdue, is a good step to take in trying to obtain payment. Always ask for payment when it is justly due.

You should never extend credit to a new customer without having them fill out a credit application and go through the credit approval policy. Once you extend credit, it is important to maintain accurate records on an accounts payment history.

Adhere to your collection policies no matter what. You cannot see the future or changing market conditions. Try to keep current with trade reports pertaining to specific companies and industries. You can try Eli Financial's *Debt Collection Compliance Alert Newsletter*, this is a paid subscription; however, if you join Credit & Collections for free, you can get a discounted rate. Visit *www.credit-and-collections.com* for details. You can subscribe to *The Collection Connection* at the same time. The *Collection Connection* is my free newsletter that goes out once a month. It will bring you ideas and techniques to help you in your collection efforts and keep you updated on laws regarding collections that may affect your in house collections, give you collection tips, and help you increase your Credit Department's efficiency.

*The Collection Connection* will help you learn about credit policies, and collections, starting your own agency or what to expect when working with a collection agency and how you can help a collection agency help you.

If you become a member of The American Collectors Association, you will get a free subscription to Collector Magazine. This is a great magazine that is always full of compliance information, collection trends, industry news and more. ACA International produces several industry publications, including brochures, educational materials, newsletters, an award–winning trade magazine and a comprehensive Web site. ACA International cooperatively purchases products and provides services at considerable savings for association members. You can check them out at *www.collector.com*.

CollectionIndustry.com is another site that can provide you with information to keep you up to date on collections. They provide Industry News, agency news, information on events and jobs, they provide News and articles and publications to help you with collections. Check them out at *www.collectionindustry.com/home.cfm*.

Change your collection letters frequently, you can make them stronger and more action oriented.

Discourage payments on account or changes in payment terms. Too many payment plans or changed payment terms can impair your cash flow.

When you receive payments "on account" be sure to follow up right away with a letter or phone call thanking the debtor for their payment and telling them what their new balance is and where and when to send the next payment. Enclose a payment envelope with this letter.

On large accounts call or send a reminder just a few days after terms if they get delinquent.

Ask to speak to a manager, or owner when making collection calls rather than speaking to a secretary or receptionist. Go right for the decision maker.

If a customer disputes the quality of merchandise, or service, price or delivery, you should attempt to resolve this right way. Insist they pay the portion of the bill that they are not disputing while you work out the disputed problem.

If all else has failed you may want to refer the account to an outside collection agency.

# Chapter 4

# Purpose

- To outline the procedure of when and how to write an account off to Bad Debt.

- To outline the procedure determining which accounts should be on hold and releasing customers that are on hold.

- To outline the procedure on how and when to send dunning letters.

- To outline the procedure on payment arrangements and payment options.

- To outline the procedure on small balances on accounts.

- To outline the procedure on setting up new accounts with an adequate credit limit.

- To outline the procedure of how to handle checks returned for insufficient funds, stopped payment or account closed.

- To define the procedure of when and how to make collection calls.

- To outline the process for orders paid by credit cards.

- To outline the procedure of when and how to place an account with an outside collection agency.

- To outline the procedure for opening a prepaid credit card account.

- To outline the procedure on posting UPS COD payments when detailed information is not provided.

# Chapter 5
# Debt Collection Training

You may want to train yourself or your collectors or Credit manager for their debt collection tasks. Some areas that you may want training in are:

**Developing a telephone voice**

- Refining Listening skills:
  When you call a debtor and you state the reason for your call or ask a question, wait for them to answer. No matter how long the pause is, let them break the silence.

- Managing the emotional side: Debtors will get upset that you are calling them. They will cry, yell, swear and hang up on you. When a debtor starts telling you his life history of despair and how this affects why they cannot pay, you need to be able to have compassion for the situation but offer a solution to get the debt paid. Such as a payment plan or different options for payment.

- Preparing the pre-call plan: Before you ever make a collection call you need to research the account. Before you dial you need to know the invoice number, date, amount that is past due, how past due it is, the payment history, details of the order and if there were any disputed items. When the debtor asks you a question you need to answer immediately whenever possible. This shows the debtor that your serious.

- Making opening statement: Your opening statement should be brief and to the point. You need to identify yourself and your company, state why you are calling and what you want. An example would be: "Hi, this is Michelle from KTM Auto calling about your balance of $500.00 on invoice # 1234 dated 4/1/05. I am calling today to take your payment over the phone to clear this balance from your account. Would you like to pay with a check over the phone, debit or credit card?" STOP! Let the debtor break the silence after your question and remember, always assume the debtor will pay.

- Asking questions with precision and making the transition to the payment arrangement. All your questions should be clear and to the point with silence after each question.
  Example: Debtor: I can't pay, I don't have any money
  *Collector:* Are you working?
  *Debtor:* Yes, but I just started a job and don't get paid for two weeks.
  *Collector:* What day will you get paid?
  *Debtor:* Friday

*Collector:* Okay, then you can mail a money order for $25 on Saturday This example can go so many different ways depending on the debtors responses. You have to be positive and get them to agree to make a payment. Once you reiterate what is going to happen, send them a confirmation letter with a payment envelope. Then call them on Friday to remind them about mailing the payment. An example of what you could say could be:

"Hi this is Michelle from KTM Auto, calling to confirm you will be mailing a money order for $25 tomorrow, Saturday. "

- Managing the emotional side
- Preparing the pre-call plan
- Making the opening statement
- Asking questions with precision
- Making the transition to the payment arrangement
- Handling Objections - You need to become familiar with common debtor objections. The best way to do this is to make collection calls. Some common objections and responses could be:

| OBJECTIONS | RESPONSES |
|---|---|
| I can't make a payment over the phone. I don't have a credit card or checking account. | You can Western Union the money to me, or mail a money order. |
| I don't have any money | How do you pay your utilities? Set up smaller payments for awhile or ask them to borrow from a family member. |
| I lost the invoice | Fax invoice if possible, and call right back or mail the invoice and follow up with a call. |
| I didn't receive the item. | Get proof of delivery from the shipper. |

- Closing the call - Your last statement should reiterate everything covered in your call. Repeat all actions that will be taken. Example: "Okay, on Saturday you will mail a money order for $25 in the envelope I send you today. Then you will send $25 a month every Saturday until May 15th."

Your collectors should be able to:

- Identify the most common forms of credit activity
- Name the three major credit reporting agencies and their function in credit extension
- List five important federal laws and their roles in governing the credit lifecycle
- Describe why listening is important and name three components of active listening
- Identify the differences between assertive and aggressive communication
- How to open and close a collection call with courtesy
- How to ask fact-finding questions based on the reason for delinquency
- Strategies for motivating debtors at different stages of delinquency

*Remember, to be a debt collector you must:*

- Be interested in people, and be a good communicator both verbally and in writing
- Be persuasive and persistent, with the sensitivity to deal fairly with people in often difficult situations
- Be able to stay calm under pressure, and be adaptable in sometimes tricky situations
- Have strong negotiation skills and the ability to explain financial matters firmly and clearly
- Have mathematical ability to explain payments, financial terms and credit services and policies
- Be able to understand relevant legislation concerning data protection and harassment
- Have office administration and computer skills

# Chapter 6

# Collection Downfalls of
# Small Business Owners

Small business owners sometimes make some common mistakes when just starting out, and trying to get paid. Some small business owners depend on that income more than someone who gets a check each week. This is because when you work for yourself, the work and therefore the payments are sporadic.

Small business owners just starting out are sometimes so eager to make a sale, that they will accept work or an order without getting a signed contract or checking credit references. They just wait and wait to be paid because they don't want to offend the customer or appear that they NEED the money.

ALWAYS have a written contract or agreement, you may also want to get half of the money up front with terms regarding the balance very specifically addressed in your agreement. If you can get the other party to sign the agreement, that is even better.

It is worth it to try and collect the money due at first. Make a couple of calls, if promises are made but no payment, think about using a collection service. It shows you are serious and don't work for free. Word will get around that you mean business.

Have patience.

# Chapter 7

# Helpful Tips

***Your Company is not protected from bad debt, so you need to protect yourself by:***
- Having a sound credit policy and sticking to it
- Getting a signed credit application
- Checking references
- Getting a signed contract or agreement
- Pulling a credit report if possible
- Setting a credit limit

You can pull credit reports online at *www.knowx.com*. KnowX Standard provides access public records, instantly and easily. Getting started on KnowX is fast, free and easy. For full access to their standard searches, you will be asked to complete a short registration. The information you provide gives you immediate access all of their standard searches. Your personal information is kept completely confidential.

KnowX works like most search engines. Just enter the search criteria (e.g. name, address, state, etc.) and click the search button. Most of their searches are FREE. If there is a charge associated with the search you chose, a price tag screen will ALWAYS be displayed giving you the price and an option to cancel your request! Be firm about being paid from the beginning. If a debtor knows you are serious, they will be more likely to pay. If they had to fill out a credit application and/or contract, it shows you're serious. If you place accounts for collection sooner than later, that also shows you mean business.

***Debtors will know you are serious if:***
- They had to fill out a Credit Application
- They had to sign a contract
- They receive invoices right away
- You send your invoices right away, as soon as items have shipped or the work is complete
- You call right away if you don't receive payment. Don't wait!
- You gather all the information you can about the debtor
- You are professional at all times
- You are persistent
- You make personal visits when you can
- You offer different payment methods
- You charge a late fee and/or finance charge

# Chapter 8
# Should I Extend Credit?

Extending credit works in your favor in many ways. It increases customer loyalty. Taking a financial risk for your customers demonstrates you trust them and are willing to accommodate them. If you extend credit be sure you have a credit policy in effect.

A credit policy also indicates your business is financially stable. A business in danger of going under does not give its customers the option of paying at a later date. A struggling business demands payments immediately. Be sure to mark your terms clearly on any invoices and statements you send out.

Credit policies increase sales for another reason. Some customers are unable to pay for a product or service in its entirety. If customers have the option to pay for items in monthly installments, they will be more inclined to make purchases which do not fall within their current budgets.

Extending credit also has downfalls such as your business could lose interest that you could have earned, even if you put it into a low interest savings account. You can't take advantage of purchase discounts from your vendors if the funds are not immediately available or they are paying on terms.

You may lack the capital to produce the next job, and may be forced to decline profitable deals from good payers.

Some reasons for extending credit are to meet or beat the competition. If your competitors are extending credit you may want to offer the same. It may be more convenient for your customers to be billed for your product or service. Extending credit may also increase sales. You can also use extending credit as a way to establish new accounts.

Keep in mind that extending credit will take more time and money than you are already extending. Someone will have to take the time to check references, process credit applications, set up new accounts and maybe collect on accounts that you do extend credit to that don't pay on time. This would be a Credit Manager or an Accounts Receivable clerk.

You will spend more money on possibly pulling credit reports, becoming a member of a credit bureau or credit reporting agency, telephone calls, postage, salaries, training and equipment. Extending credit can be risky, and you must be thorough with researching possible applicants. Research that is less than thorough is useless.

You may want to research how you are handling past receivables and if your control over them has been effective. A common way to do this is to use the Days Sales Outstanding (D.S.O.) formula.

D.S.O. = Current End of Month A/R Balance x 90
Total Sales for Past 3 Months

If you multiply your current end of month accounts receivables balance by 90 and divide that number by total sales for the past 3 months, you will get the number of days sales outstanding. For example, if your current month end receivables are $12,000 and your total sales for the past 3 months are $30,000, using the DSO formula the result would be:

$12,000 x 90 = D.S.O. of 36 Days
$30,000

When you decide to extend credit to your customers, you need to decide on how you want to extend credit. You don't want to be too lenient or to strict. If you are too lenient you could create a credit loss. If you are too strict this could affect sales. You will want your terms to be acceptable to your customers, whether your terms are net 30, net 45 etc. You and your staff must stand behind your credit policy and enforce the terms you set. You credit department must have backup and reinforcement from their supervisors and sales force in order to make this work.

All departments must support and abide by the credit rules or your credit policy will not work. This includes Upper Management and your Sales force.

# Chapter 9
# How to Go About Extending Credit

*Get the following information from a business and/or consumer seeking credit:*
- Business' and owner's name
- Length they have been in business
- Address, length of time at that address and a former address
- Balance sheets and/or IRS returns
- Phone numbers of business and principal's or residence
- Bank name, address, phone numbers
- Credit references, Personal and business
- Employer name, address and phone numbers
- Length of time at current employment
- Marital status, name and employment information on spouse
- Total monthly household income
- Social Security number and/or Federal ID#

This information can be in the form of a credit application or contract you may have drawn up. Be sure to have the business owner or consumer sign the document and date it. Keep the original and always give the consumer a copy.

You will then need to verify the information that has been supplied to you. You can run a report with Dun & Bradstreet if the applicant is a business (*www.dnb.com/us/*). You can call all references listed, the applicant's bank and place of employment. If you are a member of a credit bureau you can check with a credit bureau on the accuracy of the information supplied to you. If you find any information is not true, you should deny credit. Check out *www.smallbusiness.dnb.com*, D & B collects, aggregates, edits and verifies data from thousands of sources daily.

Once you decide you will grant credit, you need to put your credit terms in writing. Always have your credit terms on your invoices and statements.

Once you have invoiced your customer you need to keep a close eye on your accounts receivables. You can print a penalty on your invoices such as charging a 1-2% penalty on invoices over 30 days past due. You can make phone calls or send reminder notices to any accounts that are past due.

Another positive thing you can do is to routinely record bank account data about the client or patient as payment is received. Then, if you have to sue the debtor, you have one more place to turn to try to satisfy your judgment.

If the letters and phone calls fail, it is time to resort to either a collection agency or the courts. Collection agencies will take a 25-50% cut of any debt collected after they become involved. Courts may be a better idea if the debt is fairly small or the debt is fairly large. If it is small, small claims court may get you a judgment against the debtor without much effort. It the debt amount is large, an attorney may be able to help you get a settlement payment or a judgment against the debtor. If the debt is too large for small claims court, but too small to justify the expense of an attorney, go to the collection agency. You should stay on top of late accounts because as the overdue account ages, the likelihood of payment decreases. My website has free information and an E-Book of Collection Letters and Forms that you can use at *www.credit-and-collections.com*. I have also included some of those letters in this book.

# Chapter 10
## Laws to Know When Extending Credit

If your business does grant credit, you must comply with federal laws affecting credit sales to consumers. Also, states are beginning to adopt consumer credit laws that mirror federal law. One of the laws you should become familiar with is The Truth In Lending Act. This law requires you to disclose your exact credit terms to credit applicants and regulates how you advertise consumer credit. Among the items you must disclose to a consumer who buys on credit are monthly finance charges, your annual interest rate, your terms or when payment is due, the total price and the price if any late fees are added.

Another law is The Fair Credit Billing Act, this law explains what to do if a customer claims you made a mistake in your billing. The customer must notify you within 60 days after you mailed the first bill containing the claimed error. You must respond within 30 days unless the dispute has already been resolved. You must also conduct a reasonable investigation and, within 90 days of getting the customer's letter, explain why your bill is correct or else correct the error.

If you don't follow this procedure, you must give the customer a $50 credit toward the disputed amount — even if your bill was correct. Until the dispute is resolved, you can't report to a credit bureau that the customer is delinquent. In addition to telling you how to handle billing disputes, the Fair Credit Billing Act requires you, in periodic mailings, to tell consumers what their rights are.

The Fair Credit Billing act only covers "open end" credit accounts, such as revolving charge accounts, like credit card accounts. It does not cover installment contracts - loans or extensions of credit you repay on a fixed schedule. Consumers often buy cars, furniture and major appliances on an installment basis, and repay personal loans in installments as well, these type of "extensions of credit" are not covered by this law.

Next is The Equal Credit Opportunity Act, this law is so that you will not discriminate against a credit applicant on the basis of race, color, religion, national origin, age, sex or marital status. The Act does leave you free to consider legitimate factors in granting credit, such as the applicant's financial status (earnings and savings) and credit record. Despite the prohibition on age discrimination, you can deny a consumer who hasn't reached the legal age for entering into contracts.

The Fair Credit Reporting Act is intended to protect consumers from having their eligibility for credit marred by incomplete or misleading credit report information. The laws gives consumers the right to a copy of their credit reports. If they see an inaccurate item, they can ask that it be corrected or removed. If the business reporting the credit problem doesn't agree to a change or deletion or if the credit bureau refuses to make it, the consumer can add a 100-word statement to the file explaining his or her side of the story. This becomes a part of any future credit report.

The Fair Debt Collection Practices Act is geared mostly toward third party collectors. Small businesses are more directly affected by state laws that apply directly to collection methods used by a creditor.

I have included each of these laws in this book for you to review.

# Chapter 11
# Example of New Revolving Credit Customers

**(This can be adjusted to suit your particular business)**

**Step 1.** Any customer that expresses an interest in becoming credit approved in order to have a revolving credit account, needs to buy over $5000 worth of product from us in a year, has to have 6 months – 1 year COD activity with us, and 20% of their annual sales cannot have been returned.

**Step 2.** If they meet this criteria, send them a credit application. Once this application is received back, run it through the credit bureau for a report. Also, check the credit references listed on the credit application. If they do not have a credit card, decline the application.

**Step 3.** If the customer is approved, a letter must be sent letting them know they have been approved. The credit limit must then be put into the computer. The minimum credit limit is $1000.00.

**Step 4.** If the customer is denied, a letter must be sent letting them know they were denied and why. There needs to be a notation on the bottom of the letter telling them where the report was pulled from and giving them a phone number and address for the credit reporting agency, if they are disputing the results of the credit check. The Credit Bureau will provide your company with a denial form to use. I have included some in this book for you. The original is sent to the customer and a copy is attached to the credit application. All credit applications need to be filed in one file cabinet in the Credit Managers office. All information is confidential. This file cabinet should be locked.

**Step 5.** Credit reports can be re-run after one year or quarterly in order to review credit limits.

**Step 6.** If a customer calls to set up a new account from a company that had a previous account, the previous account needs to be terminated and a new account opened for the new owner, and a credit application sent to them.

**Step 7.** If there is a balance on the terminated account, the previous owner is responsible. If you cannot find them, place them for collection. The new business owner cannot use the same account as the previous owner, since all transactions are a credit history for another individual, and they may still owe you money.

Following are two examples of hypothetical customer situations:

*HYPOTHETICAL CUSTOMER*

**Criteria for evaluation, terms extended, filing requirements**

**When application is denied**

**Step 1.** Jon from Video Games Central has come in and wants to fill out a credit application. Since Jon has been a customer for over 4 years we just need to check his history for returns and yearly purchase amount. Jon just makes the $5000 annual sales and makes quite a few returns but below the 20% mark. We send him a credit application.

**Step 2.** We receive Jon's credit application and run it through the credit bureau for a copy of his credit report. While we wait for that information we call the references listed on the application. We call his bank and have to fax over a request for information on our letterhead, we then call the bank back and ask:

How long has Video Games Central had this account?

What is the average daily balance?

Have there been any NSF checks?

We take notes to attach to the credit application, with the credit report. The credit report has printed out and we see that the address and social security numbers all match. Video Games Central rents their storefront but have made all payments on time. They have a supplier listed on their credit report who had them on an open account at one time. They were current for 6 months, then started being 45-60 days past due with the balance growing each month. This vendor put them on COD and Jon is still past due with them and has a fairly large balance due.

The bank lets us know that Video Games Central has had this account for 2 years, and it has a negative balance and averages 4 NSF checks a month in the past 6 months.

**Step 3 & 4.** We deny the application and send out a Credit Denied notice. We file all paperwork in the a locked file cabinet.

## HYPOTHETICAL CUSTOMER

### Criteria for evaluation, terms extended, filing requirements

### When application is approved

**Step 1.**     Jon from Video Games Central has come in and wants to fill out a credit application. Since Jon has been a customer for over 4 years we just need to check his history for returns and yearly purchase amount. Jon purchases more than the required $5000 worth of product in a year and his return ratio is very low. We send him a credit application.

**Step 2.** We receive Jon's credit application and run it through the credit bureau for a copy of his credit report. While we wait for that information we call the references listed on the application. We call his bank and have to fax over a request for information on our letterhead, we then call the bank back and ask:

How long has Video Games Central had this account?

What is the average daily balance?

Have there been any NSF checks?

We take notes to attach to the credit application, with the credit report. The credit report has printed out and we see that the address and social security numbers all match. Video Games Central has very good credit, they show that they own the building they run their store from. They have current open accounts with their vendors, and have no history of being past due.

**Step 3.** We approve the application and send out a Credit Approved Letter and set the credit limit to $1500.00 in our computer.

**Step 4.** Since we approved this credit application, we skip this part.

**Step 5.** Make a note so that one year from the date you ran the credit report you will run the report again and review the credit limit on this account.

Since this account was approved, you are ready to file your credit application, credit report and any notes you have in a locked file cabinet.

# Chapter 12
# State Laws on Adding Interest or Late Fees

*This information is provided only as a guide and is not intended as legal advice; consult your attorney for the most accurate information on the legal interest rates in each state.

### ALABAMA

There are no requirements more restrictive than the FDCPA. Legal rate of interest is 6%. Except as otherwise provided by law, the maximum rate of interest you may add to a loan or good, money owed etc, except by written contract is $6.00 on $100.00 for one year. If you do have a contract the rate is 8%.

### ALASKA

Legal rate permitted by law without an agreement is 10.5%. If you have a signed contract the rate is 10.5%.

### ARIZONA

Legal rate permitted by law without an agreement is 10%. If you have a signed contract the rate must be agreed to in writing.

### ARKANSAS

Legal rate permitted by law without an agreement is 6%. Contract rate is 5% above the Federal Reserve Discount rate at the time of the contract.

### CALIFORNIA

Legal rate is 7% without a contract. With an oral contract the rate is 7% or 10% with a written contract.

### COLORADO

Legal rate is 8% compounded annually. Contract rate is as set in the contract and limited annually.

## CONNECTICUT

Legal rate is 8% a year without an agreement. In computing interest 360 days may be considered to be a year. With a contract the rate is 12% per annum.

## DELAWARE

Legal rate is anything not in excess of 5% over the Federal Reserve discount rate. If you have a contract the rate is as agreed upon in writing, not to exceed 5% over the Federal Reserve discount rate.

## DISTRICT OF COLUMBIA

Legal rate is 6% without an agreement. If you have a contract the rate is 24%.

## FLORIDA

Legal rate is 11%. With a contract the rate is 18%.

## GEORGIA

Legal rate is 7% without an agreement. Contract rate is 16% on amounts of $3,000 and less. Any rate is allowed on an amount more than $3,000.

## HAWAII

Legal rate is 10% without an agreement. Contract rate is 12% per year.

## IDAHO

Legal rate is 12% without an agreement and if you have a contract it is whatever you agreed upon.

## ILLINOIS

Legal rate is 5% without an agreement. Contract fee is 9% with any rate allowed for residential, state, bank or business loans.

## INDIANA

Legal rate is 8% without an agreement. Contract rate is greater of 21% on all unpaid balances or the total of 36% on balances of less than $870.00 or less. It is 21% on balances over $870.00 and less than $2900.00; or 15% on balances over $2900.00.

## IOWA

Legal rate is 5%. Contract rate is 2% above the monthly average ten year constant maturity interest rate of the US Government notes and bonds as published by the board of governors of the federal reserve system for the calendar month second preceding the month during which the maximum rate based thereon will be effective, rounded to the nearest one-fourth of 1% per year.

## KANSAS

Legal rate is 10% per annum, when no other rate of interest is agreed upon, for any money after it becomes due; for money lent or money due on settlement of account, from the day of liquidating the account and ascertaining the balance, for money received for the use of another and retained without the owner's knowledge of the receipt; for money due and withheld by an unreasonable and vexatious delay of payment or settlement of accounts, for all other money due and to become due for the forbearance of payment whereof an express promise to pay interest has been made and for money due from corporations and individuals to their daily or monthly employees from and after the end of each month, unless paid within 15 days.

If you have a contract, it is subject to the following provision, the parties to any bond, bill, promissory note or other instrument of writing at a rate not to exceed 15% per annum, unless otherwise specifically authorized by law.

## KENTUCKY

Legal rate is 8% without an agreement. But any party may agree, in writing, for the payment of interest in excess of that rate.

Contract rate must be agreed by parties in writing, for any payment in excess of 8% at a per annum rate not to exceed 4% in excess of the discount rate on 90 day commercial paper in effect at the Federal Reserve Bank in the Federal Reserve District where the transaction is consummated or 19%, whichever is less, on money due or to become due upon any contract or other obligation in writing where the original principal amount is $15,000.00 or less AND at any rate on money due or to become due upon any contract or other obligation in writing where the original principal amount is in excess of $15,000.00. Also, any state or national bank may charge $10 for any loan negotiated at the bank in Kentucky, even if the legal interest does not equal that sum.

## LOUISIANA

Legal rate is 12% without an agreement and with a contract.

## MAINE

Legal rate is 6% without an agreement. If you have a contract the rate is 30% on unpaid balances of $1000.00 or less, 21% on unpaid balances over $1000.00 but not over $2800.00 and 15% on balances over $2800.00.

## MARYLAND

Legal rate is 6% without an agreement and 8% with a contract.

## MASSACHUSETTS

Legal rate is 6% without an agreement. Contract rate has no limit.

## MICHIGAN

Legal rate is 5% and Contract rate is 7%.

## MINNESOTA

Legal rate is 6% and Contract rate is 8%.

## MISSISSIPPI

Legal rate is 8% without an agreement. For a contract rate, any rate is allowed and agreed to if principal balance or proposed amount exceeds $2000.00

## MISSOURI

Legal rate is 9% when no other rate is agreed upon. Contract rate is 10% but parties may agree, in writing, to an interest rate not exceeding 10% per annum.

## MONTANA

Legal rate is 10% with the following exceptions:
Mont. Code Ann 31-1-106 (1999) reprinted below:
1)      Except as otherwise provided by the Uniform Commercial Code, 31-1-111 and 31-1-112, or 31-1-817, unless there is an express contract in writing fixing a different rate or a law or ordinance or resolution of a public body fixing a different rate on its obligations, interest is payable on all money at the rate of 10% a year after it becomes due on:
a)      any instrument of writing, except a judgment
b)      an account stated

c)      money lent or due on any settlement of accounts from the date on which the balance is ascertained; and

d)      money received for the use of another person and detained from that person. Contract rate is not more than 15% or an amount 6% points per year above the prime rate.

## NEBRASKA

Legal rate is 6% without an agreement. Contract rate is 16% per annum. 18% on installment contracts.

## NEVADA

Legal rate is 2% over the prime rate at the largest bank in the state on the January 1 or July 1 immediately preceding judgment and adjusted accordingly each January 1 and July 1.

## NEW HAMPSHIRE

Legal rate is 10% without an agreement. There is no limit for Contract rate.

## NEW JERSEY

The maximum rate of interest to be charged is 6% per annum or 16% per annum when there is a written contract specifying a rate of interest, unless as provided by law. Contracts are at any rate of interest which the parties agree to.

## NEW MEXICO

Legal rate is 15% without an agreement. Contract rate is whatever rate is agreed upon in writing agreed upon by both parties.

## NEW YORK STATE

Legal rate is 16% without an agreement. Contract rate is also 16%.

## NORTH CAROLINA

Legal rate is 8%. Contract rate is 16% for $25000.00 or less. For anything over that amount see N.C. Gen. Stat 24-1.1 and 24-1.2 (1998).

## NORTH DAKOTA

Legal rate is 6% without an agreement. Contract rate is 5.5% over the average rate for 6 month US treasury bills, but not less than 7%.

## OHIO

Legal rate is not to exceed 8% per annum. Either party may agree to pay a rate of interest in excess of 8% when the original amount of the principal indebtedness exceeds $100,000.00 or when the instrument evidences a loan secured by a mortgage or deed of trust on real estate where the loan has been approved, insured, guaranteed, purchased or for which an offer or commitment to insure, guarantee or purchase has been received, in whole or in part, by the federal government or any agency or by the state.

## OKLAHOMA

Legal rate is 6% without an agreement. Contract rate is any rate agreed to as may be authorized by law.

## OREGON

Legal rate is 9% without an agreement. Contract rate is agreed to by both parties in the contract.

## PENNSYLVANIA

Legal rate is 6% without an agreement. Contract rate is equal to the Monthly Index of Long Term US Government Bond Yields for the second preceding calendar month, plus an additional 2.5% per annum rounded off to the nearest quarter of 1% per annum.

## RHODE ISLAND

Legal rate is 12% without an agreement. Contract rate is 21%.

## SOUTH CAROLINA

Legal rate is 6% or 8.75% when the phrase "legal rate" or "lawful rate" is used in a contract or other document. Contract rate is any rate or as provided in Consumer Protection Code.

## SOUTH DAKOTA

Category A is 4 ½% per year
Category B is 10% per year
Category C is 12% per year
Category D is 1% per month
Category E is 4% per year
Category F is 15% per year
Category G is 5/6 of 1% per month or fraction thereof. Unless a maximum interest rate or charge is specifically established elsewhere in the code, there is no maximum interest rate or charge the interest rate is established by written agreement.

## TENNESSEE

Legal rate is 10% without an agreement. Contract rate is 4% over average weekly prime rate.

## TEXAS

Legal rate is 6% without an agreement. Contract rate is 10% a year.

## UTAH

Legal rate is 10% without an agreement. Contract rate that is agreed upon in a contract.

## VERMONT

Legal rate is 12% without an agreement. Contract rate is 12%.

## VIRGINIA

Legal rate is 8% without an agreement. Contract rate is 12%.

## WASHINGTON STATE

Legal rate is 12% without a written agreement. Contract rate is 12%.

## WEST VIRGINIA

Legal rate is 6% without an agreement. Contract rate is 8%.

## WISCONSIN

Legal rate is 5% without a written agreement. Contract ate not exceeding the rate allowed in Wis. Stat. Ann 138.041 to 138.056, 138.09 to 138.12, 218. 0101 to 218.0163 or 422.201 in which case the rate will be expressed in writing.

## WYOMING

Legal rate is 7% per annum with no agreement or provisions by law of a different rate. Contract rate is 18% per year calculated according to the actuarial method on the unpaid balances of the amount financed on the assumption that the debt will be paid according to the agreed amount and will not be paid before the end of the agreed term.

# Chapter 13
# Credit Grantors and the FDCPA

The Fair Debt Collections Practices Act covers the collection practices of third-party debt collectors and attorneys who regularly collect debts for others. The Fair Debt Collection Practices Act became effective March 20, 1978.

### *Credit grantors should know this law regardless because:*
- Credit grantors collection practices are covered by the law under certain conditions.
- Credit grantors should know what their collection services and attorneys may and may not do under the law especially if they hire them to do collection work for them as it is a reflection on them and their business.
- Creditors may be liable with respect to the collection practices of third-party debt collectors under Section 5 of the Federal Trade Commission Act and in some cases under their states laws.
- Credit grantors must comply with FDCPA when they collect their own debts using a name other than their own. For example, Dunn's Oil Company uses the name The Dunn Collection Service to collect its own debts, they must comply. If several hospitals or doctor's offices join in a "shared hospital/medical services" concept and collect their own debts through a collection service they set up and gave a name to other than that of the hospital or doctors office, they must comply. If a credit grantor mails a series of collection letters that carry a business name other than the company's and that are not clearly showing that they are affiliated with the creditor, then the credit grantor must comply. Also, some financial institutions, such as banks and credit unions, become debt collectors when they ask for help from another bank when a debtor has relocated, then the bank must comply.

## *SKIPTRACING*
## *WHAT IS SKIP TRACING?*

Skip Tracing is the process of tracking down someone who owes you money. In order to successfully collect on a delinquent account, you have to locate the debtor. A debtor may relocate and/or have his telephone disconnected, believing they are leaving creditors with no immediate means of contact.

A skip trace can be done for current address and phone, fictitious business names, social security death index, bankruptcies, judgements, liens, national property and deed transfers.

### When should you skip trace?
- When mail is returned
- When the phone is disconnected

### Some information needed to Skip Trace:
- Full name (first, middle, last)
- Social Security Number
- Date of Birth
- Former address
- Employment information
- Vehicle and drivers license information
- Spouse information

You should have this information in your locked file cabinet, with your credit application.

To get started with skip tracing you need to know where to go to look for and find your debtors. You need to get all the information together that you have on the debtor. There are many ways to try to find a debtor, you can look in a local telephone book, or if they are in another state or were in the past, you can use an online service such as *www.555-1212.com/* or *www.411locate.com/.* You can also call directory assistance if you have an idea of what town the debtor might be in. You can also pull a new credit report on the debtor, you may find a wealth of information here! It could list the last known address and employment, if they own property and/or a vehicle. You can also call any creditors that are listed on the credit report and ask if they have an address for your debtor.

Other places you can check by going to your local courthouse or town hall in some cases:
- Traffic records
- Circuit civil records
- County civil records
- Circuit criminal records
- County criminal records
- Voter registration
- Marriage records
- Occupational license
- Property tax rolls

- Hunting and fishing licenses
- Property records
- Automobile registration

You can search online for debtor using various methods. You can search by name, phone number, address, state or email address. You can do reverse lookups and more. Some sites offer this service free, other charge a fee. I have had better luck with fee based services. We have a large listing of free and fee based skip tracing tools at *www.credit-and-collections.com* under Resources. Here are some of the places you can try:

**FREE lookups:**
411 Locate  *www.411locate.com/*
411 Locate in Canada  *http://canada411.sympatico.ca/*
Free Email address directory  *www.emailaddresses.com/*
Telephone Directories on the Web  *www.teldir.com/eng/*
The Ultimate Yellow Pages  *www.theultimates.com/yellow/*
Worldpages Phone Search  *www.worldpages.com/*

**FEE based skip tracing:**
Flat Rate Info.com  *www.flatrateinfo.com*
Search America  *www.searchamerica.com*
*www.merlindata.com*
*www.accurint.com*

In regards to skip tracing a collector may communicate once with any third party, anyone other than the debtor, in order to obtain the address, phone number and work address of the debtor. Under certain conditions, such as to correct erroneous information, the collector may communicate with a third party more than once. An example might be a friend or neighbor or family member. **Remember: The collector cannot disclose to a third party any information about the debt. You are just trying to locate them so you may then try to collect. You can tell the friend or neighbor you are looking for them regarding a business or personal matter.**

## COMMUNICATIONS WITH THE DEBTOR

In the law, the word "consumer" is used rather than "debtor". A Collector may communicate with the consumer or debtor between 8 a.m. and 9 p.m. local time of the debtor. If the collector knows this is an inconvenient time for the debtor, the collector may set up another time for communication.

The collector may communicate with the debtor at work, except when the employer prohibits such communication.

If the debtor notifies the collector in writing that the debtor refuses to pay and wants communication to stop, the collector MUST stop communicating with the debtor except to advise the debtor of possible actions:

- That you are closing the account and won't continue to try and collect
- That you may take legal/collection action
- That this may be reported to a credit bureau

## HARASSMENT/ABUSE

The collector may not:

Harass, oppress or abuse the debtor in any way. These words are not defined by the courts when cases arise under the law but this practice is not practiced or condoned by ethical businesses or collection services.

## FALSE OR MISLEADING REPRESENTATIONS

- Collectors cannot use any false or deceptive representations when trying to collect debts.
- Collectors are forbidden to represent that they are affiliated with the United States or any state or that the collector is an attorney or works for a credit reporting agency.
- False representation of the amount owed or legal status of any debt.
- Threats to take any action that is illegal or that the debt collector does not intend to take. This is why when you send a letter saying you will place an account for collection in 15 days, for example, you must follow through.
- Collectors can not make a claim that the debtor committed a crime by not paying their debt.
- You cannot tell the debtor that you have started a legal process unless you have.
- You cannot tell a debtor that consumers or debtors that do not pay will be arrested or imprisoned or that their property will be seized unless such action is legal and you intend to take it.

# Chapter 14

## Federal Credit Laws

If your business extends credit to its customers, you'll need to comply with federal consumer credit laws.

### 1. The Truth in Lending Act

This statute attempts to ensure that customers know what they're getting into. It requires you to disclose your exact credit terms to credit applicants and regulates how you advertise consumer credit. Among the items you must disclose to a consumer who buys on credit are the following:

- The monthly finance charge
- The annual interest rate
- When payments are due
- The total sale price — cash price of the item or service plus all other charges
- The amount of any late payment charges and when they'll be imposed.
- Any other charges they may be responsible for if they don't pay on time such as court or attorney fees

### 2. The Fair Credit Billing Act

This law dictates what you must do if a customer claims you made a mistake in your billing. The customer must notify you within 60 days after you mailed the first bill containing the claimed error. You must respond within 30 days unless the dispute has already been resolved. You must also conduct a reasonable investigation and, within 90 days of getting the customer's letter, explain why your bill is correct or correct the error. If you don't follow this procedure, you must give the customer a $50 credit toward the disputed amount — even if your bill was correct. Until the dispute is resolved, you can't report to a credit bureau that the customer is delinquent.

State laws may also deal with billing disputes. Generally, if a state law on this subject conflicts with the federal statute, the federal statute will control — but there's one exception: a state law will prevail if it gives a consumer more time to notify a creditor about a billing error. For example, as explained above, the federal law gives a consumer 60 days after receiving a bill to notify you of a billing error. If a state law gives a consumer 90 days to notify you, the consumer will be entitled to the extra 30 days. It is very important for you to be familiar with any state laws for this reason.

In addition to telling you how to handle billing disputes, the Fair Credit Billing Act requires you, in periodic mailings, to tell consumers what their rights are. This could be included on invoices or the back of statements. You can also include this on your credit applications that the applicant must sign.

### 3. The Equal Credit Opportunity Act

You may not discriminate against a credit applicant on the basis of race, color, religion, national origin, age, sex or marital status. The Act does leave you free to consider legitimate factors in granting credit, such as the applicant's financial status (earnings and savings) and credit record. Despite the prohibition on age discrimination, you can reject a consumer who hasn't reached the legal age in your state for entering into contracts. In such a case you can request a co-signer. Legal age in most states is 18 years old.

### 4. The Fair Credit Reporting Act

This law deals primarily with credit reports issued by credit reporting agencies. It's intended to protect consumers from having their eligibility for credit thwarted by inaccurate or obsolete credit report information. The law gives consumers the right to a copy of their credit reports. If they feel something is inaccurate, they can ask that it be corrected or removed. If the business reporting the credit problem doesn't agree to a change or deletion or if the credit bureau refuses to make it, the consumer can add a 100-word statement to the file explaining his or her side of the story. This becomes a part of any future credit report.

### 5. The Fair Debt Collection Practices Act

This statute addresses abusive methods used by third-party collectors — bill collectors you hire to collect overdue bills. Small businesses are more directly affected by state laws that apply directly to collection methods used by a creditor. Some states require creditors to follow the FDCPA as well. It is a good idea to make yourself very familiar with the FDCPA.

# Chapter 15

# Things You Can Do To
# Help You Comply With the FDCPA

If you add interest, late fees or delinquency charges on account, your collection agency should be aware of this. Under FDCPA, your collectors are allows to add interest and other charges to the past due amount if the agreement or contract creating the debt allows it or it if is permitted by state law.

The law permits you to contact a third party in order to locate a skip. If you have good information on the original credit application, you may contact anyone on the credit application to obtain information on the debtor without disclosing why you are looking for them and that this is about a past due balance.

If you receive a payment on an account you have placed with an outside collection agency, you should immediately notify the collection service. An agency that continues to try and collect on a debt that has been paid could be charged with harassment or use of false representation. You, as a credit grantor, could be held jointly responsible.

## PENALTIES FOR VIOLATING THE FDCPA

Debt collectors can be fined up to $1,000.00 plus actual damages for violating the FDCPA. A Collector who acted in good faith and made a bona fide error is not liable for such penalties.

As of this writing credit grantors are covered by the following Federal Debt Collection Laws:

Section 5 of the FTC Act

The Magnuson-Moss FTC Improvements Act, which allows the FTC to apply an action taken against a credit grantor to other credit grantors who were not involved in that action when such actions are adjudicative or litigative in nature or are the result of a final FTC order. The author of FDCPA has said that if an when his subcommittee finds credit grantors are following abusive, misleading or deceptive debt collection practices, they will be included in future legislation.

# Chapter 16

# Unfair Practices

*The following are prohibited by law:*
- You may not charge debtors for collect telephone calls or telegrams made.
- You may not solicit a postdated check for the purpose of threatening criminal prosecution.
- You may add certain charge to the account if state law permits or the agreement or contract creating the debt allows you to.
- You may accept post dated checks. If a check is postdated by more than 5 days, you must send the debtor a written notice of intent to deposit that check not more than 10 or less than 3 business days prior to depositing the check.

## VALIDATION OF DEBTS

You must send the debtor written notice of his right to dispute the debt within 5 days of the initial communication with the debtor. In response to a written notice of dispute from the debtor, you must give the debtor verification of that debt or a copy of a judgment if you have one. Acceptable forms of verification are:
- Invoices
- Statements
- Agreement or Contract, signed or unsigned (signed is better!)
- Other types of verification depending on the debt might be a proof of order, proof of delivery from the shipper etc.

# Chapter 17

# Credit Applications

The best way to get credit information is to have a customer fill out a credit application. We have included a sample Credit Application that you can use. The main reason you will want to use a credit application is to gather the credit information that you can check to decide if you want to extend credit. You may also use the credit application to help you collect on the account if it ever becomes past due.

*On your credit application you will want to have a statement such as:*

"The undersigned herby agrees that should a credit account be opened, and in the event of default in the payment of any amount due, and if such account is submitted to a collection authority, to pay an additional charge equal to the cost of collection including court costs.

"The undersigned individual who is either a principal of the credit applicant or a sole proprietorship of the credit applicant, recognizing that his or her individual credit history may be a factor in the evaluation of the credit history of the applicant, hereby consents to and authorizes the use of a consumer credit report on the undersigned by the above named business credit grantor, from time to time as may be needed, in the credit evaluation process."

OR

"My signature indicates that I understand and agree to comply fully with the terms and conditions enumerated in this credit application." (You would want to use this if you have included your credit terms on the application).

"My signature certifies that everything I have stated in the application is correct to the best of my knowledge."

You can have credit applications printed to suit your business, you can create your own or you can purchase them at an office supply store. Some companies use a carbon form and then can keep the original signed copy and give one copy to their customer. If you create your own, consult with your attorney since there are certain questions that credit granters are not allowed to ask consumers.

*Some of the questions you cannot ask a consumer are:*
- **Marital status**, unless the account will be a joint account.

- You cannot deny credit based on marital status. Applicants do not have to tell you if they receive income from welfare, child support, or alimony. You cannot discriminate against applicants on the basis of sex, marital status, race, color, religion, national origin and/or age.

***If your application is for a business rather than a consumer you will want to ask the following:***
- The company's legal name, it should be officially registered with the state the company does business in.
- The names, addresses and social security numbers of the principals of the company.
- The companies address, length of time there and the previous address if they have been there less than one year.
- How many years the company has been in business.
- The companies bank name, address, type of account and account number.
- Three or four trade references.
- The type of service or product the company supplies.
- Federal ID#

You might also want to include a personal guarantee on a business account. Then an officer or owner of a company could be held personally responsible for any business debts.

You will also want to update your credit applications you have on file, maybe once a year. If you think a company may be in financial trouble you might want to update the credit application quarterly.

In some cases you may allow a Co-signer on the application. If you do, you must get the same information as you do for the main contact. Check all references and if you do approve credit and the main contact defaults, you would go after the co-signer for your money. When approving a co-signer remember that co-signers should be able to pay the loan.

Studies show that for co-signed credit or loans that go unpaid by the original customer, 3-4 co-signers are asked to repay the loan.

The credit application is the most important part of a new customer. This will help you to decide what credit limit to extend and if not paid it will help you to collect your money. You should be looking for stable income or employment, someone who does not have a lot of debt, good existing credit, and no NSF checks, judgments, or collection accounts.

If you pull a credit report on the person who has filled out the credit application, here are some things to look for when deciding whether to approve them for credit:

- Have they paid their bills on time?
- What is their outstanding debt?
- How long is their credit history?
- Have they applied for new credit recently and often?
- What types of "credit" accounts to they currently have and how many?

## SAMPLE OF INFORMATION

## WHICH MAY BE ON A CREDIT APPLICATION

### PERSONAL INFORMATION

Name:
Date:
Present Address:
No. Years:
Own or Rent:
No. of Dependents:
Name and address of employer:
Years employed in this type of work or profession:
Years on this job:
Position/Title:
Type of business:
Home phone:
Business phone:
Gross monthly income:
Base employment income:
Overtime:
Bonuses:
Commissions:
Dividends/Interest:
Net Rental Income:
Other Sources:
(Alimony, child support or separate maintenance income need not be revealed if the Borrower does not choose to have it considered as a basis for repaying this loan.)
If employed in present position less than two years state:
Previous employer:
Type of business:
Position:
Dates from/to:

Monthly income:

Have you declared or been declared bankruptcy in the past five years?:

Are you a party to any lawsuit?:

## ASSETS

Checking and Savings Accounts

Stocks and Bonds

## DEBTS

Loans

Notes

Credit Cards

Real Estate Owned

Retirement Fund

Net Worth of Business Owned

Automobile (make and year)

Other Assets

## OTHER

_____

BORROWER SIGNATURE

Borrower Signature Line

# Chapter 18
# How to Read a Credit Report

An explanation usually accompanies any report you receive. It describes legal rights and other helpful information. You can also always call the credit bureau that supplied the report for an explanation. This information is also available on line or a representative from the Credit Bureau can come to your office to explain how to read the credit report to you.

Credit histories come from public records or organizations that have granted credit to someone. An asterisk by an account indicates that the item may require further review by a prospective creditor when checking the credit history.

To pull someone's credit report you must have a permissible purpose.

The federal Fair Credit Reporting Act (FCRA) requires that this notice be provided to inform users of consumer reports of their legal obligations. State law may impose additional requirements. This first section of this summary sets forth the responsibilities imposed by the FCRA on any users of consumer reports. The subsequent sections discuss the duties of users of reports that contain specific types of information, or that are used for certain purposes, and the legal consequences of violations. The FCRA, 15 U.S.C. §§1681 -1681u , is set forth in full at the Federal Trade Commission's Internet web site (*www.ftc.gov*).

I. OBLIGATIONS OF ALL USERS OF CONSUMER REPORTS
   A.   Users Must Have a Permissible Purpose Congress has limited the use of consumer reports to protect consumers' privacy. A user must have a permissible purpose under the FCRA to obtain a consumer report. Section 604 of the FCRA contains a list of the permissible purposes under the law. These are:
   As ordered by a court or a federal grand jury subpoena. Section 604(a)(1)
   As instructed by the consumer in writing. Section 604(a)(2)
   For the extension of credit as a result of an application from a consumer, or the review or collection of a consumer's account. Section 604(a)(3)(A) (Be sure to have a signed credit application).
   For employment purposes, including hiring and promotion decisions, where the consumer has given written permission. Sections 604(a)[3](B) and 604(b)
   For the underwriting of insurance as a result of an application from a consumer. Section 604(a)(3)(C)
   When there is a legitimate business need, in connection with a business transaction that is initiated by the consumer. Section 604(a)(3)(F)( i )

To review a consumer's account to determine whether the consumer continues to meet the terms of the account. Section 604(a)(3)(F)(ii)

To determine a consumer's eligibility for a license or other benefit granted by a governmental instrumentality required by law to consider an applicant's financial responsibility or status. Section 604(a)(3)(D)

For use by a potential investor or servicer, or current insurer, in a valuation or assessment of the credit or prepayment risks associated with an existing credit obligation. Section 604(a)(3)(E)

For use by state and local officials in connection with the determination of child support payments, or modifications and enforcement thereof. Sections 604(a)(4) and 604(a)(5)

In addition, creditors and insurers may obtain certain consumer report information for the purpose of making unsolicited offers of credit or insurance. The particular obligations of users of this "prescreened" information are described in Section V below.

B.  Users Must Provide Certifications

Section 604(f) of the FCRA prohibits any person from obtaining a consumer report from a consumer reporting agency (CRA) unless the person has certified to the CRA (by a general or specific certification, as appropriate) the permissible purpose(s) for which the report is being obtained and certifies that the report win not be used for any other purpose.

C.  Users Must Notify Consumer When Adverse Actions Are Taken

The term "adverse action" is defined very broadly by Section 603 of the FCRA. "Adverse actions" include all business, credit, and employment actions affecting consumers that can be considered to have a negative impact - such as unfavorably changing credit or contract terms or conditions, denying or canceling credit or insurance, offering credit on less favorable terms than requested, or denying employment or promotion.

1.  Adverse Actions Based on Information Obtained From a CRA

If a person takes any type of adverse action that is based at least in part on information contained in a consumer report, the user is required by Section 615(a) of the FCRA to notify the consumer. The notification may be done in writing, orally, or by electronic means. It must include the following:

The name, address, and telephone number of the CRA (including a toll-free telephone number, if it is a nationwide CRA) that provided the report.

A statement that the CRA did not make the adverse decision and is not able to explain why the decision was made.

A statement setting forth the consumer's right to obtain a free disclosure of the consumer's file from the CRA if the consumer requests the report within 60 days.

A statement setting forth the consumer's right to dispute directly with the CRA the accuracy or completeness of any information provided by the CRA.

2. **Adverse Actions Based on Information Obtained From Third Parties Who Are ~ Consumer Reporting Agencies**
   If a person denies (or increases the charge for) credit for personal, family, or household purposes based either wholly or partly upon information from a person other than a CRA, and the information is the type of consumer information covered by the FCRA, Section 615(b)(1) of the FCRA requires that the user clearly and accurately disclose to the consumer his or her right to obtain disclosure of the nature of the information that was relied upon by making a written request within 60 days of notification. The user must provide the disclosure within a reasonable period of time following the consumer's written request.

3. **Adverse Actions Based on Information Obtained From Affiliates**
   If a person takes an adverse action involving insurance, employment, or a credit transaction initiated by ~e consumer, based on information of the type covered by the FCRA, and this information was obtained from an entity affiliated with the user of the information by common ownership or control, Section 615(b)(2) requires the use: to notify the consumer of the adverse action. The notification must inform the consumer that he or she may obtain a disclosure of the nature of the information relied upon by making a written request within 60 days of receiving the adverse action notice. If the consumer makes such a request, the user must disclose the nature of the information not later than 30 days after receiving the request. (Information that is obtained directly from an affiliated entity relating solely to its transactions or experiences with the consumer, and information from a consumer report obtained from an affiliate are not covered by Section[615](b)(2).)

II.  OBLIGATIONS OF USERS WHEN CONSUMER REPORTS ARE OBTAINED FOR EMPLOYMENT PURPOSES

If information from a CRA is used for employment purposes, the user has specific duties, which are set forth in Section 604(b) of the FCRA. The user must:

Make a clear and conspicuous written disclosure to the consumer before the report is obtained, in a document that consists solely of the disclosure, that a consumer report may be obtained.

Obtain prior written authorization from the consumer .

Certify to the CRA that the above steps have been followed, that the information being obtained will not be used in violation of any federal or state equal opportunity law or regulation, and that, if any adverse action is to be taken based on the consumer report, a copy of the report and a summary of the consumer's rights will be provided to the consumer .

Before taking an adverse action, provide a copy of the report to the consumer as well as the summary of the consumer's rights. (The user should receive this summary from the CRA, because Section 604(b)(1)(B) of the FCRA requires CRAs to provide a copy of the summary)' with each consumer report obtained for employment purposes.)

III.     OBLIGATIONS OF USERS OF INVESTIGATIVE CONSUMER REPORTS

Investigative consumer reports are a special type of consumer report in which information about a consumer's character, general/ reputation, personal characteristics, and mode of living is obtained through personal interviews. Consumers who) are' the subjects of such reports are given special rights under the FCRA. If a user intends to obtain an investigative consumer report, Section 606 of the FCRA requires the following:

The user must disclose to the consumer that an investigative consumer report may be obtained. This must be done in a written disclosure that is mailed, or otherwise delivered, to the consumer not later than three days after the date on which the report was first requested. The disclosure must include a statement informing the consumer of his or her right to request additional disclosures of the nature and scope of the investigation as described below, and must include the summary of consumer rights required by Section 609 of the FCRA. (The user should be able to obtain a copy of the notice of consumer rights from the CRA that provided the consumer report.)

The user must certify to the CRA that the disclosures set forth above have been made and that the user will make the disclosure described below.

Upon the written request of a consumer made within a reasonable period of time after the disclosures required above, the user must make a complete disclosure of the nature and scope of the investigation that was requested. This must be made in a written statement that is mailed, or otherwise delivered, to the consumer no later than five days after the date on which the request was received from the consumer or the report was first requested, whichever is later in time.

## IV. OBLIGATIONS OF USERS OF CONSUMER REPORTS CONTAINING MEDICAL INFORMATION

Section 604(g) of the FCRA prohibits consumer reporting agencies from providing consumer reports that contain medical information for employment purposes, or in connection with credit or insurance transactions, without the specific prior consent of the consumer who is the subject of the report. In the case of medical information being sought for employment purposes, the consumer must explicitly consent to the release of the medical information in addition to authorizing the obtaining of a consumer report generally.

## V. OBLIGATIONS OF USERS OF "PRESCREENED" LISTS

The FCRA permits creditors and insurers to obtain limited consumer report information for use in connection with unsolicited offers of credit or insurance under certain circumstances. Sections 603(1), 604(c), 604(e), and 615(d) This practice is known as "prescreening" and typically involves obtaining a list of consumers from a CRA who meet certain pre-established criteria. If any person intends to use prescreened lists, that person must (1) before the offer is made, establish the criteria that will be relied upon to make the offer and to grant credit or insurance, and (2) maintain such criteria on file for a three-year period beginning on the date on which the offer is made to each consumer. In addition, any user must provide with each written solicitation a clear and conspicuous statement that:

Information contained in a consumer's CRA file was used in connection with the transaction.

The consumer received the offer because he or she satisfied the criteria for credit worthiness or insurability used to screen for the offer.

Credit or insurance may not be extended if, after the consumer responds, it is determined that the consumer does not meet the criteria used for screening or any applicable criteria bearing on credit worthiness or insurability , or the consumer does not furnish required collateral.

The consumer may prohibit the use of information in his or her file in connection with future prescreened offers of credit or insurance by contacting the notification system established by the CRA that provided the report. This statement must include the address and taller telephone number of the appropriate notification system.

## VI.    OBLIGATIONS OF RESELLERS

Section 607(e) of the FCRA requires any person who obtains a consumer report for resale to take the following steps: Disclose the identity of the end-user to the source CRA.

Identify to the source CRA each permissible purpose for which the report will be furnished to the end-user.

Establish and follow reasonable procedures to ensure that reports are resold only for permissible purposes, including procedures to obtain: (1) the identity of all end-users; (2) certifications from all users of each purpose for which reports will be used; and (3) certifications that reports will not be used for any purpose other than the purpose(s) specified to the reseller. Resellers must make reasonable efforts to verify this information before selling the report.

## VII.    LIABILITY FOR VIOLATIONS OF THE FCRA

Failure to comply with the FCRA can result in state or federal enforcement actions, as well as private lawsuits. Sections 616, 617, and 621. In addition, any person who knowingly and willfully obtains a consumer report under false pretenses may face criminal prosecution. Section 619

What is a credit score or risk?

A credit score is a number you use to help decide if you extend credit to this person, will you be paid back in a timely manner or be paid at all. Credit scores are also called risk scores because they help you predict the risk that the customer will not be able to repay the debt as agreed. Scores are generated by statistical models using elements from a credit report, and sometimes from other sources, such as credit applications. However, scores are not stored as part of a credit history. Rather, scores are generated at the time you request a credit report and then included with the report.

Credit scores are fluid numbers that change as the elements in a credit report change. For example, payment updates or a new account could cause scores to fluctuate. There are many different credit scores used in the financial service industry. Scores may be different from lender to lender (or from car loan to mortgage loan) depending on the type of credit scoring model that was used. The Credit Bureau you pull your reports from can tell you more about the scores, what is good or bad etc.

# Chapter 19

# Credit Scores

*How credit scores are calculated*

Designers of credit scoring review a set of consumers – often over a million. The credit profiles of the consumers are examined to identify common variables they exhibited. The designers then build statistical models that assign weights to each variable, and these variables are combined to create a credit score.

Models for specific types of loans, such as auto or mortgage, more closely consider consumer payment statistics related to these loans. Model builders strive to identify the best set of variables from a consumer's past credit history that most effectively predict future credit behavior. This way you can try to "predict" how their credit with your company will be.

*What's in a credit score?*

The information that impacts a credit score varies depending on the score being used. Credit scores are <u>only</u> affected by elements in a credit report, such as:
- Number of late payments
- Type, number and age of accounts
- Total debt
- Recent inquiries
- How late payments are or were at any time

If a business card/corporate card or gas card does not appear on your credit report, it will not affect your score. Credit scores do not consider:
- Your race, color, religion, national origin, sex or marital status. U.S. law prohibits credit scoring from considering these facts, as well as any receipt of public assistance, or the exercise of any consumer right under the Consumer Credit Protection Act.
- Age.
- Salary, occupation, title, employer, date employed or employment history. However, you will consider this information in making their approval decisions.
- Where the applicant lives.
- Any interest rate being charged on a particular credit card or other account.
- Any items reported as child/family support obligations or rental agreements.

- Certain types of inquiries (requests for credit reports). The score does not count "consumer disclosure inquiry" requests made for credit reports in order to check it. It also does not count "promotional inquiry" requests made by lenders in order to make a "pre-approved" credit offer – or "account review inquiry" requests made by lenders to review an account with them. Also, inquiries for employment purposes are not counted.

## Types of credit scores

There are primarily two types of scores – generic scores and custom scores. Custom scores are generated by individual lenders, who rely on credit reports and other information, such as account history, from their own portfolios. Generic scores are for general use in making lending decisions and are based on credit data only. The lower the score the greater the risk of default.

## Why you should use credit scores

Before credit scores, lenders physically looked over each applicant's credit report to determine whether to grant credit. A lender might deny credit based on a subjective judgment that a consumer already held too much debt, or had too many recent late payments. Not only was this time consuming, but also human judgment was prone to mistakes and bias. Lenders used personal opinion to make a decision about an applicant that may have had little bearing on the applicant's ability to repay debt. You would be doing this if you don't pull a credit report but rather call the references on the credit application.

Credit scores help you assess risk more fairly because they are consistent and objective. They also consider information you don't have access to with out pulling a credit report.

## Credit score factors

Score factors are the elements from a credit report that drive credit scores. For example, total debt, income, types of accounts, number of late payments and age of accounts affect credit scores. Score factors indicate what elements of a credit history most affected the credit score at the time it was calculated.

You will be required to provide applicants with the most significant score factors when they are declined credit. This needs to be on the denial letter you send.

Derogatory things to look for on a credit report when deciding whether or not to extend credit are:

- Bankruptcy filings within the past 10 years
- Open tax liens and judgments, regardless of the amount of the lien, or any filing released within the past five years
- Total number of UCC filings with one or more of the following pledged collateral:
    - (a)   Accounts receivable
    - (b)   Inventory
    - (c)   Contracts
    - (d)   Proceeds
    - (e)   Hereafter acquired property
    - (f)   Leases
    - (g)   Notes receivable
    - (h)   Reported collection accounts
    - (i)   Telecommunications accounts that are reported as service disconnect, write off or skip.

Also look for:
- Accounts placed for collection
- Repossessions
- Unpaid student loans

# Chapter 20
# Credit Manager Tools

The following tools are essential for a Credit manager to effectively do his or her job. Without even one of these tools, there will be a crack for a debtor to slip through.

- Signed Credit Application
- Full knowledge of The Fair Debt Collection Practices Act and additional laws particular to the state in which you are collecting
- Communication skills
- Negotiation skills
- Skip tracing or locating skills
- Mediation skills
- Organization skills

Without the tools above you will have a hard time doing your job as a credit manager or collector.

I have included some helpful websites you can browse for more information. You can also use any search engine to find many more useful websites.

- Fair Debt Collection Practices Act:
  *www.credit-and-collections.com/resources-fairdebt.html*
- State laws listed by state:  *www.lawdog.com/state/laws.htm*
- Information on communication skills:
  *www.inc.com/guides/growth/23032.html*
- Information on negotiating:
  *www.salestrainingamerica.com/negotiations_training.htm*
- Great site full of information on mediation:  *www.mediate.com/*
- Sites with tools to help you be organized:
  *www.shopgetorganized.com/*
  *www.viking.com/*
  *www.staples.com*
  *www.officedepot.com*
  *www.officemax.com*
- Printed products such as small or large payment envelopes:
  *www.challengebp.com/search.asp?keyword=Pay%20Envelope*
  You can also have these printed at any printers office or office supply store.
- Past due stickers:  *www.rentons.com*

# Chapter 21
# New Customer Procedures

When a new customer calls or comes in to set up an account, you should set up the account on a COD or cash only basis. The customer should be sent or given a credit application if they wish to become a charge customer. I have provided you with a sample credit application you can use. You can create your own or purchase pre-printed applications at office supply stores such as Staples. You can also have them custom printed with your logo or with carbon if you want to keep a copy easily on file. You can create this yourself or have your printer, who does your business cards or letterhead create them for you. Carbon is a VERY good idea. This way you can give the customer a copy and you keep the original with the signature.

Once the application is received back, you need to run the credit application and make a decision on a credit limit. If the customer is approved, a letter must be sent letting the customer know that they are credit approved and for how much. If the customer is denied credit, a letter must be sent letting them know they were denied and what the reasons are. There needs to be a notation on the bottom of the letter telling them where they can call or write to obtain a free copy of their credit report if they disagree with any of the information. The Credit Bureau will provide you with a sample letter to have printed with your company information on it. It needs to be a two-part letter and the original is mailed to the customer and the copy attached to the credit application. All credit applications need to be filed in one file cabinet that can be locked. All information is confidential. Usually this file cabinet is in the Credit managers office.

Credit reports can be re-run after one year or quarterly in order to review credit limits.

There are many ways to run a credit application. You can become a member of a credit bureau and run credit reports. You can find a credit bureau near you by looking in the yellow pages. Call them and tell them you are a business owner and want to join so you can run credit reports to approve customers for credit. There is usually a sign up fee, a monthly fee and sometimes you might have to purchase software where you can run the social security number and have the report print on your printer in your office. Prices can range from $150-$250 in my experience. If you don't want to spend that much money, you can just check the references the customer has provided for you. You should call all personal and business references and the bank reference. You want to ask the bank if the customer has had any NSF checks and what the average daily balance is. You may have to fax over a copy of the signed credit application for the bank to give you this information. Also call the references, although it is highly unlikely someone would use a reference that was not good. You will want to ask the business references how long they have been doing business with this customer, how much they spend a month, if they are current and if they have ever been past due or had any NSF checks. You should ask the personal references how long they have known the customer, how they know them and if they would recommend them as a good credit risk.

TAKE NOTES! Any notes you take should be attached to the credit application. You can also do this online by going to *www.equifax.com*, *www.transunion.com* or *www.experian.com*, you can inquire about credit reporting and also pulling credit reports.

# Chapter 22

# NSF Check Procedures

If a check is returned from the bank, you need to send the customer a letter telling them that the check was returned for insufficient funds, or stopped payment or account closed, or whatever the case may be. The letter should include a statement that they have been charged an NSF check fee and they need to remit this immediately. You need to post the check back to the account along with the NSF fee. A note needs to be made on the account stating that there was an NSF check and the date. The account should be put on hold until the check clears. A good idea is to call them immediately and let them know the check was returned, then I would still send out the NSF letter.

If you receive the check back a second time, you need to call the customer and make a payment arrangement. Regardless of your conversation, you need to send a Demand For Payment by certified mail. Once you receive the signed return receipt back, you need to wait 14 days for the payment. If you do not receive the payment within the 14 days, you need to call the authorities in the town where the check originated. You will need to provide them with a copy of the demand for payment letter, the original check and the original return receipt.

The account needs to be on hold and if you do business with them again, after they have repaid this debt, it needs to be a cash only or prepaid transaction. You can also consider money orders or cashiers checks.

In most cases, the authorities will recover the money, if not, the account should be placed with a collection agency. You can also file a small claims complaint.

# Chapter 23
# Communications with the Debtor

In the law, the word "consumer" is used rather than "debtor". A Collector may communicate with the consumer or debtor between 8 a.m. and 9 p.m. local time of the debtor. If the collector knows this is an inconvenient time for the debtor, the collector may set up another time for communication.

The collector may communicate with the debtor at work, except when the employer prohibits such communication.

If the debtor notifies the collector in writing that the debtor refuses to pay and wants communication to stop, the collector MUST stop communicating with the debtor except to advise the debtor of possible actions:
- That you are closing the account and won't continue to try and collect
- That you may take legal/collection action
- That this may be reported to a credit bureau

## HARASSMENT/ABUSE

### The collector may not:

Harass, oppress or abuse the debtor in any way. These words are not defined by the courts when cases arise under the law but this practice is not practiced or condoned by ethical businesses or collection services.

## FALSE OR MISLEADING REPRESENTATIONS

Collectors cannot use any false or deceptive representations when trying to collect debts. Collectors are forbidden to represent that they are affiliated with the United States or any state or that the collector is an attorney or works for a credit reporting agency. False representation of the amount owed or legal status of any debt. You cannot make threats to take any action that is illegal or that you do not intend to take. When you send a letter saying you will place an account for collection in 15 days, for example, you must follow through. The collector can also not make a claim that the debtor committed a crime by not paying their debt. You cannot tell the debtor that you have started a legal process unless you have. You cannot tell a debtor that consumers or debtors that do not pay will be arrested or imprisoned or that their property will be seized unless such action is legal and you intend to take it.

## UNFAIR PRACTICES

### The following are prohibited by law:
- You may not charge debtors for collect telephone calls or telegrams made.
- You may not solicit a postdated check for the purpose of threatening criminal prosecution.
- You may add certain charges to the account if state law permits or the agreement or contract creating the debt allows you to.
- You may accept post dated checks. If a check is postdated by more than 5 days, you must send the debtor a written notice of intent to deposit that check not more than 10 or less than 3 business days prior to depositing the check.

## VALIDATION OF DEBTS

You must send the debtor written notice of his right to dispute the debt within 5 days of the initial communication with the debtor. In response to a written notice of dispute from the debtor, you must give the debtor verification of that debt or a copy of a judgment if you have one. Acceptable forms of verification are:
- Invoices
- Statements
- Agreement or Contract, signed or unsigned (signed is better!)
- Other types of verification, depending on the debt might be a proof of order, proof of delivery from the shipper etc.

# Chapter 24
## Dunning Letter Procedure

**(When terms are net 30)**

A customer should receive their first dunning letter when their account is over thirty days past due terms. This should be a friendly reminder. The second letter is sent when the customer is over 45 days past due. This should be another friendly reminder. Phone calls should start to be made at this point. The third letter is sent when the account is 60 days past due. The account should be put on hold and a letter telling the customer that they are on hold should be sent. The fourth letter is sent at 90 days, this letter tells the customer that if they do not respond immediately, further action will be taken. The final letter is sent at 120 days past due. This letter states that payment must be received by a certain date or their account will be placed with an outside collection agency.

Throughout this procedure, collection calls are made at least once a week. The letters that are being sent are put in the tickler file and followed up on daily. You can use a tickler file in your computer or make your own. One idea is to write Monday-Friday on tabbed manilla folders. Stand them upright in a file holder, then follow up each day with the corresponding folder.

Once you send a letter telling the customer that you will be placing their account with a collection agency, you must do it on that day unless some kind of arrangement has been made. It is a violation of the FDCPA to say you will take a specific action and then not follow through.

# Chapter 25

# How to Make Your

# Credit Forms and Letters Work!

When you create your credit forms, and collection letters or notices, you need to remember that there a certain state and federal requirements you must follow.

*Some tips for making your forms "work":*
- Speak in simple terms, rather than big words and legal "jargon" if you can avoid it
- Don't ramble on or repeat yourself.
- Make sure after reading the notice or form, the customer knows everything you want them to know about your credit policy.
- Did you include everything you needed to include to be compliant with all laws?
- Is your language clear?
- Is the type easy to read?
- Is it organized?
- Does your letter have "white space" or is it crowded?

Be sure to review any credit or collection forms with your attorney to be sure you are in compliance with any laws or if necessary under the U.C.C.C. (Uniform Consumer Credit Code).

Be sure your applications or forms relate to your customers. Depending on the education, average age, education level, or income of your customers you may need to adjust your forms so they are easily understood. Words you may want to avoid in your contracts might be:
- Heretofore
- Hereinafter
- Hereinabove
- Herein
- Foregoing
- Aforesaid
- Aforementioned
- Thereof
- Hereby
- Assent

*Simplify your words*

| ORIGINAL WORD | CAN BE |
|---|---|
| Complicated | Simple |
| Shall be deemed | is |
| Under the provisions of | under |
| Is required to | must |
| Indebtedness | debt |
| Liability | debt |
| In and to | in |
| Due and payable | due |
| In excess of | more than |
| In the event of | if |
| Each of the undersigned | you |

# Chapter 26
# Collection Calls Procedure

Before you ever make a collection call, you need to look in the comments screen of the computer to see what has been done. Any time you speak to a customer, you need to make a note in the comments screen. You should always put the date first and then what was said. Then if you call a customer or they call you, you have the information instantly. Some programs have a notes section you can add notes to, some programs also will automatically put in the user and date and time in when you begin to type. This is very important. This way, if you leave a message and the debtor calls back, anyone who answers the phone will see who spoke to them last, on what day and time and what was said.

Once you place the call, you must only speak to the owner of the business or an authorized bookkeeper if the account is a business. If the account is a consumer debt, only speak to the person who owes the money or a spouse. NEVER discuss past due accounts with an unauthorized person, such as a receptionist, neighbor, friend, or relative, other than a spouse.

Once you have the owner or debtor on the phone, identify yourself and your company, and state the purpose of your call. If the customer tells you they cannot pay anything, listen to their story and then explain that you understand that they cannot pay the whole balance at this time, but that you do need a payment. (Start at 80% and go down from there).

At the end of the call, repeat the payment schedule to the debtor and make a note in the comments screen. Whenever you make a payment arrangement like this, you need to send a follow up letter the same day with the same information in the letter. A good idea is to include a payment envelope with the letter. The easier you make it for the debtor to make a payment, the better your chances of being paid. You may even want to provide a postage paid envelope or at least an envelope pre-printed with your company address.

These letters need to be kept in a tickler file with a follow up date written on them, usually a week later. Then on that day you need to pull the letters and check to see if the customer has paid you. If they have not, you need to call them again. If they have made a partial payment, you need to send a letter thanking them for that payment and telling them when you expect the next payment. Put a copy of the letter in your tickler file with a date of a week later to follow up. If possible, fax or email the invoice so they have it immediately then call right back, to verify they received it and get a date the check will be sent. Always try to get a check number. Call back the day they say they are going to mail it and verify it was mailed that day.

## WHEN TO MAKE A COLLECTION CALL

The first collection call should be made when an account is 45 days old. (Based on terms of net 30) This should be a friendly call to remind them about the bill and make sure they have a copy of the invoice. You will also ask them when the check will be mailed or if it has been already. If it has been mailed, get a check number, amount and date.

The second call would be made if payment is not received within a week or two. This call would refer back to the first call, where there wasn't a problem and they were going to send out the payment.

The third and any following calls will be made if payment is not received within a week of the second call. These calls would be made weekly until there is a satisfactory payment schedule.

## HOW TO MAKE A COLLECTION CALL

Before making any collection calls, check the comments screen of the computer to see if there are any comments that could be helpful with the call.

Any time there is any interaction with a customer, a notation must be put in the comments screen. Always put the date first and then what was said. This way, if a customer calls you back, you have the information instantly, and it is available to anyone else who may get the call.

Once the call is placed to the business, only speak to the owner or an authorized bookkeeper. NEVER discuss past due accounts with unauthorized personnel, such as a receptionist.

Once the owner or bookkeeper is on the phone, identify yourself and your company, then state the purpose of your call. If the customer tells you that they cannot pay anything, listen to their story and explain that you understand that they cannot pay the whole balance at this time, but that you do need a payment. Give them options, such as, paying by credit card. When trying to get them to make a payment, start at 80% of the balance and go down from there. Having payment options is very helpful, such as check by phone, credit or debit card payments, or a place they can pay online.

At the end of the call, repeat the payment schedule to the debtor and make a note in the comments screen. Whenever a payment arrangement is made, a follow up letter must be sent confirming the payment schedule. You can also enclose a payment envelope, the easier you can make it for the debtor the better your chances of being paid.

These letters will be kept in a tickler file with a follow up date written on them, a week later. Each day the letters for that day will be pulled and followed up on. If the customer has not paid, they will be called again. If they have made a partial payment, a new letter will be sent, thanking them for their payment and confirming the next payment. If the balance has been paid in full the letter will be filed in the general file.

# Chapter 27
# Collection Calls Tips and Examples

Making collection calls is somewhat of an art. Once you do it long enough you can almost anticipate what the debtor is about to say. You need to be on top of things and know what to say to every response while maintaining professionalism and staying within the law.

*Collection Call Tips*
- Inexpensive - Compared to personal visits and individually typed letters
- Immediate - Produces some sort of answer the moment the contact is made
- Personal - Allows an exchange between two people
- Informative - Allows you to ask questions, obtain information and take appropriate action
- Flexible - Approach can be varied as changing situations demand
- It Should Result In Agreement As To What Is To Be Done!
- Use voice mail or answering machines if available. Leave detailed complete messages and speak slowly
- Always be courteous
- When asked why you are calling, never say it is in regards to a debt, regarding an invoice is better
- Create a sense of Urgency by leaving a deadline time to hear from them
- Get the name of a person in charge of issuing checks or paying bills
- Ask for the best time to call them in the future
- Leave complete messages, your name, company name, phone number, and the request for a return call
- Get the name of the person taking the message
- Ask when the person you need to speak with will be back, and call at that time

The following are some examples of common replies debtors give when on the phone with a bill collector and how you can or should respond. Bob will be the collector.

**Bob:** *Mr. Smith, this is Bob from Acme tools, we have not received your monthly payment on your account.*

*Mr. Smith: You didn't send me an envelope.*

*Bob: Whether we send you an envelope or not you must make your monthly payments to avoid further action. I can take your payment now over the phone and give you the mailing address for further payments. I will also send you a confirmation letter with your new balance after today's payment, with a payment envelope.*

*No matter how ridiculous this may sound, this happens a lot more than you think. Bob took care of every aspect of the situation and left the debtor no way out of this phone call or making a payment.*

*Mr. Smith: I never received a bill*

*Bob: What is your address?*

*This way you can verify it was sent to the correct address and also you can ask for a fax number and fax it then and there or mail a copy immediately with a payment envelope.*

*Mr. Smith: We sent a check*

*Bob: What date did you send the check? What was the check number and amount? Where did you mail the check from and what address did you send it to?*

*This makes the debtor look up the information if it was in fact mailed and if it was not, it prompts the debtor to send a check since he is now giving you a check number.*

You must be ready to ask questions about whatever answer the debtor may give you. You must be ready to provide a solution so they do not have a way out of paying. If you don't have an answer ready, they will just give you another excuse.

# Chapter 28
## Payment Arrangement Procedures

When a customer cannot pay in full, payment arrangements can be made. The amount must be reasonable in comparison to the debt, and must include finance charges. The arrangements are made over the phone with the customer and confirmed in writing once the call is complete.

Once the arrangements have been made with the customer, a letter must be sent confirming the arrangement. The arrangements must then be put into the comments screen of the computer.

If the arrangements are on a piece of equipment only and for an extended period of time, the computer must be adjusted to no finance charge is accrued.

Send a payment confirmation letter to the customer.

# Chapter 29
# Posting UPS/COD Payments

When a UPS check is received with a payment you cannot identify, the cash receipts clerk will call UPS and obtain more information regarding the payment. Such as, the company name or zip code or any other information they can give you.

Once you have this information and have identified the account that paid, the money is posted to the correct account.

# Chapter 30
# Credit Card Procedures

Any customer that wants to have a credit card number on file to have orders charged as ordered will need to sign a document which authorizes your company to charge their card at the time they place the order. This document will expire one year after they sign it. These forms need to be filed in the Credit Managers office, as this information is confidential. You may want to keep them with the customer's credit application in a locked file cabinet.

When a customer calls in to place an order and the order will be charged to a credit card, customer service will take the order and fill out a credit card slip which will then be forwarded to accounting. You may also want the 3 digit security code found on the back of the credit card.

Accounting gets approval on the credit card and then processes the payment.

This procedure will ensure that all credit cards are charged appropriately with customer authorization.

## *CREDIT CARD ON FILE FOR PREPAID CUSTOMERS*

When a customer wants a prepaid account, you must get the type of credit card, the credit card number and expiration date.

Send them a credit card authorization form to be filled out and returned to you.

I have provided one for you to use in this book.

Fill out a credit card slip to be given to accounts receivable to be processed.

Once the credit card authorization form is returned they are kept on file. Once a year, the forms are reviewed to make sure the expiration date is valid. If not, call the customer and update the form.

# Chapter 31
## Small Balance Report Procedures

Once a month a report should be run that shows all balances $10.00 and under. The accounts that have these small balances need to be reviewed and addressed.

If an account has a balance under $10.00 that is only finance charges, this needs to be written off.

If there is a legitimate charge for under $10.00, a letter should be sent to the customer asking them to pay this small balance. If it is someone you are continuing doing business with, this should be enough to get him or her to pay it. If it is a customer that is not buying from you anymore, you can make one phone call after your initial letter then write the balance off. It is not worth the collection effort for such a small amount of money. A note should be made in the computer that this balance was written off in case the customer does ever place another order.

This should be done towards the end of each month.

# Chapter 32
## Account on Hold Procedures

Each day run a report of all accounts on hold. You must review each account to see why they are on the report. If they have a past due balance, you need to make sure some action has been taken and if not, take some. If you decide you are going to hold an order, you need to call the customer and let them know the order is being held. A Hold letter must then be sent the same day. Try to get a payment over the phone and then you can release the order.

If there is another reason why the account is on the Hold Report and you are not going to hold the order, you need to review why the account is showing up on the report and correct it. This may mean you want to review the credit limit or maybe there is a disputed balance or some other problem. These should be rectified as soon as possible so the Hold Report does not have accounts on there that don't need to be and to minimize repetitious reviewing of accounts on the report.

A report showing all accounts on Hold needs to be run daily and reviewed to make sure that when someone has paid, they come off Hold and their order is shipped.

The Hold report should be run two times a day. First thing in the morning, and again, before 2:00. The Credit Manager runs this report.

If the order is not going to be held, release the order in the computer, and review why the account is showing up on the report. The credit limit may need to be reviewed or maybe there is a disputed balance etc. The problem should be rectified as soon as possible to as to minimize repetitious reviewing of accounts on the report.

Remember, this is just a guide, you can change this to fit your business.

# Chapter 33

# If a Business is Sold

If a customer calls to set up a new account from a business that had a previous account, the previous account needs to be terminated and a new account opened for the new owner. You must have them fill out a credit application just like any new customer.

If there is a balance on the terminated account, you must attempt to collect it from the owner. If they have left the area and do not pick up certified mail and you cannot obtain a phone number for them, place them for collection. Make sure the new owner did not also purchase the Accounts Receivable balances. If they did, they may be responsible for the balance that is due.

The new owner cannot use the same account as the previous owner, since all transactions are a credit history for another individual.

# Chapter 34
# Bad Debt Write Off Procedure

You should have a bad debt write off sheet that has 3 copies. One should go to the Credit Manager, one to the Credit Managers Supervisor and one to general file.

*The sheet needs to contain the following:*
1) Account number
2) Name and address of debtor
3) Last pay date
4) Last payment amount
5) Amount now owing
6) Comments (this would be the reason you are without the balance)

The bad debt write off's should be done quarterly and approved by a manager. Once the sheet has been approved the account can be written off to the bad debt GL#. (General ledger #). Any portion of the balance that is a finance charge needs to be written off to the finance charge GL# and not added to the sheet.

The accounts that are written off need to be reported to the Credit Bureau so it will appear on the customers credit report.

The accounts then need to be terminated and a notation made in the computer that his was a bad debt write off.

## WHEN TO WRITE AN ACCOUNT OFF TO BAD DEBT
- The account has already been placed with a collection agency
- The debtor died and the debt is over one year old
- The debtor has filed bankruptcy

## BAD DEBTS RECOVERED

If you receive a payment for a bad debt that has been written off, the payment should NOT be posted to the customers account, it needs to be posted to the GL# for bad debt recovered, this will offset the write off. A note needs to be made on the file copy of the bad debt write off sheet and also in the computer.

You need to notify the Credit Bureau that the debt was paid, so that they can reflect that on the credit report.

# Chapter 35
# Placing Accounts with an
# Outside Collection Agency

*Place an account with a collection agency when:*
- The phone is disconnected
- Mail is being returned and certified mail is unclaimed
- The debtor has moved and is out of business
- All in house collection efforts have been exhausted

## *HOW TO PLACE AN ACCOUNT WITH A COLLECTION AGENCY*

Once a collection agency has been decided on, the information on the debtor can be faxed, mailed or called in, using the form provided to you by the agency. If you have many accounts some agencies will accept spreadsheets of debtors.

Once the account has been placed for collection, the account must be terminated or closed and coded so no finance charges are assessed. Do not continue to send invoices or statements once you place the account with a collection agency.

A note must be made in the comments screen that the account has been placed for collection and the date on which it was placed.

If a debtor calls, they MUST be referred back to the collection agency, and the agency must be made aware that the debtor contacted you. The agency will send you a statement with any payments monthly. Most agencies will keep you updated with phone calls or reports throughout the month. Some agencies have websites where you can check the status of your accounts online.

To find an agency in your state, visit *www.credit-and-collections.com/members.html*, scroll down to the map and click on your state for agencies in your area. You can also do a search on Yahoo or Google.

# Chapter 36
## Place for Collection Procedure

*An account should be placed with an outside collection agency if:*
1) The phone is disconnected
2) Mail is being returned and certified letters are unclaimed
3) You can't find a debtor (most agencies do skip tracing)
4) You are spending an excessive amount of time pursuing an account and are not getting any results

Once you have decided on a collection agency, you can fax, mail or call in your accounts. The agency will provide you with a form that tells you what information they require.

Once you have placed an account with an agency, you want to terminate the account in your system and you want to code the account so that no more finance charges are added to the balance.

There should be a note in the computer indicating that the account has been placed for collection and the date on which they were placed. If the debtor calls you, you MUST refer them back to the collection agency, and let the agency know that the debtor has contacted you.

The agency will send you a statement with any payments monthly.

# Chapter 37
# Choosing a Collection Agency

This chapter will help you decide when to place accounts with an outside collection agency and how to choose an agency.

*Selecting a Qualified Service*

Choosing a professional collection service to manage delinquent accounts and other related tasks is a wise decision. The agency should represent your organization in a responsible and professional manner, and provide a satisfactory rate of recovery while maintaining your public image. This decision involves more that just giving your business to the lowest bidder - it requires careful consideration.

Consider the following qualifications and credentials when choosing a collection service:

- Is the agency a member of a national trade association? Membership is an indication of professional integrity.
- Does the agency belong to a local Chamber of Commerce or Rotary Club?
- Does the agency charge fees that are clearly stated?
- Is the agency prepared to give the best possible service? An agency cannot guarantee results on any specific date, but will often estimate an average recovery rate that one can expect.
- Will the agency be sensitive to a consumer's individual situation? The agency should promptly notify you when it discovers a consumer who is a hardship case and recommend a proper procedure to follow.
- Make sure the agency complies with all state laws and the FDCPA.
- Check to see if the agency holds memberships in state or national trade associations or is a member of a chamber of commerce or listed with the Better Business Bureau.

## WHEN TO PLACE AN ACCOUNT WITH A COLLECTION AGENCY
- The customer does not respond to the first invoice
- Payment is not made within terms
- The customer makes repetitious, unfounded complaints
- The customer denies responsibility
- The customer is a skip
- The customer fails to keep in contact

The longer you keep an account on the books, the less chance there is of collecting it.

*More Credit Problem Indicators:*
- Non- sufficient funds check (NSF)
- Debtor never available
- Extreme changes in payment habits
- Broken promises
- Unfounded disputes
- Operating at a loss
- Biggest Customer went bankrupt
- Changed banks
- Growing faster than planned
- Facing cash flow problems
- Disputes with partners or principals
- Poor working capital position
- Heavy indebtedness

*A Collection Agency is needed if a customer is:*
- Habitually slow paying
- Skips, runs away from debt
- Tries to reduce debt through complaints
- Changes jobs frequently
- Does not return calls
- Rude and will not work with you
- Mail returned & phone disconnected

*Once you place an account...*

Once an account is placed with an outside Collection Agency, you cannot continue to add interest or any other fees. Cease sending out statements and any other collection efforts. If the debtor contacts you in any way, refer them back to the agency and let the agency know they have contacted you.

*As a credit grantor, you should be aware of some basic principals:*
- Granting credit carries an unavoidable element of risk. You will have some losses regardless of how closely you screen applicants.
- A clear understanding by both parties of the terms of the credit transactions when it is initiated. Thus a signed credit application or contract that clearly spells out your terms.
- A systematic and diligent follow up of every account.

## Extending Credit

As a credit grantor, your business is one of many that allows consumers to use goods and services immediately and pay for them later. While extending credit increases your gross sales, it also puts you at risk of some losses due to nonpayment.

Most businesses that write-off a percentage of sales to bad debts have an established rate of procedure for this action. In most businesses, this rate runs from 0.5% to 1% on low-profit transactions, and up to 5% on high-profit sales and services. When the charge-off rate exceeds 5%, it becomes necessary to find ways to improve controls over bad debt losses.

You don't have to accept excessive losses as an inherent part of doing business and extending credit. The fundamentals of establishing and maintaining effective controls over bad debt are comparatively simple, and it is possible to reduce these loses.

## Identifying Bad Debt

You can keep bad debts to a minimum and have more success recovering them if you identify them early on. Your actions at this point of your credit and collections procedures are very important. Your reaction can mean the difference between recovery or loss. When you identify a potential bad debt, you need to act quickly and decisively. The more time that passes, the less chance you have of obtaining payment.

Accounts that are carried indefinitely usually originate with creditors who do a limited amount of business, have the highest credit losses or the lowest debt recovery.

## Reducing Bad Debt

You should have a standard, in-house written policy on handling accounts. The policy should include when to call new customers, when to call established customers and when to send letters. You can use the examples in this book for that.

Assuming that there is regular billing, you will find that most debtors will pay as agreed. A certain number will pay after a friendly reminder. Some will encounter a change in economic situation that makes it difficult to pay, such as illness or loss of job. After a regular follow-up with these consumers, they will usually give insight into their financial situation, their reason for nonpayment, a promise to pay and eventually they will fulfill this promise. A small number of consumers, rarely over 5%, will require more attention, but will eventually pay.

This can usually only be achieved by giving each account proper and constant attention. You need to keep on top of all accounts, even those that are "just a little bit" past due.

### A successful in-house policy must:
- Be tough yet flexible
- Have specific guidelines of action
- Be consistently enforced

Proper and consistent attention involves developing a collection procedure or policy and following each step fully before moving on to the next step. It means that you never move backward or repeat a step in the hope of salvaging an account. You need to be firm and on top of things.

### When to Hire a Professional Collector

As an account ages, the chances of collecting on it decreases dramatically. It's expensive to carry accounts that you will not be able to collect using the methods at your disposal. It's often a better use of your company's time and resources to concentrate on other aspects of your business. This is why some agencies charge more the older an account is. They are usually much harder to collect.

A professional collection service can assist you in collecting accounts that remain delinquent. Collectors have a vast knowledge of collection techniques, technology and compliance issues. Using a professional collection service will save time and likely yield better results than you can.

When accounts reach 90-120 days past due you may want to consider placing them with a collection agency. Some people place accounts at 60 days, it is totally up to you. The sooner you place accounts with an agency, the better your chances of recovery.

### Look for the following signs that you may need to work with a collection service:
- A new customer does not respond to the first letter. For some unknown reason, the consumer will not or cannot pay. Potential losses could be kept to a minimum by prompt referral to a collection service.
- Payment terms fail. In some cases irresponsible consumers pay when and if they want to. This group is responsible for 25 to 50% of the cost of collections. Cost and potential losses are reduced by quick action.
- The consumer makes repetitious, unfounded complaints. Such consumers are often better handled by collection agencies.
- The consumer totally denies responsibility. Without professional help, these accounts are usually written off as total losses. This is when it is

good to have a signed credit application or contract and also if possible, proof of the order and who placed it.

- Delinquency coexists with serious marital difficulties. These also require professional collection help, with the added urgency of obtaining payment before the disappearance of one or both of the responsible parties. If divorced people say the other is responsible. Get a copy of the divorce decree which will state who is responsible.
- Repeated delinquencies occur along frequent changes of address or jobs. This group is responsible for 90% of all "skips". A skip is a consumer who has moved without informing creditors or leaving a forwarding address. The chance of finding a consumer and collecting a debt will decrease over time, so quick action is important. Most agencies provide a skip tracing service.
- Obvious financial irresponsibility is apparent. In such cases, little hope exists for voluntary payments and a quick settlement.
- There is an unauthorized transfer or disposal of goods delivered in a conditional sales contract.

### Working with a Collection Agency

List collection agency accounts on special listing forms. Accurate information about the account will improve collections.

### In all cases, the minimum information should include:
- The correct name, address & telephone number of the debtor
- Name of debtors spouse
- Whether mail has been returned
- Debtors and/or spouses occupation or last known occupation & phone number
- Names of relatives, friends, neighbors and references
- Summary of any disputes
- Date of last transaction, order or payment
- Cellular phone, fax, email address
- Nick names or aliases, maiden name

Cooperate with your collection service. Rely on the experience, diligence and judgment of your collection service for the best and quickest results and promptly refer any developments on the assigned accounts to the collector.

See that your collection service is fully acquainted with the nature of the goods or services involved. If the collection service is familiar with the goods and services your company provides, it will be better suited to handle the complex situations that arise during collection.

Do not place an account with more than one collection agency. Make sure that if you change collection agencies, the account is only being worked on by one agency.

Collection agencies fees are based on results, not on time spent on the account. Don't expect payments to be made immediately.

# Chapter 38

# Doing Business Online
# Electronic Contract & Electronic Signatures

Thanks to federal legislation enacted in 2000, electronic contracts and electronic signatures are just as legal and enforceable as signed paper contracts. The law, known as the Electronic Signatures in Global and International Commerce Act, helps with online contracts.

An electronic contract is an agreement created and "signed" in electronic form — in other words, no paper or other hard copies are used. For example, you write a contract on your computer, email it to a business associate and the business associate emails it back with an electronic signature indicating acceptance. This can also be a page on your Website in the form of a "Click to Agree" contract, the user clicks an "I Agree" button on a page containing the terms of the software license before the transaction can be completed. A lot of Websites have this type of contract on sites that sell membership services or a service where they do not ship a product.

One of the electronic contract issues has been whether agreements made in a purely online environment were "signed" and therefore legally binding. Since a traditional ink signature isn't possible on an electronic contract, people have used several different ways to indicate their electronic signatures, including typing the signer's name into the signature area, pasting in a scanned version of the signer's signature, clicking an "I Accept" button or using cryptographic "scrambling" technology. Some businesses have software that lets them capture a customers IP address, which tells them where the computer order was placed from.

The federal electronic signature law won't override any state laws on electronic transactions provided the state law is "substantially similar" to the federal law or the state has adopted the Uniform Electronic Transactions Act (UETA), which also establishes the legal validity of electronic signatures and contracts. In other words, if the state's law is more or less the same as the new federal law, it will remain in force - but if not, it will be trumped by the federal law. This ensures that electronic contracts and electronic signatures will be valid in all states, regardless of where the parties live or where the contract is executed.

While the e-signature law makes paper unnecessary in many situations, it also gives consumers and businesses the right to continue to use paper where desired.

The most significant legal effect of the e-signature law is to make electronic contracts and signatures as legally valid as paper contracts. For example, an unhappy party to an electronic contract cannot challenge its validity simply because it's not on paper - or because an electronic signature was used to sign it.

The fact that electronic contracts have been endowed with solid legal support is great news for companies that conduct business online, particularly companies that provide financial, insurance and household services to consumers. Under the law, consumers can now buy almost any goods or services without placing pen to paper.

# Chapter 39
# Small Claims Court

If you have tried to collect your money from a customer with no results and you don't want to place the account with an outside collection agency, you can always file a claim with small claims court depending on the dollar amount that is owed. Small claims balances vary by state. The first thing you should do before filing is try and settle the debt with your customer. You can do this by sending letters, making phone calls or even making a personal visit. If it is a business you can contact the Better Business Bureau in your state. You can also check to see if the business is a member of any associations such as a Rotary Club or The Chamber of Commerce. You might even offer to settle the debt for less than what is owed in order to just get it paid.

You will need to fill out a small claims complaint form in the appropriate district courthouse. The court clerk will provide you with a copy of the completed forms. In the Plaintiff section you will put your company name.

You will have to fill out a brief explanation of why you are suing. Then fill out the Defendant section with all information you have.

You will also have to fill out a Military Affidavit, which the clerk will provide you with. You must submit these completely filled out forms and the filing fee to the court. The court will then send the defendant a copy of the complaint. Usually, within 30 days a hearing to contest the claim may be requested by the defendant. The court will notify both of you of the hearing date.

**NOTE:** It is very important for you to notify the court in writing if the case is settled before you go to court.

When a hearing is requested you should bring ALL paperwork you have in relation to the debt. You can also bring witnesses if they can help explain why you are owed the money. Remember, wait until the judge asks you a question before you speak. You will need to explain exactly why the debtor owes you the money, the judge may ask you questions and you should not stray in your answers. Answer the judge very clearly and be direct. The debtor will then have a chance to speak and the judge will notify you in writing, with a court decision usually, within 14 days.

If the debtor does not appear, you will be granted a default judgment. If you do not appear, the case will be dismissed.

### I have a judgment, now what?

If you receive a judgment you will still need to collect your money, the court does not do that for you. Once the debtor receives their copy of the judgment, they may just pay.

If they don't pay, you can file a motion for periodic payments with the court. Your courthouse can provide you with the forms to do this. If you don't want to continue trying to collect once you have obtained a judgment you can hire a Judgment Recovery Service. I have some listed on *www.credit-and-collections.com* and you can also check out:

*www.wecollect.com/*
*www.tjr.biz/*
*www.judgmentrecovery.ws/*
*http://pages.prodigy.net/sgramer/*
*www.ncjcorp.com/*

# Chapter 40
# Small Claims Court for the 50 States

The following information is for reference only and based on my own personal research and should be researched through your local Courthouse. Visit or call your local Small Claims clerk for up to date information. As of this writing this information is as accurate as I could make it but laws may have changed since this writing.

## ALABAMA
**Dollar limit:** $3000
**Where to sue:** County or District where the defendant resides, or injury or property damage occurred. A Corporation should be sued wherever it is doing business.
**Service of Process:** Sheriff, court approved server or certified mail
**Attorneys:** Allowed, but required for collection agencies
**Appeals:** Allowed by either party within 14 days to Circuit court for new trial
**Evictions:** Must be done through regular district court docket.
Additional Information:
- The defendant must file a written answer within 14 days of service or they lose by default.
- Equitable relief is available
- Director of Courts publishes guide to Alabama Small Claims Rules

## ALASKA
**Dollar limit:** $7,500
**Where to sue:** Court nearest to the defendant's residence or place of employment, district which injury or property damage occurred or the district where the defendant does business.
**Service of Process:** Peace officer or registered or certified mail. Certified or registered mail service is binding on defendant who refuses to accept and sign for the letter. After such a refusal, the small claims clerk re-mails it regular first class, and service is assumed.
**Transfer:** Defendant (or plaintiff, if there is a counterclaim) or a judge may transfer a case to regular District court.
**Attorneys:** Allowed, but required for collection agencies
**Evictions:** Not allowed
*Additional Information:*
The defendant must file a written answer within 20 days of service or they lose by default.

## ARIZONA

**Dollar limit:** Small Claims courthouse $2,500, Regular Justice Court $5,000

**Where to sue:** Precinct where any defendant resided, where the act or omission occurred or where the obligation was to be performed.

**Service of process:** Sheriff, adult approved by court, registered or certified mail with return receipt.

**Transfer:** To regular Justice Court if defendant in Small claims Division counterclaims over $2,500 or objects at least 10 days before the hearing. For counterclaims over $5,000, transfer is allowed to Superior court.

**Attorneys:** Allowed only if both parties agree in writing

**Appeals:** Not allowed in Small Claims, allowed in Justice Court.

**Evictions:** Not allowed in Small Claims, allowed in Justice Court.

*Additional Information:*

- Defendant must answer in writing within 20 days or lose by default
- Equitable relief is available
- No right to Jury trial in Small Claims Division, this is allowed in Justice Court
- Collection Agencies are not allowed to sue in Small Claims Court. They are allowed in Justice Court

## ARKANSAS

**Dollar Limit:** $5,000

**Where to sue:** County where the defendant resides, or where the act or omission occurred or where the obligation was to be performed.

**Service of Process:** Sheriff, constable (Justice of the Peace Court ONLY), certified mail in Small Claims Court only.

**Transfer:** In Small Claims, if the judge learns that any party is represented by an attorney, he or she must transfer to regular Municipal Court. No transfer provision is provided for Justice of the Peace Courts.

**Attorneys:** Not allowed in Small Claims Court but are allowed in Justice of the Peace.

**Appeals:** Allowed by either party within 30 days to Circuit Court for a new trial.

Additional Information:

- No collection agencies
- Defendant must file a written answer within 20 days of service if within the state, 30 days if outside the state.
- No right of jury trial in Small Claims Division, but this is allowed in Justice Court.

## CALIFORNIA

**Dollar limit:** $5,000, except that a plaintiff may not file a claim over $2,500 more than twice a year $2,500 is also the limit for suits involving a surety company.

**Where to sue:** Judicial district where the defendant resides, or resided when promise was made, act or omission occurred, or obligation was to be performed.

**Service of process:** Sheriff, disinterested adult, or certified or registered mail.

**Transfer:** If defendant counterclaims over $5,000, case will be heard in higher court if the Small Claims Court agrees to the transfer.

**Attorneys:** Not allowed

**Appeals:** Allowed by defendant or a plaintiff who lost a counterclaim, within 30 days to Superior court for a new trial. Plaintiff may not appeal on the claim, but can make a motion to correct clerical errors or where a decision is based on a legal mistake.

**Evictions:** Not allowed

Additional Information:

- Collection agencies cannot sue in Small Claims Court
- No jury trials allowed
- Equitable relief is available
- Small Claims advisor is available at no cost.
- List of interpreters may be available, call your local courthouse.
- Judge may make a "conditional judgment" to order the performance of actions by a party.

## *COLORADO*

**Dollar Limit:** $5,000

**Where to sue:** County where defendant resided, is employed, is a student at an institution of higher learning or has an office for the transactions of business.

**Service of Process:** Sheriff, disinterested adult or certified mail.

**Transfer:** Allowed by defendant who has a counterclaim over $5,000

**Attorneys:** Allowed only if the attorney is a plaintiff, or defendant or a full time employee or one of the following with respect to these types of plaintiffs or defendants: general partner, officer, or active member. If an attorney does appear as permitted above, the other party may have an attorney also.

**Appeals:** Allowed by either party within 15 days to District Court, on law-not facts. Parties may agree before or at the trial that there will be no appeals.

**Evictions:** Not allowed

Additional Information:

- Collection agencies cannot sue in small claims court
- No plaintiff may file more than 2 claims per month in Small Claims Court and no more than 18 claims per year are allowed
- No jury trials are allowed

## *CONNECTICUT*

**Dollar limit:** $2,500

**Where to sue:** County or geographical location where the defendant resided or does business or where the act or omission occurred or where the obligation occurred.

**Service of Process:** Peace Officer, disinterested adult, registered mail or regular first-class mail.

**Transfer:** Allowed by defendant to regular Superior Court, if there is a counter claim over $2,500.

**Attorneys:** Allowed, required for corporations

**Appeals:** Not allowed

**Evictions:** Not allowed

## DELAWARE

**Dollar limit:** $15,000

**Where to sue:** Anywhere

**Service of Process:** Sheriff, constable or certified mail

**Transfer:** No provision

**Attorneys:** allowed

**Appeals:** Allowed by either party within 15 days to Superior court for new trial.

**Evictions:** allowed

*Additional Information:*

- A jury trial can be demanded if right to trial provided by statute
- Interest due on any cause of action may be added to the claim, even if adding it will make the amount exceed the $15,000
- If defendants counterclaim against the Plaintiff exceeds $15,000, the plaintiff can still pursue the counterclaim in Small Claims Court

## DISTRICT OF COLUMBIA

**Dollar limit:** $5,000

**Service of Process:** U.S. Marshal, adult approved by court or certified with return receipt or registered mail. Service is assumed if letter refused.

**Transfer:** Transferable to regular Superior Court if justice required, defendants counterclaim affects interest in land or housing or either party demands a jury trial. Attorneys or Certified Law Students are allowed and required for corporations.

**Appeals:** To court of appeal by either party within 3 days.

**Evictions:** not allowed

*Additional Information:*

Mandatory mediation is required for contested cases

## FLORIDA

**Dollar limit:** $2,500

**Where to sue:** County where the defendant resides, where the act or omission occurred or contract entered into.

Service of process: Peace officer, adult approved by the court, or for FL residents only, registered mail with return receipt.

**Transfer:** allowed only if defendant counterclaims over $2,500

**Attorneys:** allowed

**Appeals:** motion must be made within 10 days after the return of verdict or filing of a judgment.

**Evictions:** allowed

*Additional information:*

- Either party may demand a jury trial, plaintiff must make the demand when filing suit, the defendant must make the demand within 5 days after service or notice of suit or at a pretrial conference
- Defendant must file counterclaim in writing at least 5 days before the appearance date

## *GEORGIA*

**Dollar Limit:** $5,000

**Where to sue:** County where the defendant resides.

**Service of process:** Constable, official or person authorized by a judge.

**Transfer:** only if defendants counterclaim is over $5,000

**Attorneys:** allowed

**Evictions:** allowed

*Additional Information:*

- Courts may adopt local rules of procedure
- No jury trials
- Defendant must answer complaint in writing or verbally within 30 days to avoid default. Equitable relief available

## *HAWAII*

**Dollar Limit:** $3,500, no limit on landlord-tenant deposit cases.

**Where to sue:** Judicial district where the defendant or a majority of defendants reside or act or omission occurred or where renal premises situated.

Service of Process: Sheriff, County Chief or Police, certified with return receipt or registered mail or by either party personally delivered.

**Transfer:** If either party demands a jury trial or the claim or counterclaim is over $5,000, otherwise only if plaintiff agrees.

**Attorneys:** allowed unless it is a landlord-tenant deposit case. Also with the courts permission, an attorney may represent another if they do not charge a fee.

**Appeals:** Not allowed.

**Evictions:** Not allowed

*Additional Information:*

- Contact the state house for a booklet on Small Claims Division Procedures
- Jury trails will be transferred to circuit court
- Cases limited to recovering money, recovering personal property, recover shopping carts or to recover damages sustained in repossessing carts
- No punitive damages
- Equitable relief available in landlord-tenant cases

## IDAHO

**Dollar Limit:** $3,000

**Where to sue:** County where the defendant resides or where the claim arose.

**Service of Process:** Sheriff, disinterested adult or certified or registered mail with return receipt.

**Attorneys:** Not allowed

**Appeals:** Allowed by either party within 30 days to Attorney Magistrate for new trial.

**Evictions:** No

*Additional Information*:

Collection agencies cannot sue in Small Claims Court and no jury trials are allowed

## ILLINOIS

**Dollar limit:** $5,000

**Where to sue:** County where the defendant resides or where the act or omission occurred.

**Service of Process:** sheriff, court approved adult, certified or registered mail with return receipt.

**Transfer:** If claim or counterclaim is over $5,000

**Attorneys:** Allowed by either party within 30 days to Appellate Court, on law- not facts.

**Evictions:** Not allowed.

*Additional Information:*

- Court may order installments on payments by judgment if debtor remains unpaid over 3 years
- Either party may demand a Jury Trial in small claims court only
- Corporations may not appear as an assignee

## INDIANA

**Dollar Limit:** $3,000

**Where to sue:** County where defendant resides is employed, act or omission occurred or obligation was incurred or was to be performed.

**Service of process:** Personal service first, if unable to serve then registered or certified mail.

**Transfer:** Defendant may transfer to regular docket by requesting a jury trail at least 3 days prior to the trail date, only in Small Claims Court.

**Attorneys:** Allowed

**Appeals:** From Small Claims docket of other courts, same as from regular circuit court.

**Evictions:** allowed if total rent due does not exceed $6,000.

*Additional Information:*

Defendant may request a jury trial within 10 days following the service of a complaint

## IOWA

**Dollar Limit:** $4,000

**Where to sue:** County where the defendant resides, act or omission occurred or obligation was to be performed.

**Service of Process:** Peace officer, disinterested adult or certified mail.

**Transfer:** At judge's discretion

**Attorneys:** allowed

**Appeals:** Allowed by either party to District court, upon oral notice at end of hearing or if filed written notice within 20 days of judgment. No new evidence may be presented on appeal.

**Evictions:** allowed

*Additional Information:*

- The defendant must file a written answer within 20 days after service, or will lose by default; a form will be included with the summons
- Any action to recover a piece of property may be granted if the value of the property is $4,000 or less
- The Small Claims Docket has jurisdiction over orders and motions relative to collecting judgments from personal property, including garnishments, where the amount involved does not exceed $4,000

## KANSAS

**Dollar limit:** $1,800

**Where to sue:** County where defendant lives or county where plaintiff resided, if the defendant was served there or the defendants place of doing business or employment.

**Service of Process:** Personal service by sheriff or adult approved by the court or certified mail.

**Transfer:** If the defendant counterclaims over $1,800 but within the dollar limit of the regular district court, the judge may decide the claim or let the defendant reserve the right to bring claim in court of competent jurisdiction.

**Attorneys:** If one party uses an attorney or is an attorney the other party may as well.

**Appeals:** allowed by either party within 10 days to District court for a new trial.

*Additional Information:*

- No person may file more than 10 claims in the same court in one year

## KENTUCKY

**Dollar Limit:** $1,500

**Where to sue:** Judicial district where the defendant resides or does business.

**Service of Process:** Certified or register mail first, then by sheriff or constable.

**Transfer:** Allowed to regular District court or circuit court if defendants counterclaim is over $1,500 or if defendant demands a jury trial, or if a judge deems matter to complex for Small claims court.

**Attorneys:** Allowed

**Appeals:** Allowed by either party within 10 days to Circuit court, on law-not fact.

**Evictions:** allowed
*Additional information:*
- Collection agencies or lenders of money cannot sue in Small Claims Court
- No person may file more than 25 claims in a year in any district court
- If a defendant makes a written request for a jury trial within 7 days before the hearing date, the case is transferred to a regular court

## LOUISIANA
**Dollar Limit:** $2,000
**Where to sue:** Parish where the defendant resided.
**Service of process:** Certified mail with return receipt or sheriff or constable only if mail is unclaimed or refused.
**Transfer:** Small claims may be transferred to city Court for any reason if defendant files a written request within the time allowed for filing an answer to the complaint.
**Attorneys:** allowed
**Appeals:** allowed by either party in Justice of the Peace Courts within 15 days to District court for a new trial.
**Evictions:** allowed
*Additional information:*
- Equitable relief is available
- Judge may award installment payments
- Default taken in Justice of the Peace Court if answer not filed within 10 days of service
- No class actions, summary proceeding or executory processing allowed
- Parties may request arbitration

## MAINE
**Dollar Limit:** $4.500
**Where to sue:** Division in which the defendant resided or has a business or where the transaction occurred.
**Service of process:** Personally or registered or certified mail.
**Transfer:** allowed
**Appeals:** allowed by either party within 10 days to Superior court
**Evictions:** allowed
*Additional information:*
- Jury trials are not allowed
- Judges have power to refer cases to mediation

## MARYLAND
**Dollar Limit:** $2,500
**Where to Sue:** County in which debtor resides, is employed, or does business, or where an injury to the debtor or property occurred.

**Service of process:** Sheriff or nonparty, personally or by certified mail, if refused the clerk re-mails and service is presumed.

**Transfer:** To regular civil docket if counterclaim exceeds $2,500 or if defendant demands jury trial.

**Attorneys:** allowed

**Appeals:** Allowed by either party within 30 days for a new trial.

**Evictions:** Allowed as long as the rent claimed does not exceed $2,500.

## MASSACHUSETTS

**Dollar limit:** $2,000

**Where to sue:** Judicial district in which the plaintiff or defendant resides, is employed, or does business. Service of process: sheriff, constable or certified mail.

**Transfer:** Allowed only at courts discretion

**Attorneys:** allowed

**Appeals:** allowed by defendant within 10 days to Superior court for a new trial

**Evictions:** no.

MICHIGAN

**Dollar limit:** $1,750

**Where to sue:** County where defendant resides, or where act occurred.

**Service of Process:** Personal service or court clerks certified mail.

**Transfer:** Either party may transfer to District court procedure.

**Attorneys:** Not allowed

**Appeals:** No allowed

**Evictions:** no

## MINNESOTA

**Dollar limit:** $7,500

**Where to sue:** County in which defendant resides

**Service of Process:** Mail or personal service by clerk of court

**Transfer:** to County court on jury demand

**Attorneys:** not allowed

**Appeals:** To County court for new trial or jury trial

**Evictions:** no

## MISSISSIPPI

**Dollar limit:** $2,500

**Where to sue:** District where defendant resides or where act occurred or obligation entered into.

**Service of Process:** Sheriff, or constable

**Attorneys:** allowed

**Appeals:** allowed by either party within 10 days

**Evictions:** No

## MISSOURI

**Dollar limit:** $3,000

**Where to sue:** County where defendant resides or where act occurred.

**Service of Process:** Certified mail or sheriff

**Transfers:** allowed if defendant counterclaims over $3,000

**Attorneys:** allowed

**Appeals:** allowed within 10 days

**Evictions:** no

## MONTANA

**Dollar limit:** $3,000

**Where to sue:** any county or judicial district

**Service of Process:** Sheriff, constable

**Transfer:** allowed by defendant to Justice Court within 10 days

**Attorneys:** not allowed unless all parties present have an attorney

**Appeals:** Allowed within 30 days

**Evictions:** No

## NEBRASKA

**Dollar limit:** $2,100

**Where to sue:** County where defendant resides

**Service of Process:** Sheriff or certified mail

**Transfer:** transferable to civil court on defendants request or with a counterclaim of over $2,100

**Attorneys:** not allowed

**Appeals:** allowed within 30 days

**Evictions:** no

## NEVADA

**Dollar limit:** $3,500

**Where to sue:** city where defendant resides

**Service of Process:** personal service by sheriff or constable or licensed process server

**Attorneys:** allowed

**Appeals:** allowed within 20 days on law not facts.

**Evictions:** No

## NEW HAMPSHIRE

**Dollar limit:** $2,500

**Where to sue:** town or district where defendant or plaintiff resides, or where act occurred.

**Service of Process:** certified mail by court

**Transfer:** To Superior Court if claim plus counterclaim exceeds $2,500

**Attorneys:** allowed

**Appeals:** allowed within 30 days
**Evictions:** no

## NEW JERSEY

**Dollar limit:** $2,000
**Where to sue:** County where defendant or corporation resides.
**Service of Process:** adult approved by the court or certified mail
**Transfer:** allowed with counterclaim of $5,000
**Attorneys:** allowed
**Appeals,** allowed within 45 days
**Evictions:** no

## NEW MEXICO

**Dollar limit:** $5,000
**Where to sue:** County where defendant resides or where act occurred
**Service of Process:** by mail or personal service
**Attorneys:** allowed
**Appeals:** allowed within 15 days
**Evictions:** yes

## NEW YORK

**Dollar limit:** $3,000
**Where to sue:** where the defendant resides, is employed or has a business office
**Service of Process:** certified mail, or regular mail, if after 21 days mail is not returned, service is presumed.
**Attorneys:** allowed
**Evictions:** no

## NORTH CAROLINA

**Dollar limit:** $3,000
**Where to sue:** County where defendant resides.
**Service of Process:** Sheriff, registered or certified mail or adult approved by the court.
**Attorneys:** allowed
**Appeals:** Allowed within 10 days of notice
**Evictions:** yes

## NORTH DAKOTA

**Dollar limit:** $5,000
**Where to sue:** County where defendant resides
**Service of process:** adult or certified mail
**Attorneys:** allowed
**Evictions:** no

## OHIO
**Dollar limit:** $3,000
**Where to sue:** County where defendant resides, or obligation occurred
**Service of Process:** sheriff, certified mail by clerk of court
**Attorneys:** allowed
**Evictions:** no

## OKLAHOMA
**Dollar limit:** $4,500
**Where to sue:** county where defendant resides or where obligation was entered into.
**Service of Process:** certified mail by clerk of court.
**Attorneys:** allowed
**Appeals:** allowed within 30 days to Supreme Court
**Evictions:** no

## OREGON
**Dollar limit:** $2,500
**Where to sue:** County where defendant resides or where contract was performed
**Service of Process:** certified mail, sheriff
**Transfer:** to regular docket if counterclaim is more than $2,500 and defendant requests transfer
**Attorneys:** not allowed
**Appeals,** allowed by defendant within 10 days

## PENNSYLVANIA
**Dollar limit:** $5,000
**Where to sue:** Where defendant can be served or where act occurred
**Service of Process:** Sheriff, constable or certified mail
**Transfer:** By defendant within 30 days.
**Attorneys:** allowed
**Appeals:** allowed within 30 days
**Evictions:** yes

## RHODE ISLAND
**Dollar limit:** $1,500
**Where to sue:** district where either party resides
**Service of process:** Certified mail, sheriff, constable or deputy
**Attorneys:** allowed
**Evictions:** no

## SOUTH CAROLINA
**Dollar limit:** $2,500
**Where to sue:** County where defendant resides

**Service of process:** sheriff
**Attorneys:** allowed
**Evictions:** yes

## SOUTH DAKOTA
**Dollar limit:** $4,000
**Where to sue:** county where defendant resides
**Service of Process:** certified mail, sheriff
**Attorneys:** **allowed**
**Evictions:** **no**

## TENNESSEE
**Dollar limit:** $15,000, $25,000 in counties with a population over 700,000
**Where to sue:** where defendant or plaintiff resides
**Service of process:** sheriff, deputy sheriff, constable or certified mail
**Attorneys:** allowed
**Evictions:** yes

## TEXAS
**Dollar limit:** $5,000
**Where to sue:** where defendant resides
**Service of process:** sheriff, constable certified mail
**Attorneys:** allowed
**Appeals:** allowed within 10 days
**Evictions:** no

## UTAH
**Dollar limit** $5,000
**Where to sue:** County where defendant resides
**Service of process:** sheriff
**Attorneys:** allowed
**Evictions:** no

## VERMONT
**Dollar limit:** $3,500
**Where to sue:** where defendant or plaintiff resides
**Service of process:** sheriff, constable or certified mail
**Attorneys:** allowed
**Appeals:** allowed by either party within 30 days to Superior court
**Evictions:** no

## VIRGINIA
**Dollar limit:** $1,000

**Where to sue:** district where defendant resides or is employed, where act occurred.
**Transfer:** allowed
**Attorneys:** not allowed
**Appeals:** allowed within 10 days
**Evictions:** yes

## WASHINGTON
**Dollar limit:** $2,500
**Where to sue:** where defendant resides
**Service of process:** sheriff or deputy, constable or certified mail
**Attorneys:** not allowed
**Evictions:** no

## WEST VIRGINIA
**Dollar limit:** $5,000
**Where to sue:** where defendant resides or where act occurred
**Service of process:** sheriff
**Attorneys:** allowed\
**Appeals:** allowed within 20 days
**Evictions:** yes

## WISCONSIN
**Dollar limit:** $5,000
**Where to sue:** County where defendant resides or where claim originated.
**Service of process:** summons mailed by clerk of court
**Attorneys:** allowed
**Evictions:** yes

## WYOMING
**Dollar limit:** $4,000
**Where to sue:** county where defendant resides or where act occurred.
**Service of process:** sheriff or deputy, certified mail.
**Transfer:** allowed
**Attorneys:** allowed
**Evictions:** yes

# Chapter 41
# Statutes of Limitations by State

Every state has different limitations on how long contract and judgments are in effect. I have listed these limitation here for you and as of this writing they are accurate to my knowledge. Use this as a guide but also check with your local courthouse or state office with any questions.

## ALABAMA
**Contracts**
10 years, Written, Under Seal
6 years, promises in writing but not under seal
6 years, simple
**Judgements - Domestic**
20 years, of record
6 years, not of record

## ALASKA
**Contracts**
3 years
10 years, Under Seal
**Judgements - Domestic**
10 years

## ARIZONA
**Contracts**
6 years, written
4 years, Written, signed outside of the state
3 years, oral
**Judgements - Domestic**
5 years

## ARKANSAS
**Contracts**
3 years, Oral
5 years, Written
**Judgements - Domestic**
10 years

## CALIFORNIA
**Contracts**
2 years, Oral
4 years, written

**Judgements - Domestic**

10 years

## COLORADO

**Contracts**

3 years, except as provided by Colo. Rev. Sta. Ann 13-80-103.5

6 years

**Judgements - Domestic**

20 years, If judgment entered before July 1, 1981

6 years, if judgment entered in county court on or after July 1, 1981, may be revived.

## CONNECTICUT

**Contracts**

3 years, Oral

6 years, Written

**Judgements - Domestic of Record**

No execution to enforce a judgment for money damages rendered in any court of this state may be issued after the expiration of twenty years from the date of the judgment was entered and no action based upon such a judgment may be instituted after the expiration of twenty-five years from the date of the judgment was entered.

No execution to enforce a judgment for money damages rendered in a small claim session may be issued after the expiration of ten years from the date the judgment was entered and no action based upon any such judgment may be instituted after the expiration of 15 years from the date the judgment was entered.

## DELAWARE

**Contracts**

3 years, oral not under Seal

6 years, Written or under Seal

**Judgements - Domestic**

10 years, can be renewed

## DISTRICT OF COLUMBIA

**Contracts**

3 years, Simple, Express or Implied

12 years, Instrument under Seal

**Judgements - Domestic**

12 years, Rendered in U.S. District Court for the District of Columbia or Superior court for the District of Columbia

At the expiration of a 12 year period, the judgment shall cease to have any operation or effect. Therefore, except in the case of a proceeding that may be then pending for the enforcement of the judgment or decree, action may not be brought on, nor may it be revived, and execution may not issue on it.

An order of revival issued upon a judgment or decree during the period of 12 years from the rendition or from the date of an order reviving the judgment or decree, extends the effect and operation of the judgment or decree with the lien thereby created and all the remedies for its enforcement for the period of 12 years from the date of the order or judgment.

## FLORIDA

**Contracts**
4 years, Oral
5 years, Written
**Judgements - Domestic**
20 years, of record
5 years, not of record

## GEORGIA

**Contracts**
4 years, Oral
6 years, Written
20, under seal
**Judgements - Domestic**
7 years

## HAWAII

**Contracts**
6 years
**Judgements - Domestic**
10 years, of record
6 years, not of record

## IDAHO

**Contracts**
4 years, Oral
5 years, Written
**Judgements - Domestic**
6 years, Idaho Code 5-215(1)

## ILLINOIS

**Contracts**
5 years, Oral
10 years, Written
**Judgements - Domestic**

Revived within 20 years, 735 Ill. Comp Stat. Ann. 5/13-218

## INDIANA

### Contracts

6 years, Oral

6 years, written contract for payment of money

10 years, written contract other than for payment of money

### Judgements - Domestic

20 years, of record.

## IOWA

### Contracts

5 years, oral

10 years, written

### Judgements - Domestic

20 years, of record

No action shall be brought upon any judgment against a defendant therein, rendered in any court of record of IOWA, within 9 years after the rendition thereof, without leave of the court for good cause shown, and, if the adverse party is a resident of IOWA, upon reasonable notice of the application therefore to the adverse party; nor on a judgment of a justice of the peace in the state within 9 years after the same is rendered, unless the docket of the justice or record of such judgment is lost or destroyed, but the time during which an action on a judgment is prohibited by this section shall not be excluded in computing the statutory period of limitation for an action thereon, Iowa Code Ann. 614.3

10 years, not of record

## KANSAS

### Contracts

3 years all actions upon contracts, obligations or liabilities expressed or implied but not in writing.

5 years all action upon any agreement, contract or promise in writing.

(a) In any case founded on contract, when any part of the principal or interest shall have been paid, or an acknowledgment of an existing liability, debtor, claim, or any promise to pay the same, shall have been made, an action may be brought in such case within the period prescribed for the same, after such payment, acknowledgment or promise, but such an acknowledgment or promise must be in writing, signed by the party to be charged thereby.

(b) If there be two or more joint contractors, no one of whom is entitled to act as the agent of the others, no such joint contractor shall lose the benefit of the statute of limitations so as to be chargeable by reason of any acknowledgment, promise of payment made by any other or others of them, unless done with the knowledge and consent of, or satisfied by the joint contractor sought to be charged.

**Judgements - Domestic**
Renewal affidavit or execution keeps judgment alive every 5 years.

## KENTUCKY

**Contracts**
5 years, Oral, Express or Implied
15 years, written after the cause of action first accrued.
5 years, an action on a merchants account for goods sold and delivered, or any articles charged in such store account must commence within 5 years from January 1 next succeeding the respective dated of the delivery of the several articles charged in the account. Judgement shall be rendered for no more than the amount of articles actually charged or delivered within 5 years preceding that in which the action was brought.

**Judgements - Domestic**
15 years after the cause of action first accrued.
**Judgements - Foreign**
15 years after the cause of action first accrued.

## LOUISIANA

**Contracts**
10 years
**Judgements - Domestic**
10 years, Money judgment

## MAINE

**Contracts**
20 years, written, under seal
6 years
**Judgements - Domestic**
Every judgment and decree of any court of record of the United States, or of any state, or justice of the peace in this State shall be presumed to be paid and satisfied at the end of 20 years after any duty or obligations accrued by virtue of such judgment or decree.

## MARYLAND

**Contracts**
3 years
12 years, Under Seal
**Judgements - Domestic**
12 years

## MASSACHUSETTS

**Contracts**

20 years, under seal

20 years, contracts not limited by any other law

6 years

**Judgements - Domestic**

A judgment or decree of a court of record of the US or of any state thereof shall be presumed to be paid and satisfied at the expiration of 20 years after it was rendered.

## MICHIGAN

**Contracts**

6 years

**Judgements - Domestic**

10 years, of record

6 years, not of record

## MINNESOTA

**Contracts**

6 years

**Judgements - Domestic**

10 years

## MISSISSIPPI

**Contracts**

3 years, oral

3 years, written

6 years, sale of goods

**Judgements - Domestic**

7 years, of record

3 years, not of record

## MISSOURI

**Contracts**

10 years, written

5 years, oral

**Judgements - Domestic**

10 years, of record

5 years, not of record

## MONTANA

**Contracts**

5 years, oral

8 years, written

**Judgements - Domestic**
10 years

## NEBRASKA
**Contracts**
4 years, oral
5 years, written
**Judgements - Domestic**
If execution is not sued out within 5 years after the date of entry of any judgment that now is or may hereafter e rendered in any court of record in Nebraska, of it 5 years have intervened between the date of the last execution issued on such judgment and the time of suing out another writ or execution thereon, such judgment, and all taxable costs in the action in which such judgment was obtained, shall become dormant and shall cease to operate as a lien in the estate of the judgment debtor.

## NEVADA
**Contracts**
4 years, oral
6 years, written
**Judgements - Domestic**
6 years

## NEW HAMPSHIRE
**Contracts**
3 years
20 years, Under Seal
**Judgements - Domestic**
Actions of debt upon judgments and recognizance's may be brought within 20 years after the cause of action accrued, and not afterward.

## NEW JERSEY
Every action at law, for recovery upon a contractual claim or liability, express or implied, not under seal, shall be commenced within 6 years next after the cause of any such action shall have accrued. This section shall not apply to any action for breach of any contract for sale governed by section 12A:2-725 of the New Jersey Statutes.

Every action at law for rent or arrears for rent, founded upon a lease under seal, every action at law upon a single or penal bill under seal for the payment of money only, upon an obligation under seal conditioned for the payment of money only, shall be commenced within 16 years next after the cause of action shall have accrued. If, however, any payment is made on any such lease, specialty, recognizance, or award within or after such period of 16 years, an action thereon may be commenced within 16 years next after such payment, and no thereafter.

This section shall not apply to any action for breach of any contract for sale governed by section 12A:2-725. This section shall also not apply to any action founded upon an instrument under seal brought by a merchant or bank, finance company, or other financial institution. Any such action shall be commenced within 6 years next after the cause of any such action shall have accrued.

An action to enforce an obligation, duty or right arising under the Uniform Commercial Code, Bank Deposits and Collections chapter must be commenced within 3 years after the cause of action accrues.

A judgment in any court of record in this state may be revived by proper proceedings or an action at law may be commenced thereon within 20 years next after the date thereof, but not thereafter. An action may be commenced on a judgment obtained in any other state of country within 20 years next after the date thereof or within the period in which a like action might be brought thereon in that state or country, whichever period is shorter, but not thereafter.

## NEW MEXICO
**Contracts**
4 years, oral
6 years, written
**Judgements - Domestic**
14 years, of record
6 years, not of record

## NEW YORK
**Contracts**
6 years
4 years, sale of goods
**Judgements - Domestic**
20 years

## NORTH CAROLINA
**Contracts**
3 years
**Judgements - Domestic**
10 years

## NORTH DAKOTA
**Contracts**
6 years
4 years, contract for sale of goods

**Judgements - Domestic**
10 years

## OHIO

**Contracts**

An action upon a contract not in writing, expressed or implied, or upon a liability created by statute other than a forfeiture or penalty, shall be brought within 6 years after the cause thereof accrued.

An action upon a specialty or an agreement, contract or promise in writing shall be brought within 15 years after the cause thereof accrued.

An action for breach of any contract for sale must be commenced within 4 years after the cause of action has accrued. By the original agreement the parties may reduce the period of limitation to not less than one year but may not extend it.

If payment has been made upon any demand founded on a contract, or a written acknowledgment thereof, or a promise to pay it has been made and signed by the party to be charged, an action may be brought thereon acknowledgment, or promise.

**Judgements - Domestic**
Revived within 21 years

## OKLAHOMA

**Contracts**
3 years, oral
5 years, written
**Judgements - Domestic**
5 years, kept alive by renewal, executions or garnishment summons every 5 years, does not apply to child support.

## OREGON

**Contracts**
6 years
4 years, contract for sale of goods
**Judgements - Domestic**
10 years

## PENNSYLVANIA

**Contracts**
20 years, written, under seal
4 years, oral
6 years, written
**Judgements - Domestic**
4 years

## RHODE ISLAND
### Contracts
20 years, under seal
10 years
### Judgements - Domestic
20 years

## SOUTH CAROLINA
### Contracts
3 years, the specific language of S.C. Code Ann 15-3-530(1) provided a statute of limitations for 3 years for "an action upon a contract, obligation, or liability, expressed or implied excepting those provided for in Section 15-3-520."
### Judgements - Domestic
10 years

## SOUTH DAKOTA
6 years, an action upon a contract, obligation, or liability, express or implied,
20 years, an action upon a sealed instrument, except a real estate mortgage.
20 years, an action upon a judgment or decree or any court of SD.
10 years, an action upon a judgment or decree of any court of the US, or any state or territory other than South Dakota within the US.
10 years, an action for relief not otherwise provided for 10 years.

## TENNESSEE
### Contracts
6 years
### Judgements - Domestic
10 years, of record

## TEXAS
### Contracts
4 years, contract for sale, an action for breach of any contract for sale must be commenced within 4 years after the cause of action has accrued. By the original agreement the parties may reduce the period of limitation to not less than 1 year but may not extend it.

4 years, debt. A person must bring suit on the following actions not later than 4 years after the day the cause of action accrues, debt Tex. Civ. Prac & Rem. Code Ann 16.004(3)
### Judgements - Domestic
10 years, of record, if a writ of execution is not issued within 10 years after the rendition of a judgment of a court of record or a justice court, the judgment is dormant and execution may not be issued on the judgment unless the judgement is revived.

A dormant judgment may be revived by scire facias (a legal proceeding instituted by a judicial writ founded upon some matter of record and requiring the party proceeded against to show cause why the record should not be enforced (as by revival of the judgment), annulled, or vacated) or by an action of debt brought not later than the second anniversary of the date that the judgment becomes dormant.

## UTAH

**Contracts**
4 years, oral
6 years, written
**Judgements - Domestic**
8 years

## VERMONT

**Contracts**
6 years
14 years, signed and witnessed promissory not
**Judgements - Domestic**
8 years, can be revived or renewed

## VIRGINIA

**Contracts**
3 years, oral
5 years, written
4 years, sale of goods.
**Judgements - Domestic**
20 years
10 years, general district court

## WASHINGTON

**Contracts**
3 years, oral, except as provided in RCW 4.16.040(2), an action upon a contract or liability, express or implied, which is not in writing, and does not arise out of any written instrument.

6 years, written, the following actions shall be commenced within 6 years:

1) An action upon a contract in writing, or liability express or implied arising out of a written agreement.

2) An action upon an account receivable incurred in the ordinary course of business.

3) An action for the rents and profits or for the use and occupation of real estate.
**Judgements - Domestic**
10 years

1. Except as provided in subsections (2) and (3) of this section, after the expiration of 10 years from the date of the entry of any judgment heretofore or hereafter rendered in this state, it shall cease to be a lien or charge against the estate or person of the judgment debtor. No suit, action or other proceeding shall ever be had on any judgment rendered in this state by which the lien shall be extended or continued in force for any greater or longer period than 10 years.

2. An underlying judgment or judgment lien entered after the effective date of this act for accrued child support shall continue in force for 10 years after the 18th birthday of the younger child named in the order for whom support is ordered. All judgments entered after the effective date of this act shall contain the birth date of the youngest child for whom support is ordered.

3. A lien based upon an underlying judgment continues in force for an additional extended under RCW 6.17.020.

## WEST VIRGINIA
**Contracts**
10 years, written under seal
5 years, oral
10 years, written
**Judgements - Domestic**
10 years

## WISCONSIN
**Contracts**
6 years, contract, obligations or liability, express or implied
10 years, personal actions on any contract not limited by this chapter or any other law of this state
**Judgements - Domestic**
20 years, of record, except for mortgage deficiencies, see Wis. Stat. Ann 846.04
6 years, not of record

## WYOMING
**Contracts**
8 years, oral
10 years, written
**Judgements**
No action shall be brought to revive a judgment after 21 years after it becomes dormant, unless the party entitled to bring the action was a minor or subject to any other legal disability at the time of the judgment became dormant, in which case the action may be brought 15 years after the disability has ceased.

# Chapter 42
## Credit Related Terms

### DAYS BEYOND TERMS (DBT)

Days Beyond Terms is the average number of days a firm pays its bills past the invoice due date. The DBT is weighted by the dollar amount of each account. The prediction is a forecast of the DBT for 60 days into the future. It is based on the trend in DBT, the type of industry of the business, derogatory public record information, collection accounts, number of inquiries, years in business/on file, and other factors.

### DBT NORMS

DBT Norms let you compare the company's DBT against the average DBT for other businesses in the same industry and the average DBT for all industries. The three most common purchasing terms for the company's industry are also listed (e.g., NET 30, 2/10N30, NET 10).

### DBT RANGES

DBT Range Based on Current Payment Behavior indicates where the business' current DBT falls in comparison to other businesses in the U. S., and shows the percentage of U.S. companies that fall into four DBT ranges (0-15, 16-50, 51-90, and over 90).

### BANKRUPT

Insolvent, gone belly up, ruined, wiped out, broke, busted, penniless, in the red.

### COLLECT

Accumulate or assemble, gather, harvest, reap, amass, hoard, save, round up, pile up, squirrel away, compile, congregate, flock, group, muster, convene, meet, cluster.

### COLLECTION

Accumulation, mass, group, assortment, assembly, pile, gathering, stockpile, store, hoard, cluster, congregation, aggregation, compilation, anthology, hodgepodge.

## CREDIT

Belief, trust, faith, honesty, credibility, praise, attribute, notice, commendation, debt on account, deferred payment, charge, time, installment plan.

## DEBT

Obligation, liability, bill, debit, arrears, deficit, pledge, due, burden, red ink

## DEFAULT

Shirk, welsh, fail, stiff, skip out, run out on, dodge.

## DUNNING

Letters that are sent from the collection agency on behalf of the creditor.

## FORWARDING

The process of transferring a debtor's account from one collection agency to another agency in a different part of the country. Forwarding occurs when an agency is not licensed to do business in the state where a debtor is located.

## MONEY

Currency, legal tender, cash, bucks, dough, bread, medium of exchange, was, loot, scratch, wampum, coin, riches.

## PAY

Remit, compensate, disburse, settle, cough up, foot the bill, spend, expend, shell out, fork over, pick up the tab, contribute, bankroll, finance.

## SKIP

Hop, spring, leap, caper, romp, jump, cavort, gambol, prance, frisk, bounce, overlook, pass over, omit, exclude, leave out, forget about, disregard, never mind, ignore.

## SKIPTRACING

A method the collection agency uses to find debtors who have moved or can no longer be reached at their billing addresses or phone numbers.

# Chapter 43
## Credit & Collections Online

There are a lot of resources available online for anyone doing credit and/or collections. There are newsgroups, newsletters, message boards, websites and discussion groups. I started a discussion group with a website to go along with it, because I couldn't find all the information I was looking for. The discussion group of over 600 members is made up of business owners, people who want to start a business, credit managers, accounts receivable clerks, owners of collection agencies and collectors for all types of businesses. The members are from all over the world so it is a great place to network or just ask a credit or collections related question and get a flood of information for free. You can join or check out the website for free information at *www.credit-and-collections.com/*

I have also listed some helpful resources for you here:

### The Fair Debt Collection Practices Act
*www.ftc.gov/os/statutes/fdcpa/fdcpact.htm*

### Equifax
*www.equifax.com/*

Equifax has been providing value-added information solutions to businesses and consumers for over 105 years. Today, Equifax is a global service provider with over $1.2 billion in annual revenue and 4600 employees in 13 countries.

From first opening its doors in 1899, Equifax has a rich heritage and a distinguished track record of market leadership. The road to success has been paved by maintaining a strong focus on strategic growth, product development, and technology innovation to deliver powerful solutions to our customers.

Throughout its history, Equifax employees have been guided by a common set of practices and values called The Equifax Way. These values have established a strong and steadfast foundation for ensuring the highest levels of integrity, trust, ethics, and privacy in all of their business activities.

### Experian
*www.experian.com/*

With approximately 30 years of experience and more than 30,000 clients in North America, Experian combines their unsurpassed data with the knowledge, expertise and creativity to help companies build successful relationships with their customers. Experian also provides U.S. consumers with the tools and services to help them understand, manage and protect their personal credit profiles.

You can sign up with Experian online to do credit reporting.

### Federal Trade Commission
www.ftc.gov/ftc/business.htm

### Lawdog Center
www.lawdog.com/

Lawdog is a GREAT site! They have all kinds of information and forms for almost anything you need.

### Trans Union
www.tuc.com/

TransUnion is a leading global provider of business intelligence services supported by more than 3600 employees, in more than 24 countries worldwide. With technology-based intelligence products, including innovative credit decisioning and fraud prevention tools, advanced target marketing products, risk and profitability models and portfolio management, TransUnion enables businesses to manage financial risk and capitalize on market opportunities.

### Eli Financial
www.elifinancial.com

### Some sites to help you find people:
Canada 411   www.canada411.ca/
AnyWho Online directory   www.anywho.com/
The Area Decoder   www.areadecoder.com/
Superior Business Network Inc.   www.sbn.com/
Accurint   www.accurint.com
Search America   www.searchamerica.com
Insight   www.e-collectinfo.com/public/index.cfm

### Some FREE sites to help you find people:
www.searchbug.com/
www.melissadata.com/Lookups/index.htm
www.zipinfo.com/search/zipcode.htm
www.mapquest.com/
www.primeris.com/

*Free legal forms including Credit applications can be found at*
*www.findforms.com*

# Chapter 44

# FAQ

**Q:** How common is it that there are consistently problems collecting money from customers?

*A: Some business owners, especially new business owners are so eager for a sale that they don't document or discuss payment, then they don't want to offend the customer by asking for their money.*

**Q:** Is it worth it for a small business to attempt to go after the money due to them?

*A: It depends on the amount of the bill and what information you already have on the customer. Such as contact information so you can get a hold of them or even take them to small claims court.*

**Q:** What legal issues are involved with collecting your money?

*A: You will have to follow the FDCPA, Fair Debt Collection Practices Act and any laws in your state. Also you should also have a contract or signed agreement to protect yourself.*

**Q:** What are some of the ways a company can protect themselves or precautions they can make? Should they change the way they do business in any way?

*A: Always get a credit application and check references if extending credit. Have a good credit policy and stick to it!*

**Q:** What are the steps that a company needs to take to collect money due to them:

*A: If your calls or letters don't prompt payment, you can sue them in small claims court or place them for collection.*

**TIP:** *Be firm about being paid from the beginning. If a debtor knows you are serious, they will be more likely to pay. If they had to fill out a credit application and/or contract, it shows you're serious. If you place accounts for collection sooner than later, that also shows you mean business.*

*Debtors will know you are serious if:*
- They had to fill out a Credit Application

- They had to sign a contract
- They receive invoices right away

# Letters and Forms

# 1. Denial Notice

Date: ___/___/___

Dear _____

Your application for an apartment at _____ has been denied.

One or more of the reasons for the denial of you application may be found in:

( ) Information contained in a consumer credit report obtained from: (See List Below)

( ) A consumer credit report containing information insufficient to our need was obtained from: (See List Below)

( ) The fact that the consumer reporting agency contacted was unable to supply any information about you. (See List)

( ) Information was received from a person or company other than a consumer reporting agency. You have a right to make a written request to within 60 days of receiving this letter for a disclosure of the nature of this information. Pursuant to federal law, we are prohibited from disclosing the source of the report

When a credit report is used in making the decision, Section 615b of the Fair Credit Reporting Act requires us to tell you where we obtained that report. The consumer reporting agency that did the credit check on you was:

Creditchecker, 123 High Street, Plymouth NH 03264 800-555-1212

That company may also have obtained information on you form one or more of the consumer reporting agencies whose names, addresses and phone numbers are listed below. They and the other agencies only provide information about your credit history. They took no part in making the decision, nor can they explain why the decision was made. **A CHECK MARK INDICATES THE AGENCY PROVIDED A REPORT ON YOU.**

RENTAL HISTORY:

( ) Credit Checker, 123 High St. Plymouth NH 03264 800-555-1212

CREDIT HISTORY:

( ) Trans Union Consumer Relations, P. O. Box 1000, 2 Baldwin Place, Chester, PA 19022 800-888-4213

( ) Experian (TRW) Consumer Assistance, P. O. Box 949, Allen, TX 75002 800-682-7654

( ) CBI/Equifax Credit Information Service, P. O. Box 740241, Atlanta, GA 30374-2041 800-685-1111

You have certain rights under federal law to get a copy of your report, dispute its accuracy and insert a consumer statement. If you believe your file contains errors, is inaccurate or incomplete call the consumer reporting agency at their toll-free number, or write to them using the information listed above for disclosure. The disclosure can be made orally, in writing , or electronically. Further...

You have a right during the 60 day period that starts ___/___/___ to receive a free copy of your consumer report from the consumer reporting agency whose name is checked off above.

You have a right to dispute the accuracy or completeness of any information contained in your consumer report, as furnished by the consumer reporting agency whose name is checked off above.

You have a right to put into your file a consumer statement up to 100 words in length to explain items in your file. Trained personnel are available to help you with the consumer statement.

You may have additional rights under the credit reporting or consumer protection laws of your state. Contact your state or local consumer protection agency or a state Attorney General's office.

You should have the following information available to promptly obtain your request:

1) A copy of this denial notice

2) Your full name and spelling

3) Your social security number

4) Your complete mailing address and zip code

5) Your daytime phone number with area code

6) Name of your employer/company, if applicable

7) Your drivers license number and state of issue (*for Bad Check Only*)

Sincerely,

# 2. Prospective Applicant Denial Letter

Date ___/___/___

Dear _____

Your application for residency at the house/apartment/condominium located at _____ in the city of _____ has been unfortunately denied.

One or more of the reasons for the denial of your application may be found in:

[ ] Information contained in a consumer credit report obtained from: (See List Below)

[ ] A consumer credit report containing information insufficient to our need was obtained from: (See List Below)

[ ] The fact that the consumer reporting agency contacted was unable to supply any information about you. (See List)

[ ] Information was received from a person or company other than a consumer reporting agency. You have a right to make a written request to within 60 days of receiving this letter for a disclosure of the nature of this information.

Pursuant to federal law, we are prohibited from disclosing the source of this report.

When a credit report is used in making the decision, the Fair Credit Reporting Act requires us to tell you where we obtained that report.

That company may also have obtained information on you from one or more of the consumer reporting agencies whose names, addresses and phone numbers are listed below. They and the other agencies only provide information about your credit history. They took no part in making the decision, nor can they explain why the decision was made. The following (checked) consumer reporting agencies supplied your credit information:

[ ] Experian (TRW) Consumer Assistance, P. O. Box 949, Allen, TX 75002 800-682-7654

[ ] Trans Union Consumer Relations, P. O. Box 1000, 2 Baldwin Place, Chester, PA 19022 800-888-4213

[ ] CBI/Equifax Credit Information Service, P. O. Box 740241, Atlanta, GA 30374-2041 800-685-1111

You have certain rights under federal law to get a copy of your report, dispute its accuracy and insert a consumer statement. If you believe your file contains errors, is inaccurate or incomplete call the consumer reporting agency that has been checked at their toll-free number, or write to them using the information listed above for disclosure. The disclosure can be made orally, in writing or electronically.

You also have a right during the 60 day period that starts ___/___/___ to receive a free copy of your consumer report from the consumer reporting agency whose name is checked off above.

You have a right to dispute the accuracy or completeness of any information contained in your consumer credit report, as furnished by the consumer reporting agency whose name is checked off above.

You have a right to put into your file a consumer statement up to 100 words in length to explain items in your file.

Customer assistance at the credit reporting agency whose name has been checked is available to help you with the consumer statement.

You may have additional rights under the credit reporting or consumer protection laws of your state. If you wish you may contact your state or local consumer protection agency or a state Attorney General's office.

Thank you for your application, I wish you the best in your future endeavors.

Sincerely,

# 3. Credit Card Authorization Form

Account# _____     Date: ___/___/___

Company name: _____

Address: _____

Phone: _____

Cardholders Name:

Type of Card:    MASTERCARD   VISA   AM EX   DISCOVER

Card number: _____

Exp. Date:  ___/___/___

I hereby authorize (your company name) to automatically charge the above credit card whenever I place an order with them, unless there is a prior written notice.

_____

Signature of cardholder: _____

Date:  ___/___/___

# 4. Check Payment

Name on check _____

Address _____

_____

Check number _____

Bank Name _____ Bank State _____

Routing # _____

Account # _____

Amount Paid $ _____

Name on check _____

Address _____

_____

Check number _____

Bank Name _____ Bank State _____

Routing # _____

Account # _____

Amount paid $_____

# 5. Credit/Debit Card Payment Form

Name _____

Address _____

_____

Card # _____ Exp. Date ___/___/___

Account # _____

Amount paid $_____

# 6. Promissory Note

(For Open Account Debt)

FOR VALUE RECEIVED, the undersigned promise to pay to the order of _____ the sum of _____ Dollars, together with interest thereon at the rate of _____ % per annum on the unpaid balance.

Said principal and interest shall be payable as follows:

(Describe Terms)

The undersigned may prepay this Note in whole or in part without penalty. In the event any payment due hereunder is not paid when due, the entire balance shall be immediately due and payable upon demand of the holder. Upon default, the undersigned shall pay all reasonable attorney fees and costs necessary for the collection of this Note.

This Note is executed to evidence an existing indebtedness due the payee from the undersigned on an open account balance as of this date, and this Note shall not be construed as a separate obligation.

Signed under seal this _____ day of _____ 20__ .

_____

(Notary Signature)

# 7. Credit Application (1)

Firm Name _____

Contact person _____

Address _____

City _____ State _____ Zip _____

Type of business _____ Year business opened _____

Phone _____ Fax _____

Email _____

Federal ID# or SS# _____

Principals name _____

Bank Reference _____

Name _____

Account # _____

Address _____

City _____ State _____ Zip: _____

Phone _____

Date account opened ___/___/___

Trade References

Firm name _____ Phone _____

Firm name _____ Phone _____

The undersigned herby agrees that should a credit account be opened, and in the event of default in the payment of any amount due, and if such account is submitted to a collection authority, to pay an additional charge equal to the cost of collection including court costs.

The undersigned individual who is either a principal of the credit applicant or a sole proprietorship of the credit applicant, recognizing that his or her individual credit history may be a factor in the evaluation of the credit history of the applicant, hereby consents to and authorizes the use of a consumer credit report on the undersigned by the above named business credit grantor, from time to time as may be needed, in the credit evaluation process.

Company _____

Date___/___/___

Signature _____

Title _____

Please print your name_____

# 8. Credit Application (2)

Name _____ Date ___/___/___

Present Address _____

Home Phone _____ Business Phone _____

No. Years _____ Own or Rent: _____ No. of Dependents _____

Name and address of employer _____

_____

Years employed in this type of work or profession _____ Years on this job

Position/Title _____

Type of business _____

Home phone _____ Business phone _____

Gross monthly income _____ Base employment income _____

Overtime _____ Bonuses _____

Commissions _____ Dividends/Interest _____

Net Rental Income _____ Other Sources _____

*(Alimony, child support or separate maintenance income need not be revealed if the Borrower does not choose to have it considered as a basis for repaying this loan.)*

If employed in present position less than two years state:

Previous employer _____

_____

Type of business _____ Position _____

Dates from/to ___/___/___ to ___/___/___ Monthly income _____

Have you declared or been declared bankruptcy in the past five years? _____

Are you a party to any lawsuit? _____

ASSETS

Checking and Savings Accounts _____

Stocks and Bonds _____

Automobile (make and year) _____

Other _____

_____

Borrower Signature _____

# 9. Commercial Credit Application

Name _____ Date___/___/___

Mailing Address _____

Legal Business Name _____

Date Established ___/___/___

Doing Business as _____


Phone No. _____ Fax No. _____

Email _____

Physical Address _____

_____

Website: _____

Type of Business (circle one)

Corporation    State-Incorporated _____

Partnership        Sole Proprietor

Federal ID Number or Social Security Number _____


Number of Employees _____

Type of Business (circle one)    MFG.    Distributor    Reseller    End User    Service

A/P Contact: Phone No. _____

 Email _____

Annual Sales $ _____ Yr this business Established _____

 D&B No. (DUNS No.)_____

Name of Principals of Firm _____

Officer(s)/Owner(s)

**Name** _____

Social Security No. _____

Home Phone _____

**Name** _____

Social Security No. _____

Home Phone _____

Parent Co. Name _____

Does Parent Company Guarantee Debts? _____

(if Yes, please give details) _____

_____

Parent Co Address _____

_____

1. Bank Name _____

Phone Number _____ Fax Number _____

Address _____

_____

Account Officer _____

Checking Account No. Savings Account No. _____

Loan Number _____

Trade References: (Please give at least one from our industry)

1. Company Name _____

Phone Number _____

Address _____

_____

Account No. _____

Number of years done business with this company _____

2. Company Name _____

Phone Number _____

Address _____

_____

Account No. _____

Number of years done business with this company _____

3 Company Name _____

Phone Number _____

Address _____

_____

Account No. _____

Number of years done business with this company _____

In signing this Application, Buyer agrees to all of the above and hereby grants permission for credit information to be verified by company(ies) and financial institution(s) that the Buyer has specified on this document and others that CO NAME Inc. becomes aware of during the credit review process and from time to time. The undersigned also understands that CO NAME will retain this Application, whether or not it is approved, and that CO NAME will consider this Application as a continuing statement of the undersigned's financial position and situation until notified otherwise by the Buyer. The terms on this credit application/agreement overrides all others,

Company Name _____

Authorized Signature _____ Date ___/___/___

Signatory Name (pls. print): _____

Title _____

**(optional) PERSONAL GUARANTEE** The individual by signing this credit application/agreement is executing this Application on behalf of Buyer and personally guarantees, and agrees to be personally liable for failure of the performance by Buyer of, any and all of Buyers' obligations under this Application with CO NAME. including timely payment of any and all sums due to CO NAME

Signature _____

Date ___/___/___

Guarantor's Name (pls. print) _____

Title _____

# 10. Request for Credit References

Name _____ Date___/___/___

Mailing Address _____

Legal Business Name _____

Date ___/___/___

Subject: _____

Manner of Payment: _____

Discounts _____

Prompt _____ Slow _____

Days _____

C.O.D. _____

Suppliers _____

Customer from __/___/___ to __/___/___

High Credit $ _____ Amount now Owing $ _____

Past Due $ _____ Terms _____

Comments _____

_____

_____

**Banks**

Average Checking Account Balance $ _____ NSF checks $ _____

Loan Experience

Since __/___/___ Amount Owing $ _____

Security Held _____

Manner of Payment: As Agreed? _____

Comments _____

_____

_____

Thank you,

Credit Department

# 11. Company to Company Consulting Agreement

This Consulting Agreement (the "Agreement") is entered into by and between _____ , a (state) corporation (the "Company"), and _____ (the "Consultant").

The Company desires to obtain the services of Consultant by means of services provided by Consultant's employees dispatched by Consultant to provide services to Company hereunder ("Agents"), on its own behalf and on behalf of all existing and future Affiliated Companies (defined as any corporation or other business entity or entities that directly or indirectly controls, is controlled by, or is under common control with the Company), and Consultant desires to provide consulting services to the Company upon the following terms and conditions.

The Company has spent significant time, effort, and money to develop certain Proprietary Information (as defined below), which the Company considers vital to its business and goodwill.

The Proprietary Information will necessarily be communicated to or acquired by Consultant and its Agents in the course of providing consulting services to the Company, and the Company desires to obtain the services of Consultant, only if, in doing so, it can protect its Proprietary Information and goodwill.

Accordingly, the parties agree as follows:

**AGREEMENT**

1.   Consulting Period.

(a)  Basic Term. The Company hereby retains the Consultant and Consultant agrees to render to the Company those services described in Section 2 for the period (the "Consulting Period") commencing on the date of this Agreement and ending upon the earlier of (i) _____ 20__ (the "Term Date"), as, and to the extent, extended under Section 1(b) and (ii) the date the Consulting Period is terminated in accordance with Section 4. The Company shall pay Consultant the compensation to which it is entitled under Section 3(a) through the end of the Consulting Period, and, thereafter, the Company's obligations hereunder shall end.

(b)  Renewal. Subject to Section 4, the Consulting Period will be automatically renewed for an additional _____ month period (without any action by either party) on the Term Date and on each anniversary thereof, unless one party gives to the other written notice thirty (30) days in advance of the beginning of any ___ month renewal period that the Consulting Period is to be terminated, provided, that in no event shall the Consulting Period extend beyond _____, 20__. Either party's right to terminate the Consulting Period under this Section 1(b), instead of renewing the Agreement, shall be with or without cause and in writing.

2.   Duties, Responsibilities.

(a)  Consultant hereby agrees to provide and perform for the Company those services set forth on Exhibit A attached hereto. Consultant shall devote its best efforts to the performance of the services and to such other services as may be reasonably requested by the Company and hereby agrees to devote, unless otherwise requested in writing by the Company, [a minimum of at least _____ hours of service per week/or assign _____ individuals to provide services to the Company].

(b) Consultant shall use its best efforts to furnish competent Agents possessing a sufficient working knowledge of the Company's research, development and products to fulfill Consultant's obligations hereunder. Any Agent of Consultant who, in the sole opinion of the Company, is unable to adequately perform any services hereunder shall be replaced by Consultant within _____ days after receipt of notice from the Company of its desire to have such Agent replaced.

(c) Consultant shall use its best efforts to comply with, and to ensure that each of its Agents comply with, all policies and practices regarding the use of facilities at which services are to be perform hereunder. Consultant agrees and shall cause each of its Agents to agree to the Acknowledgment and Inventions Assignment attached hereto as Exhibit B, and Consultant shall deliver a signed original of such Acknowledgment and Inventions Assignment to Company prior to such Agent's commencement of the provision of services for the Company.

(d) Consultant shall obtain for the benefit of the Company, as an intended third-party beneficiary thereof, prior to the performance of any services hereunder by any of the Agents, the written agreement of Agent to be bound by terms no less restrictive than the terms of Sections 2(c), 5(a), 6, and 7 of this Agreement.

(e) Personnel supplied by Consultant to provide services to Company under this Agreement will be deemed Consultant's employees or agents and will not for any purpose be considered employees or agents of Company. Consultant assumes full responsibility for the actions of such personnel while performing services pursuant to this Agreement, and shall be solely responsible for their supervision and payment of salary (including all required withholding of taxes).

3. Compensation, Benefits, Expenses.

(a) Compensation. In consideration of the services to be rendered hereunder, including, without limitation, services to any Affiliated Company, Consultant shall be paid _____ payable at the time and pursuant to the procedures regularly established, and as they may be amended, by the Company during the course of this Agreement.

(b) Benefits. Other than the compensation specified in this Section 3, neither Consultant nor its Agents shall not be entitled to any direct or indirect compensation for services performed hereunder.

(c) Expenses. The Company shall reimburse Consultant for reasonable travel and other business expenses incurred by its Agents in the performance of the duties hereunder in accordance with the Company's general policies, as they may be amended from time to time during the course of this Agreement.

4. Termination of Consulting Relationship.

(a) By the Company or the Consultant. At any time, either the Company or the Consultant may terminate, without liability, the Consulting Period for any reason, with or without cause, by giving _____ days' advance written notice to the other party. If the Consultant terminates its consulting relationship with the Company pursuant to this Section 4(d), the Company shall have the option, in its complete discretion, to terminate Consultant immediately without the running of any notice period. The Company shall pay Consultant the compensation to which the Consultant is entitled pursuant to Section 3(a) through the end of the Consulting Period, and thereafter all obligations of the Company shall terminate.

(b) <u>Termination Due to Bankruptcy, Receivership</u>. The Consulting Period shall terminate and the Company's obligations hereunder (including the obligation to pay Consultant compensation under Section 3(a)) shall cease upon the occurrence of: (i) the appointment of a receiver, liquidator, or trustee for the Company by decree of competent authority in connection with any adjudication or determination by such authority that the Company is bankrupt or insolvent; (ii) the filing by the Company of bankruptcy; or (iii) any formal action of the Board to terminate the Company's existence or otherwise to wind up the Company's affairs.

5.   Termination Obligations.

(a) Consultant hereby acknowledges and agrees that all property, including, without limitation, all books, manuals, records, reports, notes, contracts, lists, blueprints, and other documents, or materials, or copies thereof, Proprietary Information (as defined below), and equipment furnished to or prepared by Consultant or its Agents in the course of or incident to its rendering of services to the Company, including, without limitation, records and any other materials pertaining to Invention Ideas (as defined below), belong to the Company and shall be promptly returned to the Company upon termination of the Consulting Period. Following termination, neither Consultant nor any of its Agents will not retain any written or other tangible material containing any Proprietary Information.

(b) The representations and warranties contained herein and Consultant's obligations under Sections 5, 6, and 7 shall survive termination of the Consulting Period and the expiration of this Agreement.

6.   Proprietary Information.

(a) <u>Defined</u>. "Proprietary Information" is all information and any idea in whatever form, tangible or intangible, pertaining in any manner to the business of the Company or any Affiliated Company, or to its clients, consultants, or business associates, unless: (i) the information is or becomes publicly known through lawful means; (ii) the information was rightfully in Consultant's or its Agents' possession or part of its general knowledge prior to the Consulting Period; or (iii) the information is disclosed to Consultant or its Agents without confidential or proprietary restrictions by a third party who rightfully possesses the information (without confidential or proprietary restriction) and did not learn of it, directly or indirectly, from the Company.

(b) <u>General Restrictions on Use</u>. Consultant agrees to hold all Proprietary Information in strict confidence and trust for the sole benefit of the Company and not to, directly or indirectly, disclose, use, copy, publish, summarize, or remove from Company's premises any Proprietary Information (or remove from the premises any other property of the Company), except (i) during the Consulting Period to the extent necessary to carry out Consultant's responsibilities under this Agreement, and (ii) after termination of the Consulting Period as specifically authorized in writing by the Company.

(c) <u>Interference with Business; Competitive Activities</u>. Consultant acknowledges that the pursuit of the activities forbidden by this Section 6(c) would necessarily involve the use or disclosure of Proprietary Information in breach of Section 6(b), but that proof of such breach would be extremely difficult. To forestall such disclosure, use, and breach, and in consideration of retaining Consultant under this Agreement, Consultant agrees that for a period of one (1) year after termination of the Consulting Period, it shall not, for itself or any third party, directly or indirectly (i) divert or attempt to divert from the Company any business of any kind in which it is engaged, including, without limitation, the solicitation of or interference with any of its suppliers or customers, (ii) employ, solicit for employment, or recommend for employment any person employed by the Company during the Consulting Period and for a period of one (1) year thereafter, or (iii) engage in any business activity that is or may be competitive with the Company.

(d) <u>Remedies</u>. Nothing in this Section 6 is intended to limit any remedy of the Company under the California Uniform Trade Secrets Act (California Civil Code Section 3426), or otherwise available under law.

7. Consultant's Inventions and Ideas.

(a) <u>Defined; Statutory Notice</u>. The term "Invention Ideas" means any and all ideas, processes, trademarks, service marks, inventions, technology, computer programs, original works of authorship, designs, formulas, discoveries, patents, copyrights, and all improvements, rights, and claims related to the foregoing that are conceived, developed, or reduced to practice by the Consultant alone or with others except to the extent that California Labor Code Section 2870 lawfully prohibits the assignment of rights in such ideas, processes, inventions, etc. Section 2870(a) provides:

Any provision in an employment agreement which provides that an employee shall assign, or offer to assign, any of his or her rights in an invention to his or her employer shall not apply to an invention that the employee developed entirely on his or her own time without using the employer's equipment, supplies, facilities, or trade secret information except for those inventions that either:

    1) Relate at the time of conception or reduction to practice of the invention to the employer's business, or actual or demonstrably anticipated research or development of the employer.

    2) Result from any work performed by the employee for the employer.

Consultant hereby acknowledges that it understands the foregoing limitations created by Section 2870.

(b) <u>Disclosure</u>. Consultant agrees to maintain adequate and current written records on the development of all Invention Ideas and to disclose promptly to the Company all Invention Ideas and relevant records, which records will remain the sole property of the Company. Consultant further agrees that all information and records pertaining to any idea, process, trademark, service mark, invention, technology, computer program, original work of authorship, design, formula, discovery, patent, or copyright that Consultant does not believe to be an Invention Idea, but is conceived, developed, or reduced to practice by Consultant (alone or with others) during the Consulting Period or during the one year period following termination of the Consulting Period, shall be promptly disclosed to the Company (such disclosure to be received in confidence). The

Company shall examine such information to determine if in fact the idea, process, or invention, etc., is an Invention Idea subject to this Agreement.

(c) <u>Assignment</u>. Consultant agrees to assign to the Company, without further consideration, its entire right, title, and interest (throughout the United States and in all foreign countries), free and clear of all liens and encumbrances, in and to each Invention Idea, which shall be the sole property of the Company, whether or not patentable. In the event any Invention Idea shall be deemed by the Company to be patentable or otherwise registrable, Consultant shall assist the Company (at its expense) in obtaining letters patent or other applicable registrations thereon and shall execute all documents and do all other things (including testifying at the Company's expense) necessary or proper to obtain letters patent or other applicable registrations thereon and to vest the Company, or any Affiliated Company specified by the Board, with full title thereto. Should the Company be unable to secure Consultant's signature on any document necessary to apply for, prosecute, obtain, or enforce any patent, copyright, or other right or protection relating to any Invention Idea, whether due to Consultant's mental or physical incapacity or any other cause, Consultant hereby irrevocably designates and appoints Company and each of its duly authorized officers and agents as Consultant's agent and attorney in fact, to act for and in Consultant's behalf and stead and to execute and file any such document, and to do all other lawfully permitted acts to further the prosecution, issuance, and enforcement of patents, copyrights, or other rights or protections with the same force and effect as if executed and delivered by Consultant.

(d) <u>Exclusions</u>. Consultant acknowledges that there are no ideas, processes, trademarks, service marks, technology, computer programs, original works of authorship, designs, formulas, inventions, discoveries, patents, copyrights, or improvements to the foregoing that it desires to exclude from the operation of this Agreement. To the best of Consultant's knowledge, there is no existing contract in conflict with this Agreement or any other contract to assign ideas, processes, trademarks, service marks, inventions, technology, computer programs, original works of authorship, designs, formulas, discoveries, patents, or copyrights that is now in existence between Consultant and any other person or entity.

(e) <u>Post-Termination Period</u>. Because of the difficulty of establishing when any idea, process, invention, etc., is first conceived or developed by Consultant, or whether it results from access to Proprietary Information or the Company's equipment, facilities, and data, Consultant agrees that any idea, process, trademark, service mark, technology, computer program, original work of authorship, design, formula, invention, discovery, patent, copyright, or any improvement, rights, or claims related to the foregoing shall be presumed to be an Invention Idea if it is conceived, developed, used, sold, exploited, or reduced to practice by Consultant or with the aid of Consultant within one (1) year after termination of the Consulting Period. Consultant can rebut the above presumption if it proves that the invention, idea, process, etc., (i) was first conceived or developed after termination of the Consulting Period, (ii) was conceived or developed entirely on Consultant's own time without using the Company's equipment, supplies, facilities, or Proprietary Information, and (iii) did not result from any work performed by Consultant for the Company. Nothing in this Agreement is intended to expand the scope of protection provided Consultant by Sections 2870 through 2872 of the California Labor Code.

8. Assignment; Successors and Assigns.

Consultant agrees that it will not assign, sell, transfer, delegate or otherwise dispose of, whether voluntarily or involuntarily, or by operation of law, any rights or obligations under this Agreement, nor shall Consultant's rights be subject to encumbrance or the claims of creditors. Any purported assignment, transfer, or delegation shall be null and void. Nothing in this Agreement shall prevent the consolidation of the Company with, or its merger into, any other corporation, or the sale by the Company of all or substantially all of its properties or assets, or the assignment by the Company of this Agreement and the performance of its obligations hereunder to any successor in interest or any Affiliated Company. Subject to the foregoing, this Agreement shall be binding upon and shall inure to the benefit of the parties and their respective heirs, legal representatives, successors, and permitted assigns, and shall not benefit any person or entity other than those enumerated above.

9. Notices.

All notices or other communications required or permitted hereunder shall be made in writing and shall be deemed to have been duly given if delivered by hand or mailed, postage prepaid, by certified or registered mail, return receipt requested, and addressed to the Company at: or to the Consultant at:

---

Notice of change of address shall be effective only when done in accordance with this Section.

10. Entire Agreement.

The terms of this Agreement are intended by the parties to be in the final expression of their agreement with respect to the retention of Consultant by the Company and may not be contradicted by evidence of any prior or contemporaneous agreement. The parties further intend that this Agreement shall constitute the complete and exclusive statement of its terms and that no extrinsic evidence whatsoever may be introduced in any judicial, administrative, or other legal proceeding involving this Agreement.

11. Amendments; Waivers

This Agreement may not be modified, amended, or terminated except by an instrument in writing, signed by a duly authorized representative of the Company and the Consultant. By an instrument in writing similarly executed, either party may waive compliance by the other party with any provision of this Agreement that such other party was or is obligated to comply with or perform, provided, however, that such waiver shall not operate as a waiver of, or estoppel with respect to, any other or subsequent failure. No failure to exercise and no delay in exercising any right, remedy, or power hereunder shall operate as a waiver thereof, nor shall any single or partial exercise of any right, remedy, or power hereunder preclude any other or further exercise thereof or the exercise of any other right, remedy, or power provided herein or by law or in equity.

12. Severability; Enforcement.

If any provision of this Agreement, or the application thereof to any person, place, or circumstance, shall be held by a court of competent jurisdiction to be invalid, unenforceable, or void, the remainder of this Agreement and such provisions as applied to other persons, places, and circumstances shall remain in full force and effect. It is the intention of the parties that the covenants contained in Sections 6 and 7 shall be enforced to the greatest extent (but to no greater extent) in time, area, and degree of participation as is permitted by the law of that jurisdiction whose law is found to be applicable to any acts allegedly in breach of these covenants. It being the purpose of this Agreement to govern competition by Consultant anywhere throughout the world, these covenants shall be governed by and construed according to that law (from among those jurisdictions arguably applicable to this Agreement and those in which a breach of this Agreement is alleged to have occurred or to be threatened) which best gives them effect.

13. Governing Law.

Subject to Section 12, the validity, interpretation, enforceability, and performance of this Agreement shall be governed by and construed in accordance with the law of the State of California.

14. Remedies.

(a) Injunctive Relief. The parties agree that in the event of any breach or threatened breach of any of the covenants in Sections 6 or 7, the damage or imminent damage to the value and the goodwill of the Company's business will be irreparable and extremely difficult to estimate, making any remedy at law or in damages inadequate. Accordingly, the parties agree that the Company shall be entitled to injunctive relief against Consultant in the event of any breach or threatened breach of any such provisions by Consultant, in addition to any other relief (including damages) available to the Company under this Agreement or under law.

(b) Exclusive. Both parties agree that this Agreement shall provide the exclusive remedies for any breach by the Company of its terms.

15. Independent Contractor.

The Consultant and its Agents shall operate at all times as an independent contractor of the Company. This Agreement does not authorize the Consultant or any of its Agents to act for the Company as its agent or to make commitments on behalf of the Company. The Company shall not withhold payroll taxes, and neither Consultant nor any of its Agents shall not be covered by health, life, disability, or worker's compensation insurance of the Company.

The parties have duly executed this Agreement as of the date first written above.

_____

CONSULTANT

By

_____

Title

_____

# EXHIBIT A

Services to be Provided

_____

_____

_____

# EXHIBIT B

## Acknowledgment and Inventions Assignment

I hereby:

1.   acknowledge that my employer,_____ ("Employer"), is bound by the terms of its agreement with ("Company") to keep confidential certain information that may be disclosed to me before or during my service to my Employer on behalf of the Company and acknowledge that under the terms of my [employment/confidentiality] agreement with Employer, I am bound and obligated by terms equally or more restrictive of such terms regarding the confidentiality of Company's information; and

2.   agree to assign to the Company, without further consideration, all of my entire right, title, and interest (throughout the United States and in all foreign countries), free and clear of all liens and encumbrances, in any and intellectual property, including but not limited to, any and all trademarks, copyrightable materials, inventions, technology, computer programs, original works of authorship, designs, formulas, and discoveries, created by me alone or working with others while providing services to my Employer for the benefit of the Company pursuant to the agreement between my Employer and the Company, which shall be the sole property of the Company, whether or not patentable, except to the extent that California Labor Code Section 2870 lawfully prohibits the assignment of rights in such ideas, processes, inventions, etc. Section 2870(a) provides:

Any provision in an employment agreement which provides that an employee shall assign, or offer to assign, any of his or her rights in an invention to his or her employer shall not apply to an invention that the employee developed entirely on his or her own time without using the employer's equipment, supplies, facilities, or trade secret information except for those inventions that either:

(1)   Relate at the time of conception or reduction to practice of the invention to the employer's business, or actual or demonstrably anticipated research or development of the employer.

(2)   Result from any work performed by the employee for the employer.

I hereby acknowledge that I understand the foregoing limitations created by Section 2870.

In the event any such intellectual property shall be deemed by Company to be patentable or otherwise registrable, I shall assist Company (at its expense) in obtaining letters patent or other applicable registrations thereon and shall execute all documents and do all other things (including testifying at the Company's expense) necessary or proper to obtain letters patent or other applicable registrations thereon and to vest the Company, or Company specified by the Company, with full title thereto. Should the Company be unable to secure my signature on any document necessary to apply for, prosecute, obtain, or enforce any patent, copyright, or other right or protection relating to any Invention Idea, whether due to my mental or physical incapacity or any other cause, I hereby irrevocably designate and appoint Company and each of its duly authorized officers and agents as my agent and attorney in fact, to act for and in my behalf and stead and to execute and file any such document, and to do all other lawfully permitted acts to further the prosecution, issuance, and enforcement of patents, copyrights, or other rights or protections with the same force and effect as if executed and delivered by me.

Signed:

_____

_____

Name (please print) _____ Date___/___/___

# 12. Consulting Agreement

This Consulting Agreement (this "Agreement") is entered into as of ___/___/___ by and between

_____ and _____

1. _____ (consultant) has expertise in the area of the Company's business and is willing to provide consulting services to the Company in the area of collections and credit.

2. The Company is willing to engage Consultant as an independent contractor, and not as an employee, on the terms and conditions set forth herein.

### AGREEMENT

In consideration of the foregoing and of the mutual promises set forth herein, and intending to be legally bound, the parties hereto agree as follows:

1.  Engagement.

(a)  The Company hereby engages Consultant to render, as an independent contractor, the consulting services described in Exhibit A hereto and such other services as may be agreed to in writing by the Company and Consultant from time to time.

(b)  Consultant hereby accepts the engagement to provide consulting services to the Company on the terms and conditions set forth herein.

2.  **Term**.

This Agreement will commence on the date first written above, and unless modified by the mutual written agreement of the parties, shall continue until the satisfactory completion of the services set forth in Exhibit A. Company may terminate this Agreement upon 10 days written notice to Consultant.

3.  Compensation.

(a)  In consideration of the services to be performed by Consultant, the Company agrees to pay Consultant in the manner and at the rates set forth in Exhibit A.

(b)  Out of pocket expenses incurred by Consultant that are authorized by the Company in advance in writing shall be reimbursed by Company to Consultant.

4.  **Confidential Information and Assignments.**

Consultant is simultaneously executing a Confidential Information and Invention Assignment Agreement for Consultants in the form of Exhibit B (the "Confidential Information and Invention Assignment Agreement"). The obligations under the Confidential Information and Invention Assignment Agreement shall survive termination of this Agreement for any reason.

5.  Interference with the Company's Business.

(a)  Notwithstanding any other provision of this Agreement, for a period of one year after termination of this Agreement, Consultant shall not, directly or indirectly, employ, solicit for employment, or advise or recommend to any other person that such other person employ or solicit for employment, any person employed or under contract (whether as a consultant, employee or otherwise) by or to the Company during the period of such person's association with the Company and one year thereafter.

(b)  Notwithstanding any other provision of this Agreement, and to the fullest extent permitted by law, for a period of one year after termination of this Agreement, Consultant shall not, directly or indirectly, solicit any clients or customers of the Company. Consultant agrees that such solicitation would necessarily involve disclosure or use of confidential information in breach of the Confidential Information and Invention Assignment Agreement.

## 6.  Representations and Warranties.

Consultant represents and warrants (i) that Consultant has no obligations, legal or otherwise, inconsistent with the terms of this Agreement or with Consultant's undertaking this relationship with the Company, (ii) that the performance of the services called for by this Agreement do not and will not violate any applicable law, rule or regulation or any proprietary or other right of any third party, (iii) that Consultant will not use in the performance of his responsibilities under this Agreement any confidential information or trade secrets of any other person or entity and (iv) that Consultant has not entered into or will enter into any agreement (whether oral or written) in conflict with this Agreement.

## 7.  Indemnification.

Consultant hereby indemnifies and agrees to defend and hold harmless the Company from and against any and all claims, demands and actions, and any liabilities, damages or expenses resulting therefrom, including court costs and reasonable attorneys' fees, arising out of or relating to the services performed by Consultant under this Agreement or the representations and warranties made by Consultant pursuant to paragraph 7 hereof. Consultant's obligations under this paragraph 8 hereof shall survive the termination, for any reason, of this Agreement.

## 8.  Attorney's Fees.

Should either party hereto, or any heir, personal representative, successor or assign of either party hereto, resort to litigation to enforce this Agreement, the party or parties prevailing in such litigation shall be entitled, in addition to such other relief as may be granted, to recover its or their reasonable attorneys' fees and costs in such litigation from the party or parties against whom enforcement was sought.

## 9.  Entire Agreement.

This Agreement, contains the entire understanding and agreement between the parties hereto with respect to its subject matter and supersedes any prior or contemporaneous written or oral agreements, representations or warranties between them respecting the subject matter hereof.

## 10. Amendment.

This Agreement may be amended only in writing signed by Consultant and by a representative of the Company duly authorized.

## 11. Severability.

If any term, provision, covenant or condition of this Agreement, or the application thereof to any person, place or circumstance, shall be held by a court of competent jurisdiction to be invalid, unenforceable or void, the remainder of this Agreement and such term, provision, covenant or condition as applied to other persons, places and circumstances shall remain in full force and effect.

## 12. Rights Cumulative.

The rights and remedies provided by this Agreement are cumulative, and the exercise of any right or remedy by either party hereto (or by its successors), whether pursuant to this Agreement, to any other agreement, or to law, shall not preclude or waive its right to exercise any or all other rights and remedies.

## 13. Remedy for Breach.

The parties hereto agree that, in the event of breach or threatened breach of this Agreement, the damage or imminent damage to the value and the goodwill of the Company's business will be inestimable, and that therefore any remedy at law or in damages shall be inadequate. Accordingly, the parties hereto agree that the Company shall be entitled to injunctive relief against Consultant in the event of any breach or threatened breach by Consultant, in addition to any other relief (including damages and the right of the Company to stop payments hereunder which is hereby granted) available to the Company under this Agreement or under law.

## 14. Agreement to Perform Necessary Acts.

Consultant agrees to perform any further acts and execute and deliver any documents that may be reasonably necessary to carry out the provisions of this Agreement.

## 15. Compliance with Law.

In connection with his services rendered hereunder, Consultant agrees to abide by all federal, state, and local laws, ordinances and regulations.

## 16. Independent Contractor.

The relationship between Consultant and the Company is that of independent contractor under a "work for hire" arrangement. All work product developed by Consultant shall be deemed owned and assigned to Company. This Agreement is not authority for Consultant to act for the Company as its agent or make commitments for the Company. Consultant will not be eligible for any employee benefits, nor will the company make deductions from fees to the consultant for taxes, insurance, bonds or the like. Consultant retains the discretion in performing the tasks assigned, within the scope of work specified.

## 17. Taxes.

Consultant agrees to pay all appropriate local, state and federal taxes.

By: _____
(signature)

Name _____
(print name)

Title _____

## Exhibit A

1. Description of Services to be Rendered

This proposal encompasses revamping a series of collection letters to be used by the collection department in pursuing delinquent accounts. This may encompass re-writing or providing new dunning notices in all accordance with the law to be used in dunning delinquent accounts. This could be up to an eleven letter series or more as determined once all notices are looked over. All letters will comply with all federal and state laws and regulations, as well as ethical standards. Collection Agency will work with the Company to ensure they are in compliance and have a series of effective dunning notices with which to use in their in house collection efforts. Dates of on site visits will be established once an agreement is made.

2. Compensation Company will pay our hourly rate of $100.00 per hour for on site visits. Normally it takes one – two 8 hour days to gather information in house to then be able to complete the work in our office at an hourly rate of $50.00 per hour. Depending on the number of letters and if they will be recreated or revamped this can take up to two weeks. All expenses will be reimbursed and travel time is billable time. These expenses include airfare, hotel, meals, car rental if needed. Payment is to be made as half down before work begins and the balance at the completion of the job.

## Exhibit B

Confidential Information and Invention Assignment

for

_____
(consultant)

## CONFIDENTIAL INFORMATION AND INVENTION ASSIGNMENT AGREEMENT FOR CONSULTANT

This CONFIDENTIAL INFORMATION AND INVENTION ASSIGNMENT AGREEMENT (the "Agreement") is made between the "Company" and the undersigned consultant.

In consideration of my relationship with the Company (which for purposes of this Agreement shall be deemed to include any subsidiaries or Affiliates** of the Company), the receipt of confidential information while associated with the Company, and other good and valuable consideration, I, the undersigned individual, agree that:

1. **Term of Agreement.** This Agreement shall continue in full force and effect for the duration of my relationship with the Company and shall continue thereafter until terminated through a written instrument signed by both parties.

2. **Confidentiality.**

(a) **Definitions.** "Proprietary Information" is all information and any idea whatever form, tangible or intangible, pertaining in any manner to the business of the Company, or any of its Affiliates, or its employees, clients, consultants, or business associates, which was produced by any employee or consultant of the Company in the course of his or her employment or consulting relationship or otherwise produced or acquired by or on behalf of the Company. All Proprietary Information not generally known outside of the Company's organization, and all Proprietary Information so known only through improper means, shall be deemed "Confidential Information." By example and without limiting the foregoing definition, Proprietary and Confidential Information shall include, but not be limited to:

(1) formulas, research and development techniques, processes, trade secrets, computer programs, software, electronic codes, mask works, inventions, innovations, patents, patent applications, discoveries, improvements, data, know-how, formats, test results, and research projects;

(2) information about costs, profits, markets, sales, contracts and lists of customers, and distributors;

(b) **Prior Actions and Knowledge.** I represent and warrant that from the time of my first contact with the Company I held in strict confidence all Confidential Information and have not disclosed any Confidential Information, directly or indirectly, to anyone outside the Company, or used, copied, published, or summarized any Confidential information, except to the extent otherwise permitted in this Agreement.

(c) **Third-Party Information.** I acknowledge that the Company has received and in the future will receive from third parties their confidential information subject to a duty on the Company's part to maintain the confidentiality of such information and to use it only for certain limited purposes. I agree that I will at all times hold all such confidential information in the strictest confidence and not to disclose or use it, except as necessary to perform my obligations hereunder and as is consistent with the Company's agreement with such third parties.

(d) **Third Parties.** I represent that my relationship with the Company does not and will not breach any agreements with or duties to a former employer or any other third party. I will not disclose to the Company or use on its behalf any confidential information belonging to others and I will not bring onto the premises of the Company any confidential information belonging to any such party unless consented to in writing by such party.

3. **Representations and Warranties.** I represent and warrant (i) that I have no obligations,

legal or otherwise, inconsistent with the terms of this Agreement or with my undertaking a relationship with the Company; (ii) that the performance of the services called for by this Agreement do not and will not violate any applicable law, rule or regulation or any proprietary or other right of any third party; (iii) that I will not use in the performance of my responsibilities for the Company any confidential information or trade secrets of any other person or entity; and (iv) that I have not entered into or will enter into any agreement (whether oral or written) in conflict with this Agreement.

## 4. **Termination Obligations.**

(a)   Upon the termination of my relationship with the Company or promptly upon the Company's request, I shall surrender to the Company all equipment, tangible Proprietary Information, documents, books, notebooks, records, reports, notes, memoranda, drawings, sketches, models, maps, contracts, lists, computer disks (and other computer-generated files and data), any other data and records of any kind, and copies thereof (collectively, "Company Records"), created on any medium and furnished to, obtained by, or prepared by myself in the course of or incident to my relationship with the Company, that are in my possession or under my control.

(b)   My representations, warranties, and obligations contained in this Agreement shall survive the termination of my relationship with the Company.

(c)   Following any termination of my relationship with the Company, I will fully cooperate with the Company in all matters relating to my continuing obligations under this Agreement.

(d)   I hereby grant consent to notification by the Company to any of my future employers or companies I consult with about my rights and obligations under this Agreement.

5.   **Injunctive Relief.** I acknowledge that my failure to carry out any obligation under this Agreement, or a breach by me of any provision herein, will constitute immediate and irreparable damage to the Company, which cannot be fully and adequately compensated in money damages and which will warrant preliminary and other injunctive relief, an order for specific performance, and other equitable relief. I further agree that no bond or other security shall be required in obtaining such equitable relief and I hereby consent to the issuance of such injunction and to the ordering of specific performance. I also understand that other action may be taken and remedies enforced against me.

6.   **Modification**. No modification of this Agreement shall be valid unless made in writing and signed by both parties.

7.   **Integration**. This Agreement sets forth the parties' mutual rights and obligations with respect to proprietary information, prohibited competition, and intellectual property. It is intended to be the final, complete, and exclusive statement of the terms of the parties' agreements regarding these subjects. This Agreement supersedes all other prior and contemporaneous agreements and statements on these subjects, and it may not be contradicted by evidence of any prior or contemporaneous statements or agreements. To the extent that the practices, policies, or procedures of the Company, now or in the future, apply to myself and are inconsistent with the terms of this Agreement, the provisions of this Agreement shall control unless changed in writing by the Company.

8.   **Not Employment**. This Agreement is not an employment agreement as I am an independent

consultant. I understand that the Company may terminate my association with it at any time, with or without cause, subject to the terms of any separate written consulting agreement executed by a duly authorized officer of the Company.

9.  **Construction**. This Agreement shall be construed as a whole, according to its fair meaning, and not in favor of or against any party. By way of example and not limitation, this Agreement shall not be construed against the party responsible for any language in this Agreement. The headings of the paragraphs hereof are inserted for convenience only, and do not constitute part of and shall not be used to interpret this Agreement.

10. **Attorneys' Fees.** Should either I or the Company, or any heir, personal representative, successor or permitted assign of either party, resort to legal proceedings to enforce this Agreement, the prevailing party in such legal proceeding shall be awarded, in addition to such other relief as may be granted, attorneys' fees and costs incurred in connection with such proceeding.

11. **Severability**. If any term, provision, covenant or condition of this Agreement, or the application thereof to any person, place or circumstance, shall be held to be invalid, unenforceable or void, the remainder of this Agreement and such term, provision, covenant or condition as applied to other persons, places and circumstances shall remain in full force and effect.

12. **Rights Cumulative**. The rights and remedies provided by this Agreement are cumulative, and the exercise of any right or remedy by either the Company or me (or by that party's successor), whether pursuant hereto, to any other agreement, or to law, shall not preclude or waive that party's right to exercise any or all other rights and remedies. This Agreement will inure to the benefit of the Company and its successors and assigns.

13. **Nonwaiver**. The failure of either the Company or me, whether purposeful or otherwise, to exercise in any instance any right, power or privilege under this Agreement or under law shall not constitute a waiver of any other right, power or privilege, nor of the same right, power or privilege in any other instance. Any waiver by the Company or by me must be in writing and signed by either myself, if I am seeking to waive any of my rights under this Agreement, or by an officer of the Company (other than me) or some other person duly authorized by the Company.

14. **Notices**. Any notice, request, consent or approval required or permitted to be given under this Agreement or pursuant to law shall be sufficient if it is in writing, and if and when it is hand delivered or sent by regular mail, with postage prepaid, to my residence (as noted in the Company's records), or to the Company's principal office, as the case may be.

15. **Agreement to Perform Necessary Acts**. I agree to perform any further acts and execute and deliver any documents that may be reasonably necessary to carry out the provisions of this Agreement.

16. **Assignment**. This Agreement may not be assigned without the Company's prior written consent.

17. **Compliance with Law.** I agree to abide by all federal, state, and local laws, ordinances and regulations.

18. **Acknowledgment**. I acknowledge that I have had the opportunity to consult legal counsel in regard to this Agreement, that I have read and understand this Agreement, that I am fully

aware of its legal effect, and that I have entered into it freely and voluntarily and based on my own judgment and not on any representations or promises other than those contained in this Agreement.

IN WITNESS WHEREOF, the undersigned have executed this Agreement as of the dates set forth below.

CAUTION: THIS AGREEMENT CREATES IMPORTANT OBLIGATIONS OF TRUST AND AFFECTS THE CONSULTANT'S RIGHTS TO INVENTIONS AND OTHER INTELLECTUAL PROPERTY THE CONSULTANT MAY DEVELOP.

This agreement will be good for 14 days from this date of (Date). If a decision has not been made in that time a new proposal can be supplied.


Dated ___/___/___ Consultant Signature _____

Printed Name of Consultant: _____

By _____

Name _____

Title _____

# 13. If You Do Your Own Credit Reporting Letter

Date ___/___/___

Dear Mr. Debtor:

Your balance is seriously past due. In order to prevent this debt from being reported to the credit bureau and thus affecting your credit history, it is imperative that you pay this balance of $500.00 in full by August 10, 2004.

Please contact this office immediately upon receipt of this letter.

Sincerely,


# 14. Placing for Collection if No Payment Letter

Date ___/___/___

Debtor name

Address

Account# _____

Balance due _____

Dear Mr. Debtor:

The services of Babs Consulting were provided with the expectation that you would pay for them.

Your check needs to be received in our office within 48 hours of your receipt of this letter or we will place your account with an outside collection agency.

Sincerely,

# 15.  Small Claims if No Payment Letter

Date ___/___/___

Debtor name

Address

Account# _____

Balance due _____

Dear Mr. Debtor:

The enclosed small claim complaint paperwork will be filed with the (town) District Court if we do not receive your payment within ten (10) days of the date of this letter.

Please call me at 603-536-4090 or toll free at 877-318-2274 if you have any questions.

This is an attempt to collect a debt and any information obtained will be used for that purpose.

Sincerely,

# 16. Legal Proceedings Letter

Date ___/___/___

Debtor name

Address

Account# _____

Balance due _____

Dear Mr. Debtor:

### Your account is seriously past due!

We have tried to reach you and have not had a response. We have no Other alternative but to inform you that unless this amount is paid in full By (DATE) we will begin legal proceeding to collect this balance.

The choice is yours, please act wisely.

Sincerely,

You may also want to include payment options or a payment envelope with the letter. You could also send it certified to show a sense of urgency.

# 17.  Partial Payment Letter

Date ___/___/___

Debtor name

Address

Account# _____

Balance due _____

Dear Mr. Debtor:

Thank you for your payment of $100.00 towards your balance. The balance due of $_____ is past due.

Please mail your check for $400.00 today. A postpaid envelope is enclosed for your payment.

Sincerely,


# 18.  Friendly Reminder Letter

Date ___/___/___

Debtor name

Address

Account# _____

Balance due _____

Dear Mr. Debtor:

This is just a reminder that your payment of $_____ has not been received in our office. If you forgot to mail us your payment, please send it today. If you have already mailed your check, please disregard this reminder.

Thank you,

# 19. Confirmation of Payment Promise Letter

Date ___/___/___

Debtor name

Address

Account# _____

Balance due _____

### Confirmation of Payment

Dear Mr. Debtor:

This letter is to confirm the commitment you made in our telephone conversation. You stated that a check would be mailed on DATE in the amount of $100.00.

Thank you in advance for your payment.

This is an attempt to collect a debt and any information obtained will be used for that purpose.

Sincerely,

# 20. Request for Payment Letter

Date ___/___/___

Debtor name

Address

Account# _____

Balance due _____

Dear Mr. Debtor:

### Request for Payment

We have extended credit to you in good faith.

You have responded by not paying your balance of «Balance» and then ignoring our letters and phone calls.

If paid in full to this office all collection activity will be stopped, so please take this opportunity and pay this balance of $_____ today.

We accept Visa, MasterCard and Discover for your convenience.

This is an attempt to collect a debt and any information obtained will be used for that purpose.

Sincerely,

# 21. Fairness Letter

Date ___/___/___

Debtor name

Address

Account# _____

Balance due _____

Dear Mr. Debtor:

On several occasions, we have called to your attention the delinquent balance on your account of $_____. We have had no response to our calls or correspondence, and as of this morning we have not received your payment.

Fairness is something that we value very highly, and we are especially appreciative when it is extended to us. At the moment, it is missing in our relationship.

Too much time has gone by during which there has been no communication. Call me when you receive this letter. I can be reached toll free at (877) 318-2274 or (603) 536-4090.

This is an attempt to collect a debt and any information obtained will be used for that purpose.

Sincerely,

# 22. Ignoring Obligations Letter

Date ___/___/___

Debtor name

Address

Account# _____

Balance due _____

Dear Mr. Debtor:

We believe that we fulfilled our obligation to you by shipping quality products . At the time and place you requested. We, in turn, expect you to fulfill your obligation by paying for the merchandise.

If there is a problem, please provide us with an explanation so we can work together to resolve this.

Your payment today will be appreciated.

Sincerely,

# 23. Return Calls Letter

Date ___/___/___

Debtor name

Address

Account# _____

Balance due _____

Dear Mr. Debtor:

Ignoring your obligations does not make them go away.

This is especially true with seriously past-due debts. Late fees and interest can cause your balance to increase and without your response, there is nothing we can do to stop this.

We are willing to work with you and would appreciate the courtesy of a return call.

Sincerely,

# 24. 7 Days Letter

Date ___/___/___

Debtor name

Address

Account# _____

Balance due _____

Dear Mr. Debtor:

### SETTLEMENT OF ACCOUNT

Because you have failed to respond to our previous letters, this is an attempt at amicable resolution of your account.

Unless your remittance reaches our office within the next seven (7) days, we will be forced to take further action. We urge you to send your payment today or call to pay by credit card or with a check by phone.

We would like to resolve this matter and put it behind us as much as you do. But we are committed to taking whatever steps are necessary and proper to enforce payment of your obligation.

If your have previously made payment arrangements and are making your payments, please disregard this notice.

Sincerely,

# 25. Notice of Non-Payment of Rent

Date ___/___/___

Debtor name

Address

Account# _____

Balance due _____

Dear Mr. Debtor:

RE: Notice to Quit Premises - Non-Payment of Rent

You are hereby notified to quit and deliver up the premises you now hold as our tenant, to wit: in or within_____ days of the receipt of this notice.

This notice is given due to non-payment of rent. The present amount due for rent arrearage is $ __

You may redeem your tenancy by full payment of said arrears within_____ days of receipt of this notice.

Very truly yours,

Landlord

# 26. Company Credit Account Denial Letter

Date ___/___/___

Company name

Address

Dear Company:

We have reviewed your application for open account terms, and at this time are unable to open an account for your company. Should circumstances change in the future, please feel free to resubmit an application. We value your business, and hope to keep you as a customer. As a cash customer you will be advised of all special sales, and we know that you will find our prices and services competitive enough to allow us to continue serving you. If you have any questions about this decision, or if I may be of any help in any way with regard to your dealings with our company, please contact me at the above office.

Sincerely,


# 27. Individual Charge Account Denial Letter

Date ___/___/___

Name

Address

Dear Client:

We regret to inform you that we are unable to open a charge account for you at present due to information obtained from the following consumer reporting agency:

We wish to advise you that you have the right under federal law to obtain full disclosure of the nature and substance of all information on you that is contained in the files of the consumer credit reporting agency, with the exception of medical data, upon the presentment of proper identification.

Although we are unable to offer you credit terms, we would be pleased to welcome you as a customer and hope that we will be able to open a charge account for you some time in the future.

Thank you for submitting your application to us.

Sincerely,

# 28. Military Letter

Date ___/___/___

Debtor name

Address

Account# _____

Balance due _____

Dear Commanding General :

Title and name of debtor, owes us $_____. Our efforts to collect have been unsuccessful, and the debt is seriously delinquent.

We would greatly value your mentioning this to Title and name of debtor, not to require him to pay but to remind him of his moral obligation.

Your assistance is truly appreciated.

Sincerely,

# 29. Bad Check Letter

**Disclaimer: Be aware that some of these sample letters have legal, financial, or other implications. If you are not sure about the use of any letter, consult with an attorney first.**

Date ___/___/___

Debtor name

Address

Account# _____

Balance due _____

Dear Debtor:

This is to inform you that your check dated _____ , payable to _____ _____ , in the amount of $_____ , has been returned to us due to insufficient funds.

We realize that such mishaps do occur and therefore are bringing this matter to your attention so that you will take the opportunity to correct this error and issue us a new check.

It is our policy to retain the old check until a new check is issued and cleared as we have unfortunately realized that there are some people who do not honor their debts. If a new check is not issued and the old check does not clear we will pursue legal action to the full extend of the law.

We are confident that you will resolve this matter and look forward to doing business with you again in the future.

Our thanks for your attention to this matter.

Very truly yours,

# 30.  NSF Checks Letter

Date ___/___/___

Debtor name

Address

Account# _____

Balance due _____

Dear Debtor:

Your check dated ___/___/___ was returned to us for Insufficient Funds.

We will redeposit this check on ___/___/___. Please make sure there are sufficient funds to cover this check., which is $_____.

Sincerely,

# 31. Notice of Dishonor of Check and Demand for Payment Letter

Date ___/___/___

Debtor name

Address

Account# _____

Balance due _____

RE: Check No._____ in the amount of $_____ NSF FEE $_____

Dear Debtor:

Your check referenced above has been dishonored by the bank. Demand is hereby made pursuant to A.S. Section 09.68.115 that you pay the undersigned this sum in full within 15 days of the date of this letter. If this amount is not paid in full within 15 days of this letter, you could be held liable for damages in the amount of $100.00, or three (3) times the face amount of the check, whichever is GREATER.

A.S. §09.68.115 provides in relevant part:

(a) In an action against a person who issues a check that is dishonored, the plaintiff may recover damages in an amount equal to $100 or triple the amount of the check, whichever is greater, except that damages recovered under this section may not exceed the amount of the check by more than $1,000...

Under A.S. §09.68.115 you may also be held liable for court costs and other costs incurred in an action to collect this debt.

Your prompt attention to this important matter would be greatly appreciated.

Sincerely,

# 32. Check Returned for Closed Account Letter

Date ___/___/___

Debtor name

Address

Account# _____

Balance due _____

RE: Check No._____ in the amount of $_____ NSF FEE $_____

Dear Debtor:

Your check #_____ in the amount of $_____ was returned to us as Account Closed. Perhaps you closed the account not realizing this check was outstanding.

Please send a new check for $_____ to replace it today.

Sincerely,

# Appendix

# Acts & Laws

# A. The Fair Debt Collection Practices Act

The Fair Debt Collection Practices Act

## § 801. Short Title [15 USC 1601 note]

This title may be cited as the "Fair Debt Collection Practices Act."

## § 802. Congressional findings and declarations of purpose [15 USC 1692]

(a) There is abundant evidence of the use of abusive, deceptive, and unfair debt collection practices by many debt collectors. Abusive debt collection practices contribute to the number of personal bankruptcies, to marital instability, to the loss of jobs, and to invasions of individual privacy.

(b) Existing laws and procedures for redressing these injuries are inadequate to protect consumers.

(c) Means other than misrepresentation or other abusive debt collection practices are available for the effective collection of debts.

(d) Abusive debt collection practices are carried on to a substantial extent in interstate commerce and through means and instrumentalities of such commerce. Even where abusive debt collection practices are purely intrastate in character, they nevertheless directly affect interstate commerce.

(e) It is the purpose of this title to eliminate abusive debt collection practices by debt collectors, to insure that those debt collectors who refrain from using abusive debt collection practices are not competitively disadvantaged, and to promote consistent State action to protect consumers against debt collection abuses.

## § 803. Definitions [15 USC 1692a]

As used in this title —

(1) The term "Commission" means the Federal Trade Commission.

(2) The term "communication" means the conveying of information regarding a debt directly or indirectly to any person through any medium.

(3) The term "consumer" means any natural person obligated or allegedly obligated to pay any debt.

(4) The term "creditor" means any person who offers or extends credit creating a debt or to whom

a debt is owed, but such term does not include any person to the extent that he receives an assignment or transfer of a debt in default solely for the purpose of facilitating collection of such debt for another.

(5) The term "debt" means any obligation or alleged obligation of a consumer to pay money arising out of a transaction in which the money, property, insurance or services which are the subject of the transaction are primarily for personal, family, or household purposes, whether or not such obligation has been reduced to judgment.

(6) The term "debt collector" means any person who uses any instrumentality of interstate commerce or the mails in any business the principal purpose of which is the collection of any debts, or who regularly collects or attempts to collect, directly or indirectly, debts owed or due or asserted to be owed or due another. Notwithstanding the exclusion provided by clause (F) of the last sentence of this paragraph, the term includes any creditor who, in the process of collecting his own debts, uses any name other than his own which would indicate that a third person is collecting or attempting to collect such debts. For the purpose of section 808(6), such term also includes any person who uses any instrumentality of interstate commerce or the mails in any business the principal purpose of which is the enforcement of security interests. The term does not include –

(A) any officer or employee of a creditor while, in the name of the creditor, collecting debts for such creditor;

(B) any person while acting as a debt collector for another person, both of whom are related by common ownership or affiliated by corporate control, if the person acting as a debt collector does so only for persons to whom it is so related or affiliated and if the principal business of such person is not the collection of debts;

(C) any officer or employee of the United States or any State to the extent that collecting or attempting to collect any debt is in the performance of his official duties;

(D) any person while serving or attempting to serve legal process on any other person in connection with the judicial enforcement of any debt;

(E) any nonprofit organization which, at the request of consumers, performs bona fide consumer credit counseling and assists consumers in the liquidation of their debts by receiving payments from such consumers and distributing such amounts to creditors; and

(F) any person collecting or attempting to collect any debt owed or due or asserted to be owed or due another to the extent such activity (i) is incidental to a bona fide fiduciary obligation or a bona fide escrow arrangement; (ii) concerns a debt which was originated by such person; (iii) concerns a debt which was not in default at the time it was obtained by such person; or (iv) concerns a debt obtained by such person as a secured party in a commercial credit transaction involving the creditor.

(7) The term "location information" means a consumer's place of abode and his telephone number at such place, or his place of employment.

(8) The term "State" means any State, territory, or possession of the United States, the District of Columbia, the Commonwealth of Puerto Rico, or any political subdivision of any of the foregoing.

## § 804. Acquisition of location information [15 USC 1692b]

Any debt collector communicating with any person other than the consumer for the purpose of acquiring location information about the consumer shall —

(1) identify himself, state that he is confirming or correcting location information concerning the consumer, and, only if expressly requested, identify his employer;

(2) not state that such consumer owes any debt;

(3) not communicate with any such person more than once unless requested to do so by such person or unless the debt collector reasonably believes that the earlier response of such person is erroneous or incomplete and that such person now has correct or complete location information;

(4) not communicate by post card;

(5) not use any language or symbol on any envelope or in the contents of any communication effected by the mails or telegram that indicates that the debt collector is in the debt collection business or that the communication relates to the collection of a debt; and

(6) after the debt collector knows the consumer is represented by an attorney with regard to the subject debt and has knowledge of, or can readily ascertain, such attorney's name and address, not communicate with any person other than that attorney, unless the attorney fails to respond within a reasonable period of time to the communication from the debt collector.

## § 805. Communication in connection with debt collection [15 USC 1692c]

(a) COMMUNICATION WITH THE CONSUMER GENERALLY. Without the prior consent of the consumer given directly to the debt collector or the express permission of a court of competent jurisdiction, a debt collector may not communicate with a consumer in connection with the collection of any debt –

(1) at any unusual time or place or a time or place known or which should be known to be inconvenient to the consumer. In the absence of knowledge of circumstances to the contrary, a debt collector shall assume that the convenient time for communicating with a consumer is after 8 o'clock antimeridian and before 9 o'clock postmeridian, local time at the consumer's location;

(2) if the debt collector knows the consumer is represented by an attorney with respect to such debt and has knowledge of, or can readily ascertain, such attorney's name and address, unless the attorney fails to respond within a reasonable period of time to a communication from the debt collector or unless the attorney consents to direct communication with the consumer; or

(3) at the consumer's place of employment if the debt collector knows or has reason to know that the consumer's employer prohibits the consumer from receiving such communication.

(b) COMMUNICATION WITH THIRD PARTIES. Except as provided in section 804, without the prior consent of the consumer given directly to the debt collector, or the express permission of a court of competent jurisdiction, or as reasonably necessary to effectuate a postjudgment judicial remedy, a debt collector may not communicate, in connection with the collection of any debt, with any person other than a consumer, his attorney, a consumer reporting agency if otherwise permitted by law, the creditor, the attorney of the creditor, or the attorney of the debt collector.

(c) CEASING COMMUNICATION. If a consumer notifies a debt collector in writing that the consumer refuses to pay a debt or that the consumer wishes the debt collector to cease further communication with the consumer, the debt collector shall not communicate further with the consumer with respect to such debt, except –

(1) to advise the consumer that the debt collector's further efforts are being terminated;

(2) to notify the consumer that the debt collector or creditor may invoke specified remedies which are ordinarily invoked by such debt collector or creditor; or

(3) where applicable, to notify the consumer that the debt collector or creditor intends to invoke a specified remedy.

If such notice from the consumer is made by mail, notification shall be complete upon receipt.

(d) For the purpose of this section, the term "consumer" includes the consumer's spouse, parent (if the consumer is a minor), guardian, executor, or administrator.

## § 806. Harassment or abuse [15 USC 1692d]

A debt collector may not engage in any conduct the natural consequence of which is to harass, oppress, or abuse any person in connection with the collection of a debt. Without limiting the general application of the foregoing, the following conduct is a violation of this section:

(1) The use or threat of use of violence or other criminal means to harm the physical person, reputation, or property of any person.

(2) The use of obscene or profane language or language the natural consequence of which is to abuse the hearer or reader.

(3) The publication of a list of consumers who allegedly refuse to pay debts, except to a consumer reporting agency or to persons meeting the requirements of section 603(f) or 604(3)[1] of this Act.

(4) The advertisement for sale of any debt to coerce payment of the debt.

(5) Causing a telephone to ring or engaging any person in telephone conversation repeatedly or continuously with intent to annoy, abuse, or harass any person at the called number.

(6) Except as provided in section 804, the placement of telephone calls without meaningful disclosure of the caller's identity.

## § 807. False or misleading representations [15 USC 1692e]

A debt collector may not use any false, deceptive, or misleading representation or means in connection with the collection of any debt. Without limiting the general application of the foregoing, the following conduct is a violation of this section:

(1) The false representation or implication that the debt collector is vouched for, bonded by, or affiliated with the United States or any State, including the use of any badge, uniform, or facsimile thereof.

(2) The false representation of –

(A) the character, amount, or legal status of any debt; or

(B) any services rendered or compensation which may be lawfully received by any debt collector for the collection of a debt.

(3) The false representation or implication that any individual is an attorney or that any communication is from an attorney.

(4) The representation or implication that nonpayment of any debt will result in the arrest or imprisonment of any person or the seizure, garnishment, attachment, or sale of any property or wages of any person unless such action is lawful and the debt collector or creditor intends to take such action.

(5) The threat to take any action that cannot legally be taken or that is not intended to be taken.

(6) The false representation or implication that a sale, referral, or other transfer of any interest in a debt shall cause the consumer to –

(A) lose any claim or defense to payment of the debt; or

(B) become subject to any practice prohibited by this title.

(7) The false representation or implication that the consumer committed any crime or other conduct in order to disgrace the consumer.

(8) Communicating or threatening to communicate to any person credit information which is known or which should be known to be false, including the failure to communicate that a disputed debt is disputed.

(9) The use or distribution of any written communication which simulates or is falsely represented to be a document authorized, issued, or approved by any court, official, or agency of the United States or any State, or which creates a false impression as to its source, authorization, or approval.

(10) The use of any false representation or deceptive means to collect or attempt to collect any debt or to obtain information concerning a consumer.

(11) The failure to disclose in the initial written communication with the consumer and, in addition, if the initial communication with the consumer is oral, in that initial oral communication, that the debt collector is attempting to collect a debt and that any information obtained will be used for that purpose, and the failure to disclose in subsequent communications that the communication

is from a debt collector, except that this paragraph shall not apply to a formal pleading made in connection with a legal action.

(12) The false representation or implication that accounts have been turned over to innocent purchasers for value.

(13) The false representation or implication that documents are legal process.

(14) The use of any business, company, or organization name other than the true name of the debt collector's business, company, or organization.

(15) The false representation or implication that documents are not legal process forms or do not require action by the consumer.

(16) The false representation or implication that a debt collector operates or is employed by a consumer reporting agency as defined by section 603(f) of this Act.

## § 808. Unfair practices [15 USC 1692f]

A debt collector may not use unfair or unconscionable means to collect or attempt to collect any debt. Without limiting the general application of the foregoing, the following conduct is a violation of this section:

(1) The collection of any amount (including any interest, fee, charge, or expense incidental to the principal obligation) unless such amount is expressly authorized by the agreement creating the debt or permitted by law.

(2) The acceptance by a debt collector from any person of a check or other payment instrument postdated by more than five days unless such person is notified in writing of the debt collector's intent to deposit such check or instrument not more than ten nor less than three business days prior to such deposit.

(3) The solicitation by a debt collector of any postdated check or other postdated payment instrument for the purpose of threatening or instituting criminal prosecution.

(4) Depositing or threatening to deposit any postdated check or other postdated payment instrument prior to the date on such check or instrument.

(5) Causing charges to be made to any person for communications by concealment of the true propose of the communication. Such charges include, but are not limited to, collect telephone calls and telegram fees.

(6) Taking or threatening to take any nonjudicial action to effect dispossession or disablement of property if –

   (A) there is no present right to possession of the property claimed as collateral through an enforceable security interest;

   (B) there is no present intention to take possession of the property; or

(C) the property is exempt by law from such dispossession or disablement.

(7) Communicating with a consumer regarding a debt by post card.

(8) Using any language or symbol, other than the debt collector's address, on any envelope when communicating with a consumer by use of the mails or by telegram, except that a debt collector may use his business name if such name does not indicate that he is in the debt collection business.

### § 809. Validation of debts [15 USC 1692g]

(a) Within five days after the initial communication with a consumer in connection with the collection of any debt, a debt collector shall, unless the following information is contained in the initial communication or the consumer has paid the debt, send the consumer a written notice containing –

(1) the amount of the debt;

(2) the name of the creditor to whom the debt is owed;

(3) a statement that unless the consumer, within thirty days after receipt of the notice, disputes the validity of the debt, or any portion thereof, the debt will be assumed to be valid by the debt collector;

(4) a statement that if the consumer notifies the debt collector in writing within the thirty-day period that the debt, or any portion thereof, is disputed, the debt collector will obtain verification of the debt or a copy of a judgment against the consumer and a copy of such verification or judgment will be mailed to the consumer by the debt collector; and

(5) a statement that, upon the consumer's written request within the thirty-day period, the debt collector will provide the consumer with the name and address of the original creditor, if different from the current creditor.

(b) If the consumer notifies the debt collector in writing within the thirty-day period described in subsection (a) that the debt, or any portion thereof, is disputed, or that the consumer requests the name and address of the original creditor, the debt collector shall cease collection of the debt, or any disputed portion thereof, until the debt collector obtains verification of the debt or any copy of a judgment, or the name and address of the original creditor, and a copy of such verification or judgment, or name and address of the original creditor, is mailed to the consumer by the debt collector.

(c) The failure of a consumer to dispute the validity of a debt under this section may not be construed by any court as an admission of liability by the consumer.

### § 810. Multiple debts [15 USC 1692h]

If any consumer owes multiple debts and makes any single payment to any debt collector with respect to such debts, such debt collector may not apply such payment to any debt which is disputed by the consumer and, where applicable, shall apply such payment in accordance with the consumer's directions.

### § 811. Legal actions by debt collectors [15 USC 1692i]

(a) Any debt collector who brings any legal action on a debt against any consumer shall –

(1) in the case of an action to enforce an interest in real property securing the consumer's obligation, bring such action only in a judicial district or similar legal entity in which such real property is located; or

(2) in the case of an action not described in paragraph (1), bring such action only in the judicial district or similar legal entity –

(A) in which such consumer signed the contract sued upon; or

(B) in which such consumer resides at the commencement of the action.

(C) Nothing in this title shall be construed to authorize the bringing of legal actions by debt collectors.

### § 812. Furnishing certain deceptive forms [15 USC 1692j]

(a) It is unlawful to design, compile, and furnish any form knowing that such form would be used to create the false belief in a consumer that a person other than the creditor of such consumer is participating in the collection of or in an attempt to collect a debt such consumer allegedly owes such creditor, when in fact such person is not so participating.

(b) Any person who violates this section shall be liable to the same extent and in the same manner as a debt collector is liable under section 813 for failure to comply with a provision of this title.

### § 813. Civil liability [15 USC 1692k]

(a) Except as otherwise provided by this section, any debt collector who fails to comply with any provision of this title with respect to any person is liable to such person in an amount equal to the sum of –

(1) any actual damage sustained by such person as a result of such failure;

(2) (A) in the case of any action by an individual, such additional damages as the court may allow, but not exceeding $1,000; or (B) in the case of a class action, (i) such amount for each named plaintiff as could be recovered under subparagraph (A), and (ii) such amount as the court may allow for all other class members, without regard to a minimum individual recovery, not to exceed the lesser of $500,000 or 1 per centum of the net worth of the debt collector; and

(3) in the case of any successful action to enforce the foregoing liability, the costs of the action, together with a reasonable attorney's fee as determined by the court. On a finding by

the court that an action under this section was brought in bad faith and for the purpose of harassment, the court may award to the defendant attorney's fees reasonable in relation to the work expended and costs.

(b) In determining the amount of liability in any action under subsection (a), the court shall consider, among other relevant factors –

(1) in any individual action under subsection (a)(2)(A), the frequency and persistence of noncompliance by the debt collector, the nature of such noncompliance, and the extent to which such noncompliance was intentional; or

(2) in any class action under subsection (a)(2)(B), the frequency and persistence of noncompliance by the debt collector, the nature of such noncompliance, the resources of the debt collector, the number of persons adversely affected, and the extent to which the debt collector's noncompliance was intentional.

(c) A debt collector may not be held liable in any action brought under this title if the debt collector shows by a preponderance of evidence that the violation was not intentional and resulted from a bona fide error notwithstanding the maintenance of procedures reasonably adapted to avoid any such error.

(d) An action to enforce any liability created by this title may be brought in any appropriate United States district court without regard to the amount in controversy, or in any other court of competent jurisdiction, within one year from the date on which the violation occurs.

(e) No provision of this section imposing any liability shall apply to any act done or omitted in good faith in conformity with any advisory opinion of the Commission, notwithstanding that after such act or omission has occurred, such opinion is amended, rescinded, or determined by judicial or other authority to be invalid for any reason.

### § 814. Administrative enforcement [15 USC 1692l]

(a) Compliance with this title shall be enforced by the Commission, except to the extend that enforcement of the requirements imposed under this title is specifically committed to another agency under subsection (b). For purpose of the exercise by the Commission of its functions and powers under the Federal Trade Commission Act, a violation of this title shall be deemed an unfair or deceptive act or practice in violation of that Act. All of the functions and powers of the Commission under the Federal Trade Commission Act are available to the Commission to enforce compliance by any person with this title, irrespective of whether that person is engaged in commerce or meets any other jurisdictional tests in the Federal Trade Commission Act, including the power to enforce the provisions of this title in the same manner as if the violation had been a violation of a Federal Trade Commission trade regulation rule.

(b) Compliance with any requirements imposed under this title shall be enforced under –

(1) section 8 of the Federal Deposit Insurance Act, in the case of –

(A) national banks, by the Comptroller of the Currency;

(B) member banks of the Federal Reserve System (other than national banks), by the Federal Reserve Board; and

(C) banks the deposits or accounts of which are insured by the Federal Deposit Insurance Corporation (other than members of the Federal Reserve System), by the Board of Directors of the Federal Deposit Insurance Corporation;

(2) section 5(d) of the Home Owners Loan Act of 1933, section 407 of the National Housing Act, and sections 6(i) and 17 of the Federal Home Loan Bank Act, by the Federal Home Loan Bank Board (acting directing or through the Federal Savings and Loan Insurance Corporation), in the case of any institution subject to any of those provisions;

(3) the Federal Credit Union Act, by the Administrator of the National Credit Union Administration with respect to any Federal credit union;

(4) subtitle IV of Title 49, by the Interstate Commerce Commission with respect to any common carrier subject to such subtitle;

(5) the Federal Aviation Act of 1958, by the Secretary of Transportation with respect to any air carrier or any foreign air carrier subject to that Act; and

(6) the Packers and Stockyards Act, 1921 (except as provided in section 406 of that Act), by the Secretary of Agriculture with respect to any activities subject to that Act.

(c) For the purpose of the exercise by any agency referred to in subsection (b) of its powers under any Act referred to in that subsection, a violation of any requirement imposed under this title shall be deemed to be a violation of a requirement imposed under that Act. In addition to its powers under any provision of law specifically referred to in subsection (b), each of the agencies referred to in that subsection may exercise, for the purpose of enforcing compliance with any requirement imposed under this title any other authority conferred on it by law, except as provided in subsection (d).

(d) Neither the Commission nor any other agency referred to in subsection (b) may promulgate trade regulation rules or other regulations with respect to the collection of debts by debt collectors as defined in this title.

### § 815. Reports to Congress by the Commission [15 USC 1692m]

(a) Not later than one year after the effective date of this title and at one-year intervals thereafter, the Commission shall make reports to the Congress concerning the administration of its functions under this title, including such recommendations as the Commission deems necessary or appropriate. In addition, each report of the Commission shall include its assessment of the extent to which compliance with this title is being achieved and a summary of the enforcement actions taken by the Commission under section 814 of this title.

(b) In the exercise of its functions under this title, the Commission may obtain upon request the views of any other Federal agency which exercises enforcement functions under section 814 of this title.

### § 816. Relation to State laws [15 USC 1692n]

This title does not annul, alter, or affect, or exempt any person subject to the provisions of this title from complying with the laws of any State with respect to debt collection practices, except to the extent that those laws are inconsistent with any provision of this title, and then only to the extent of the inconsistency. For purposes of this section, a State law is not inconsistent with this title if the protection such law affords any consumer is greater than the protection provided by this title.

### § 817. Exemption for State regulation [15 USC 1692o]

The Commission shall by regulation exempt from the requirements of this title any class of debt collection practices within any State if the Commission determines that under the law of that State that class of debt collection practices is subject to requirements substantially similar to those imposed by this title, and that there is adequate provision for enforcement.

### § 818. Effective date [15 USC 1692 note]

This title takes effect upon the expiration of six months after the date of its enactment, but section 809 shall apply only with respect to debts for which the initial attempt to collect occurs after such effective date.

Approved September 20, 1977

END NOTES

1. So in original; however, should read "604(a)(3)."

**LEGISLATIVE HISTORY:**

Public Law 95-109 [H.R. 5294]

HOUSE REPORT No. 95-131 (Comm. on Banking, Finance, and Urban Affairs).

SENATE REPORT No. 95-382 (Comm. on Banking, Housing, and Urban Affairs).

CONGRESSIONAL RECORD, Vol. 123 (1977):

Apr. 4, considered and passed House.

Aug. 5, considered and passed Senate, amended.

Sept. 8, House agreed to Senate amendment.

WEEKLY COMPILATION OF PRESIDENTIAL DOCUMENTS, Vol. 13, No. 39:

Sept. 20, Presidential statement.

**AMENDMENTS:**

SECTION 621, SUBSECTIONS (b)(3), (b)(4) and (b)(5) were amended to transfer certain administrative enforcement responsibilities, pursuant to Pub. L. 95-473, § 3(b), Oct. 17, 1978. 92 Stat. 166; Pub. L. 95-630, Title V. § 501, November 10, 1978, 92 Stat. 3680; Pub. L. 98-443, § 9(h), Oct. 4, 1984, 98 Stat. 708.

SECTION 803, SUBSECTION (6), defining "debt collector," was amended to repeal the attorney at law exemption at former Section (6)(F) and to redesignate Section 803(6)(G) pursuant to Pub. L. 99-361, July 9, 1986, 100 Stat. 768. For legislative history, *see* H.R. 237, HOUSE REPORT No. 99-405 (Comm. on Banking, Finance and Urban Affairs). CONGRESSIONAL RECORD: Vol. 131 (1985): Dec. 2, considered and passed House. Vol. 132 (1986): June 26, considered and passed Senate.

SECTION 807, SUBSECTION (11), was amended to affect when debt collectors must state (a) that they are attempting to collect a debt and (b) that information obtained will be used for that purpose, pursuant to Pub. L. 104-208 § 2305, 110 Stat. 3009 (Sept. 30, 1996).

# B. FAIR CREDIT REPORTING ACT

(Reprinted with permission Federal Trade Commission *www.ftc.gov*)

## § 601. Short title

This title may be cited as the Fair Credit Reporting Act.

## § 602. Congressional findings and statement of purpose [15 U.S.C. § 1681]

(a) Accuracy and fairness of credit reporting. The Congress makes the following findings:

(1) The banking system is dependent upon fair and accurate credit reporting. Inaccurate credit reports directly impair the efficiency of the banking system, and unfair credit reporting methods undermine the public confidence which is essential to the continued functioning of the banking system.

(2) An elaborate mechanism has been developed for investigating and evaluating the credit worthiness, credit standing, credit capacity, character, and general reputation of consumers.

(3) Consumer reporting agencies have assumed a vital role in assembling and evaluating consumer credit and other information on consumers.

(4) There is a need to insure that consumer reporting agencies exercise their grave responsibilities with fairness, impartiality, and a respect for the consumer's right to privacy.

(b) Reasonable procedures. It is the purpose of this title to require that consumer reporting agencies adopt reasonable procedures for meeting the needs of commerce for consumer credit, personnel, insurance, and other information in a manner which is fair and equitable to the consumer, with regard to the confidentiality, accuracy, relevancy, and proper utilization of such information in accordance with the requirements of this title.

## § 603. Definitions; rules of construction [15 U.S.C. § 1681a]

(a) Definitions and rules of construction set forth in this section are applicable for the purposes of this title.

(b) The term "person" means any individual, partnership, corporation, trust, estate, cooperative, association, government or governmental subdivision or agency, or other entity.

(c) The term "consumer" means an individual.

(d) Consumer report.

(1) In general. The term "consumer report" means any written, oral, or other communication of any information by a consumer reporting agency bearing on a consumer's credit worthiness, credit standing, credit capacity, character, general reputation, personal characteristics, or mode of living which is used or expected to be used or collected in whole or in part for the purpose of serving as a factor in establishing the consumer's eligibility for

(A) credit or insurance to be used primarily for personal, family, or household purposes;

(B) employment purposes; or

(C) any other purpose authorized under section 604 [§ 1681b].

(2) Exclusions. The term "consumer report" does not include

(A) any

(i) report containing information solely as to transactions or experiences between the consumer and the person making the report;

(ii) communication of that information among persons related by common ownership or affiliated by corporate control; or

(iii) communication of other information among persons related by common ownership or affiliated by corporate control, if it is clearly and conspicuously disclosed to the consumer that the information may be communicated among such persons and the consumer is given the opportunity, before the time that the information is initially communicated, to direct that such information not be communicated among such persons;

(B) any authorization or approval of a specific extension of credit directly or indirectly by the issuer of a credit card or similar device;

(C) any report in which a person who has been requested by a third party to make a specific extension of credit directly or indirectly to a consumer conveys his or her decision with respect to such request, if the third party advises the consumer of the name and address of the person to whom the request was made, and such person makes the disclosures to the consumer required under section 615 [§ 1681m]; or

(D) a communication described in subsection (o).

(e) The term "investigative consumer report" means a consumer report or portion thereof in which information on a consumer's character, general reputation, personal characteristics, or mode of living is obtained through personal interviews with neighbors, friends, or associates of the consumer reported on or with others with whom he is acquainted or who may have knowledge concerning any such items of information. However, such information shall not include specific factual information on a consumer's credit record obtained directly from a creditor of the consumer or from a consumer reporting agency when such information was obtained directly from a creditor of the consumer or from the consumer.

(f) The term "consumer reporting agency" means any person which, for monetary fees, dues, or on a cooperative nonprofit basis, regularly engages in whole or in part in the practice of assembling or evaluating consumer credit information or other information on consumers for the purpose of furnishing consumer reports to third parties, and which uses any means or facility of interstate commerce for the purpose of preparing or furnishing consumer reports.

(g) The term "file," when used in connection with information on any consumer, means all of the information on that consumer recorded and retained by a consumer reporting agency regardless of how the information is stored.

(h) The term "employment purposes" when used in connection with a consumer report means a report used for the purpose of evaluating a consumer for employment, promotion, reassignment or retention as an employee.

(i) The term "medical information" means information or records obtained, with the consent of the individual to whom it relates, from licensed physicians or medical practitioners, hospitals, clinics, or other medical or medically related facilities.

(j) Definitions relating to child support obligations.

(1) Overdue support. The term "overdue support" has the meaning given to such term in section 666(e) of title 42 [Social Security Act, 42 U.S.C. § 666(e)].

(2) State or local child support enforcement agency. The term "State or local child support enforcement agency" means a State or local agency which administers a State or local program for establishing and enforcing child support obligations.

(k) Adverse action.

(1) Actions included. The term "adverse action"

(A) has the same meaning as in section 701(d)(6) of the Equal Credit Opportunity Act; and

(B) means

(i) a denial or cancellation of, an increase in any charge for, or a reduction or other adverse or unfavorable change in the terms of coverage or amount of, any insurance, existing or applied for, in connection with the underwriting of insurance;

(ii) a denial of employment or any other decision for employment purposes that adversely affects any current or prospective employee;

(iii) a denial or cancellation of, an increase in any charge for, or any other adverse or unfavorable change in the terms of, any license or benefit described in section 604(a)(3)(D) [§ 1681b]; and

(iv) an action taken or determination that is

(I) made in connection with an application that was made by, or a transaction that was initiated by, any consumer, or in connection with a review of an account under section 604(a)(3)(F)(ii)[§ 1681b]; and

(II) adverse to the interests of the consumer.

(2) Applicable findings, decisions, commentary, and orders. For purposes of any determination

of whether an action is an adverse action under paragraph (1)(A), all appropriate final findings, decisions, commentary, and orders issued under section 701(d)(6) of the Equal Credit Opportunity Act by the Board of Governors of the Federal Reserve System or any court shall apply.

(l) Firm offer of credit or insurance. The term "firm offer of credit or insurance" means any offer of credit or insurance to a consumer that will be honored if the consumer is determined, based on information in a consumer report on the consumer, to meet the specific criteria used to select the consumer for the offer, except that the offer may be further conditioned on one or more of the following:

(1) The consumer being determined, based on information in the consumer's application for the credit or insurance, to meet specific criteria bearing on credit worthiness or insurability, as applicable, that are established

(A) before selection of the consumer for the offer; and

(B) for the purpose of determining whether to extend credit or insurance pursuant to the offer.

(2) Verification

(A) that the consumer continues to meet the specific criteria used to select the consumer for the offer, by using information in a consumer report on the consumer, information in the consumer's application for the credit or insurance, or other information bearing on the credit worthiness or insurability of the consumer; or

(B) of the information in the consumer's application for the credit or insurance, to determine that the consumer meets the specific criteria bearing on credit worthiness or insurability.

(3) The consumer furnishing any collateral that is a requirement for the extension of the credit or insurance that was

(A) established before selection of the consumer for the offer of credit or insurance; and

(B) disclosed to the consumer in the offer of credit or insurance.

(m) Credit or insurance transaction that is not initiated by the consumer. The term "credit or insurance transaction that is not initiated by the consumer" does not include the use of a consumer report by a person with which the consumer has an account or insurance policy, for purposes of

(1) reviewing the account or insurance policy; or

(2) collecting the account.

(n) State. The term "State" means any State, the Commonwealth of Puerto Rico, the District of Columbia, and any territory or possession of the United States.

(o) Excluded communications. A communication is described in this subsection if it is a communication

    (1) that, but for subsection (d)(2)(D), would be an investigative consumer report;

    (2) that is made to a prospective employer for the purpose of

        (A) procuring an employee for the employer; or

        (B) procuring an opportunity for a natural person to work for the employer;

    (3) that is made by a person who regularly performs such procurement;

    (4) that is not used by any person for any purpose other than a purpose described in subparagraph (A) or (B) of paragraph (2); and

    (5) with respect to which

        (A) the consumer who is the subject of the communication

            (i) consents orally or in writing to the nature and scope of the communication, before the collection of any information for the purpose of making the communication;

            (ii) consents orally or in writing to the making of the communication to a prospective employer, before the making of the communication; and

            (iii) in the case of consent under clause (i) or (ii) given orally, is provided written confirmation of that consent by the person making the communication, not later than 3 business days after the receipt of the consent by that person;

        (B) the person who makes the communication does not, for the purpose of making the communication, make any inquiry that if made by a prospective employer of the consumer who is the subject of the communication would violate any applicable Federal or State equal employment opportunity law or regulation; and

        (C) the person who makes the communication

            (i) discloses in writing to the consumer who is the subject of the communication, not later than 5 business days after receiving any request from the consumer for such disclosure, the nature and substance of all information in the consumer's file at the time of the request, except that the sources of any information that is acquired solely for use in making the communication and is actually used for no other purpose, need not be disclosed other than under appropriate discovery procedures in any court of competent jurisdiction in which an action is brought; and

            (ii) notifies the consumer who is the subject of the communication, in writing, of the consumer's right to request the information described in clause (i).

(p) Consumer reporting agency that compiles and maintains files on consumers on a nationwide basis. The term "consumer reporting agency that compiles and maintains files on consumers on a nationwide basis" means a consumer reporting agency that regularly engages in the practice of assembling or evaluating, and maintaining, for the purpose of furnishing consumer reports to third parties bearing on a consumer's credit worthiness, credit standing, or credit capacity, each of the following regarding consumers residing nationwide:

(1) Public record information.

(2) Credit account information from persons who furnish that information regularly and in the ordinary course of business.

## § 604. Permissible purposes of consumer reports [15 U.S.C. § 1681b]

(a) In general. Subject to subsection (c), any consumer reporting agency may furnish a consumer report under the following circumstances and no other:

(1) In response to the order of a court having jurisdiction to issue such an order, or a subpoena issued in connection with proceedings before a Federal grand jury.

(2) In accordance with the written instructions of the consumer to whom it relates.

(3) To a person which it has reason to believe

(A) intends to use the information in connection with a credit transaction involving the consumer on whom the information is to be furnished and involving the extension of credit to, or review or collection of an account of, the consumer; or

(B) intends to use the information for employment purposes; or

(C) intends to use the information in connection with the underwriting of insurance involving the consumer; or

(D) intends to use the information in connection with a determination of the consumer's eligibility for a license or other benefit granted by a governmental instrumentality required by law to consider an applicant's financial responsibility or status; or

(E) intends to use the information, as a potential investor or servicer, or current insurer, in connection with a valuation of, or an assessment of the credit or prepayment risks associated with, an existing credit obligation; or

(F) otherwise has a legitimate business need for the information

(i) in connection with a business transaction that is initiated by the consumer; or

(ii) to review an account to determine whether the consumer continues to meet the terms of the account.

(4) In response to a request by the head of a State or local child support enforcement agency (or a State or local government official authorized by the head of such an agency), if the person making the request certifies to the consumer reporting agency that

(A) the consumer report is needed for the purpose of establishing an individual's capacity to make child support payments or determining the appropriate level of such payments;

(B) the paternity of the consumer for the child to which the obligation relates has been established or acknowledged by the consumer in accordance with State laws under which the obligation arises (if required by those laws);

(C) the person has provided at least 10 days' prior notice to the consumer whose report is requested, by certified or registered mail to the last known address of the consumer, that the report will be requested; and

(D) the consumer report will be kept confidential, will be used solely for a purpose described in subparagraph (A), and will not be used in connection with any other civil, administrative, or criminal proceeding, or for any other purpose.

(5) To an agency administering a State plan under Section 454 of the Social Security Act (42 U.S.C. § 654) for use to set an initial or modified child support award.

(b) Conditions for furnishing and using consumer reports for employment purposes.

(1) Certification from user. A consumer reporting agency may furnish a consumer report for employment purposes only if

(A) the person who obtains such report from the agency certifies to the agency that

(i) the person has complied with paragraph (2) with respect to the consumer report, and the person will comply with paragraph (3) with respect to the consumer report if paragraph (3) becomes applicable; and

(ii) information from the consumer report will not be used in violation of any applicable Federal or State equal employment opportunity law or regulation; and

(B) the consumer reporting agency provides with the report, or has previously provided, a summary of the consumer's rights under this title, as prescribed by the Federal Trade Commission under section 609(c)(3) [§ 1681g].

(2) Disclosure to consumer.

(A) In general. Except as provided in subparagraph (B), a person may not procure a consumer report, or cause a consumer report to be procured, for employment purposes with respect to any consumer, unless—

(i) a clear and conspicuous disclosure has been made in writing to the consumer at any time before the report is procured or caused to be procured, in a document that consists solely of the disclosure, that a consumer report may be obtained for employment purposes; and

(ii) the consumer has authorized in writing (which authorization may be made on the document referred to in clause (i)) the procurement of the report by that person.

(B) Application by mail, telephone, computer, or other similar means. If a consumer described in subparagraph (C) applies for employment by mail, telephone, computer, or other similar means, at any time before a consumer report is procured or caused to be procured in connection with that application—

(i) the person who procures the consumer report on the consumer for employment purposes shall provide to the consumer, by oral, written, or electronic means, notice that a consumer report may be obtained for employment purposes, and a summary of the consumer's rights under section 615(a)(3); and

(ii) the consumer shall have consented, orally, in writing, or electronically to the procurement of the report by that person.

(C) Scope. Subparagraph (B) shall apply to a person procuring a consumer report on a consumer in connection with the consumer's application for employment only if—

(i) the consumer is applying for a position over which the Secretary of Transportation has the power to establish qualifications and maximum hours of service pursuant to the provisions of section 31502 of title 49, or a position subject to safety regulation by a State transportation agency; and

(ii) as of the time at which the person procures the report or causes the report to be procured the only interaction between the consumer and the person in connection with that employment application has been by mail, telephone, computer, or other similar means.

(3) Conditions on use for adverse actions.

(A) In general. Except as provided in subparagraph (B), in using a consumer report for employment purposes, before taking any adverse action based in whole or in part on the report, the person intending to take such adverse action shall provide to the consumer to whom the report relates—

(i) a copy of the report; and

(ii) a description in writing of the rights of the consumer under this title, as prescribed by the Federal Trade Commission under section 609(c)(3).

(B) Application by mail, telephone, computer, or other similar means.

(i) If a consumer described in subparagraph (C) applies for employment by mail, telephone, computer, or other similar means, and if a person who has procured a consumer report on the consumer for employment purposes takes adverse action on the employment application based in whole or in part on the report, then the person must provide to the consumer to whom the report relates, in lieu of the notices required under subparagraph (A) of this section and under section 615(a), within 3 business days of taking such action, an oral, written or electronic notification—

(I) that adverse action has been taken based in whole or in part on a consumer report received from a consumer reporting agency;

(II) of the name, address and telephone number of the consumer reporting agency that furnished the consumer report (including a toll-free telephone number established by the agency if the agency compiles and maintains files on consumers on a nationwide basis);

(III) that the consumer reporting agency did not make the decision to take the adverse action and is unable to provide to the consumer the specific reasons why the adverse action was taken; and

(IV) that the consumer may, upon providing proper identification, request a free copy of a report and may dispute with the consumer reporting agency the accuracy or completeness of any information in a report.

(ii) If, under clause (B)(i)(IV), the consumer requests a copy of a consumer report from the person who procured the report, then, within 3 business days of receiving the consumer's request, together with proper identification, the person must send or provide to the consumer a copy of a report and a copy of the consumer's rights as prescribed by the Federal Trade Commission under section 609(c)(3).

(C) Scope. Subparagraph (B) shall apply to a person procuring a consumer report on a consumer in connection with the consumer's application for employment only if—

(i) the consumer is applying for a position over which the Secretary of Transportation has the power to establish qualifications and maximum hours of service pursuant to the provisions of section 31502 of title 49, or a position subject to safety regulation by a State transportation agency; and

(ii) as of the time at which the person procures the report or causes the report to be procured the only interaction between the consumer and the person in connection with that employment application has been by mail, telephone, computer, or other similar means.

(4) Exception for national security investigations.

(A) In general. In the case of an agency or department of the United States Government which seeks to obtain and use a consumer report for employment purposes, paragraph (3) shall not apply to any adverse action by such agency or department which is based in part on such consumer report, if the head of such agency or department makes a written finding that—

(i) the consumer report is relevant to a national security investigation of such agency or department;

(ii) the investigation is within the jurisdiction of such agency or department;

(iii) there is reason to believe that compliance with paragraph (3) will—

(I) endanger the life or physical safety of any person;

(II) result in flight from prosecution;

(III) result in the destruction of, or tampering with, evidence relevant to the investigation;

(IV) result in the intimidation of a potential witness relevant to the investigation;

(V) result in the compromise of classified information; or

(VI) otherwise seriously jeopardize or unduly delay the investigation or another official proceeding.

(B) Notification of consumer upon conclusion of investigation. Upon the conclusion of a national security investigation described in subparagraph (A), or upon the determination that the exception under subparagraph (A) is no longer required for the reasons set forth in such subparagraph, the official exercising the authority in such subparagraph shall provide to the consumer who is the subject of the consumer report with regard to which such finding was made—

(i) a copy of such consumer report with any classified information redacted as necessary;

(ii) notice of any adverse action which is based, in part, on the consumer report; and

(iii) the identification with reasonable specificity of the nature of the investigation for which the consumer report was sought.

(C) Delegation by head of agency or department. For purposes of subparagraphs (A) and (B), the head of any agency or department of the United States Government may delegate his or her authorities under this paragraph to an official of such agency or department who has personnel security responsibilities and is a member of the Senior Executive Service or equivalent civilian or military rank.

(D) Report to the congress. Not later than January 31 of each year, the head of each agency and department of the United States Government that exercised authority under this paragraph during the preceding year shall submit a report to the Congress on the number of times the department or agency exercised such authority during the year.

(E) Definitions. For purposes of this paragraph, the following definitions shall apply:

(i) Classified information. The term 'classified information' means information that is protected from unauthorized disclosure under Executive Order No. 12958 or successor orders.

(ii) National security investigation. The term 'national security investigation' means any official inquiry by an agency or department of the United States Government to determine the eligibility of a consumer to receive access or continued access to classified information or to determine whether classified information has been lost or compromised.

(c) Furnishing reports in connection with credit or insurance transactions that are not initiated by the consumer.

    (1) In general. A consumer reporting agency may furnish a consumer report relating to any consumer pursuant to subparagraph (A) or (C) of subsection (a)(3) in connection with any credit or insurance transaction that is not initiated by the consumer only if

        (A) the consumer authorizes the agency to provide such report to such person; or

        (B) (i) the transaction consists of a firm offer of credit or insurance;

            (ii) the consumer reporting agency has complied with subsection (e); and

            (iii) there is not in effect an election by the consumer, made in accordance with subsection (e), to have the consumer's name and address excluded from lists of names provided by the agency pursuant to this paragraph.

    (2) Limits on information received under paragraph (1)(B). A person may receive pursuant to paragraph (1)(B) only

        (A) the name and address of a consumer;

        (B) an identifier that is not unique to the consumer and that is used by the person solely for the purpose of verifying the identity of the consumer; and

        (C) other information pertaining to a consumer that does not identify the relationship or experience of the consumer with respect to a particular creditor or other entity.

    (3) Information regarding inquiries. Except as provided in section 609(a)(5) [§ 1681g], a consumer reporting agency shall not furnish to any person a record of inquiries in connection with a credit or insurance transaction that is not initiated by a consumer.

(d) Reserved.

(e) Election of consumer to be excluded from lists.

    (1) In general. A consumer may elect to have the consumer's name and address excluded from any list provided by a consumer reporting agency under subsection (c)(1)(B) in connection with a credit or insurance transaction that is not initiated by the consumer, by notifying the agency in accordance with paragraph (2) that the consumer does not consent to any use of a consumer report relating to the consumer in connection with any credit or insurance transaction that is not initiated by the consumer.

    (2) Manner of notification. A consumer shall notify a consumer reporting agency under paragraph (1)

        (A) through the notification system maintained by the agency under paragraph (5); or

        (B) by submitting to the agency a signed notice of election form issued by the agency for purposes of this subparagraph.

(3) Response of agency after notification through system. Upon receipt of notification of the election of a consumer under paragraph (1) through the notification system maintained by the agency under paragraph (5), a consumer reporting agency shall

(A) inform the consumer that the election is effective only for the 2-year period following the election if the consumer does not submit to the agency a signed notice of election form issued by the agency for purposes of paragraph (2)(B); and

(B) provide to the consumer a notice of election form, if requested by the consumer, not later than 5 business days after receipt of the notification of the election through the system established under paragraph (5), in the case of a request made at the time the consumer provides notification through the system.

(4) Effectiveness of election. An election of a consumer under paragraph (1)

(A) shall be effective with respect to a consumer reporting agency beginning 5 business days after the date on which the consumer notifies the agency in accordance with paragraph (2);

(B) shall be effective with respect to a consumer reporting agency

(i) subject to subparagraph (C), during the 2-year period beginning 5 business days after the date on which the consumer notifies the agency of the election, in the case of an election for which a consumer notifies the agency only in accordance with paragraph (2)(A); or

(ii) until the consumer notifies the agency under subparagraph (C), in the case of an election for which a consumer notifies the agency in accordance with paragraph (2)(B);

(C) shall not be effective after the date on which the consumer notifies the agency, through the notification system established by the agency under paragraph (5), that the election is no longer effective; and

(D) shall be effective with respect to each affiliate of the agency.

(5) Notification system.

(A) In general. Each consumer reporting agency that, under subsection (c)(1)(B), furnishes a consumer report in connection with a credit or insurance transaction that is not initiated by a consumer, shall

(i) establish and maintain a notification system, including a toll-free telephone number, which permits any consumer whose consumer report is maintained by the agency to notify the agency, with appropriate identification, of the consumer's election to have the consumer's name and address excluded from any such list of names and addresses provided by the agency for such a transaction; and

(ii) publish by not later than 365 days after the date of enactment of the Consumer Credit Reporting Reform Act of 1996, and not less than annually thereafter, in a publication of general circulation in the area served by the agency

(I) a notification that information in consumer files maintained by the agency may be used in connection with such transactions; and

(II) the address and toll-free telephone number for consumers to use to notify the agency of the consumer's election under clause (I).

(B) Establishment and maintenance as compliance. Establishment and maintenance of a notification system (including a toll-free telephone number) and publication by a consumer reporting agency on the agency's own behalf and on behalf of any of its affiliates in accordance with this paragraph is deemed to be compliance with this paragraph by each of those affiliates.

(6) Notification system by agencies that operate nationwide. Each consumer reporting agency that compiles and maintains files on consumers on a nationwide basis shall establish and maintain a notification system for purposes of paragraph (5) jointly with other such consumer reporting agencies.

(f) Certain use or obtaining of information prohibited. A person shall not use or obtain a consumer report for any purpose unless

(1) the consumer report is obtained for a purpose for which the consumer report is authorized to be furnished under this section; and

(2) the purpose is certified in accordance with section 607 [§ 1681e] by a prospective user of the report through a general or specific certification.

(g) Furnishing reports containing medical information. A consumer reporting agency shall not furnish for employment purposes, or in connection with a credit or insurance transaction, a consumer report that contains medical information about a consumer, unless the consumer consents to the furnishing of the report.

## § 605. Requirements relating to information contained in consumer reports [15 U.S.C. § 1681c]

(a) Information excluded from consumer reports. Except as authorized under subsection (b) of this section, no consumer reporting agency may make any consumer report containing any of the following items of information:

(1) Cases under title 11 [United States Code] or under the Bankruptcy Act that, from the date of entry of the order for relief or the date of adjudication, as the case may be, antedate the report by more than 10 years.

(2) Civil suits, civil judgments, and records of arrest that from date of entry, antedate the report by more than seven years or until the governing statute of limitations has expired, whichever is the longer period.

(3) Paid tax liens which, from date of payment, antedate the report by more than seven years.

(4) Accounts placed for collection or charged to profit and loss which antedate the report by more than seven years.[1]

(5) Any other adverse item of information, other than records of convictions of crimes which antedates the report by more than seven years.[1]

(b) Exempted cases. The provisions of subsection (a) of this section are not applicable in the case of any consumer credit report to be used in connection with

(1) a credit transaction involving, or which may reasonably be expected to involve, a principal amount of $150,000 or more;

(2) the underwriting of life insurance involving, or which may reasonably be expected to involve, a face amount of $150,000 or more; or

(3) the employment of any individual at an annual salary which equals, or which may reasonably be expected to equal $75,000, or more.

(c) Running of reporting period.

(1) In general. The 7-year period referred to in paragraphs (4) and (6)[2] of subsection (a) shall begin, with respect to any delinquent account that is placed for collection (internally or by referral to a third party, whichever is earlier), charged to profit and loss, or subjected to any similar action, upon the expiration of the 180-day period beginning on the date of the commencement of the delinquency which immediately preceded the collection activity, charge to profit and loss, or similar action.

(2) Effective date. Paragraph (1) shall apply only to items of information added to the file of a consumer on or after the date that is 455 days after the date of enactment of the Consumer Credit Reporting Reform Act of 1996.

(d) Information required to be disclosed. Any consumer reporting agency that furnishes a consumer report that contains information regarding any case involving the consumer that arises under title 11, United States Code, shall include in the report an identification of the chapter of such title 11 under which such case arises if provided by the source of the information. If any case arising or filed under title 11, United States Code, is withdrawn by the consumer before a final judgment, the consumer reporting agency shall include in the report that such case or filing was withdrawn upon receipt of documentation certifying such withdrawal.

(e) Indication of closure of account by consumer. If a consumer reporting agency is notified pursuant to section 623(a)(4) [§ 1681s-2] that a credit account of a consumer was voluntarily closed by the consumer, the agency shall indicate that fact in any consumer report that includes information related to the account.

(f) Indication of dispute by consumer. If a consumer reporting agency is notified pursuant to section 623(a)(3) [§ 1681s-2] that information regarding a consumer who was furnished to the agency is disputed by the consumer, the agency shall indicate that fact in each consumer report that includes the disputed information.

## § 606. Disclosure of investigative consumer reports [15 U.S.C. § 1681d]

(a) Disclosure of fact of preparation. A person may not procure or cause to be prepared an investigative consumer report on any consumer unless

(1) it is clearly and accurately disclosed to the consumer that an investigative consumer report including information as to his character, general reputation, personal characteristics and mode of living, whichever are applicable, may be made, and such disclosure

(A) is made in a writing mailed, or otherwise delivered, to the consumer, not later than three days after the date on which the report was first requested, and

(B) includes a statement informing the consumer of his right to request the additional disclosures provided for under subsection (b) of this section and the written summary of the rights of the consumer prepared pursuant to section 609(c) [§ 1681g]; and

(2) the person certifies or has certified to the consumer reporting agency that

(A) the person has made the disclosures to the consumer required by paragraph (1); and

(B) the person will comply with subsection (b).

(b) Disclosure on request of nature and scope of investigation. Any person who procures or causes to be prepared an investigative consumer report on any consumer shall, upon written request made by the consumer within a reasonable period of time after the receipt by him of the disclosure required by subsection (a)(1) of this section, make a complete and accurate disclosure of the nature and scope of the investigation requested. This disclosure shall be made in a writing mailed, or otherwise delivered, to the consumer not later than five days after the date on which the request for such disclosure was received from the consumer or such report was first requested, whichever is the later.

(c) Limitation on liability upon showing of reasonable procedures for compliance with provisions. No person may be held liable for any violation of subsection (a) or (b) of this section if he shows by a preponderance of the evidence that at the time of the violation he maintained reasonable procedures to assure compliance with subsection (a) or (b) of this section.

(d) Prohibitions.

(1) Certification. A consumer reporting agency shall not prepare or furnish investigative consumer report unless the agency has received a certification under subsection (a)(2) from the person who requested the report.

(2) Inquiries. A consumer reporting agency shall not make an inquiry for the purpose of preparing an investigative consumer report on a consumer for employment purposes if the making of the inquiry by an employer or prospective employer of the consumer would violate any applicable Federal or State equal employment opportunity law or regulation.

(3) Certain public record information. Except as otherwise provided in section 613 [§ 1681k], a consumer reporting agency shall not furnish an investigative consumer report that includes information that is a matter of public record and that relates to an arrest, indictment, conviction, civil judicial action, tax lien, or outstanding judgment, unless the agency has verified the

accuracy of the information during the 30-day period ending on the date on which the report is furnished.

(4) Certain adverse information. A consumer reporting agency shall not prepare or furnish an investigative consumer report on a consumer that contains information that is adverse to the interest of the consumer and that is obtained through a personal interview with a neighbor, friend, or associate of the consumer or with another person with whom the consumer is acquainted or who has knowledge of such item of information, unless

(A) the agency has followed reasonable procedures to obtain confirmation of the information, from an additional source that has independent and direct knowledge of the information; or

(B) the person interviewed is the best possible source of the information.

## § 607. Compliance procedures [15 U.S.C. § 1681e]

(a) Identity and purposes of credit users. Every consumer reporting agency shall maintain reasonable procedures designed to avoid violations of section 605 [§ 1681c] and to limit the furnishing of consumer reports to the purposes listed under section 604 [§ 1681b] of this title. These procedures shall require that prospective users of the information identify themselves, certify the purposes for which the information is sought, and certify that the information will be used for no other purpose. Every consumer reporting agency shall make a reasonable effort to verify the identity of a new prospective user and the uses certified by such prospective user prior to furnishing such user a consumer report. No consumer reporting agency may furnish a consumer report to any person if it has reasonable grounds for believing that the consumer report will not be used for a purpose listed in section 604 [§ 1681b] of this title.

(b) Accuracy of report. Whenever a consumer reporting agency prepares a consumer report it shall follow reasonable procedures to assure maximum possible accuracy of the information concerning the individual about whom the report relates.

(c) Disclosure of consumer reports by users allowed. A consumer reporting agency may not prohibit a user of a consumer report furnished by the agency on a consumer from disclosing the contents of the report to the consumer, if adverse action against the consumer has been taken by the user based in whole or in part on the report.

(d) Notice to users and furnishers of information.

(1) Notice requirement. A consumer reporting agency shall provide to any person

(A) who regularly and in the ordinary course of business furnishes information to the agency with respect to any consumer; or

(B) to whom a consumer report is provided by the agency;

a notice of such person's responsibilities under this title.

(2) Content of notice. The Federal Trade Commission shall prescribe the content of notices under paragraph (1), and a consumer reporting agency shall be in compliance with this

subsection if it provides a notice under paragraph (1) that is substantially similar to the Federal Trade Commission prescription under this paragraph.

(e) Procurement of consumer report for resale.

(1) Disclosure. A person may not procure a consumer report for purposes of reselling the report (or any information in the report) unless the person discloses to the consumer reporting agency that originally furnishes the report

(A) the identity of the end-user of the report (or information); and

(B) each permissible purpose under section 604 [§ 1681b] for which the report is furnished to the end-user of the report (or information).

(2) Responsibilities of procurers for resale. A person who procures a consumer report for purposes of reselling the report (or any information in the report) shall

(A) establish and comply with reasonable procedures designed to ensure that the report (or information) is resold by the person only for a purpose for which the report may be furnished under section 604 [§ 1681b], including by requiring that each person to which the report (or information) is resold and that resells or provides the report (or information) to any other person

(i) identifies each end user of the resold report (or information);

(ii) certifies each purpose for which the report (or information) will be used; and

(iii) certifies that the report (or information) will be used for no other purpose; and

(B) before reselling the report, make reasonable efforts to verify the identifications and certifications made under subparagraph (A).

(3) Resale of consumer report to a federal agency or department. Notwithstanding paragraph (1) or (2), a person who procures a consumer report for purposes of reselling the report (or any information in the report) shall not disclose the identity of the end-user of the report under paragraph (1) or (2) if—

(A) the end user is an agency or department of the United States Government which procures the report from the person for purposes of determining the eligibility of the consumer concerned to receive access or continued access to classified information (as defined in section 604(b)(4)(E)(i)); and

(B) the agency or department certifies in writing to the person reselling the report that nondisclosure is necessary to protect classified information or the safety of persons employed by or contracting with, or undergoing investigation for work or contracting with the agency or department.

## § 608. Disclosures to governmental agencies [15 U.S.C. § 1681f]

Notwithstanding the provisions of section 604 [§ 1681b] of this title, a consumer reporting agency may furnish identifying information respecting any consumer, limited to his name, address, former addresses, places of employment, or former places of employment, to a governmental agency.

### § 609. Disclosures to consumers [15 U.S.C. § 1681g]

(a) Information on file; sources; report recipients. Every consumer reporting agency shall, upon request, and subject to 610(a)(1) [§ 1681h], clearly and accurately disclose to the consumer:

(1) All information in the consumer's file at the time of the request, except that nothing in this paragraph shall be construed to require a consumer reporting agency to disclose to a consumer any information concerning credit scores or any other risk scores or predictors relating to the consumer.

(2) The sources of the information; except that the sources of information acquired solely for use in preparing an investigative consumer report and actually used for no other purpose need not be disclosed: Provided, That in the event an action is brought under this title, such sources shall be available to the plaintiff under appropriate discovery procedures in the court in which the action is brought.

(3)(A) Identification of each person (including each end-user identified under section 607(e)(1) [§ 1681e]) that procured a consumer report

(i) for employment purposes, during the 2-year period preceding the date on which the request is made; or

(ii) for any other purpose, during the 1-year period preceding the date on which the request is made.

(B) An identification of a person under subparagraph (A) shall include

(i) the name of the person or, if applicable, the trade name (written in full) under which such person conducts business; and

(ii) upon request of the consumer, the address and telephone number of the person.

(C) Subparagraph (A) does not apply if—

(i) the end user is an agency or department of the United States Government that procures the report from the person for purposes of determining the eligibility of the consumer to whom the report relates to receive access or continued access to classified information (as defined in section 604(b)(4)(E)(i)); and

(ii) the head of the agency or department makes a written finding as prescribed under section 604(b)(4)(A).

(4) The dates, original payees, and amounts of any checks upon which is based any adverse characterization of the consumer, included in the file at the time of the disclosure.

(5) A record of all inquiries received by the agency during the 1-year period preceding the request that identified the consumer in connection with a credit or insurance transaction that

was not initiated by the consumer.

(b) Exempt information. The requirements of subsection (a) of this section respecting the disclosure of sources of information and the recipients of consumer reports do not apply to information received or consumer reports furnished prior to the effective date of this title except to the extent that the matter involved is contained in the files of the consumer reporting agency on that date.

(c) Summary of rights required to be included with disclosure.

(1) Summary of rights. A consumer reporting agency shall provide to a consumer, with each written disclosure by the agency to the consumer under this section

(A) a written summary of all of the rights that the consumer has under this title; and

(B) in the case of a consumer reporting agency that compiles and maintains files on consumers on a nationwide basis, a toll-free telephone number established by the agency, at which personnel are accessible to consumers during normal business hours.

(2) Specific items required to be included. The summary of rights required under paragraph (1) shall include

(A) a brief description of this title and all rights of consumers under this title;

(B) an explanation of how the consumer may exercise the rights of the consumer under this title;

(C) a list of all Federal agencies responsible for enforcing any provision of this title and the address and any appropriate phone number of each such agency, in a form that will assist the consumer in selecting the appropriate agency;

(D) a statement that the consumer may have additional rights under State law and that the consumer may wish to contact a State or local consumer protection agency or a State attorney general to learn of those rights; and

(E) a statement that a consumer reporting agency is not required to remove accurate derogatory information from a consumer's file, unless the information is outdated under section 605 [§ 1681c] or cannot be verified.

(3) Form of summary of rights. For purposes of this subsection and any disclosure by a consumer reporting agency required under this title with respect to consumers' rights, the Federal Trade Commission (after consultation with each Federal agency referred to in section 621(b) [§ 1681s]) shall prescribe the form and content of any such disclosure of the rights of consumers required under this title. A consumer reporting agency shall be in compliance with this subsection if it provides disclosures under paragraph (1) that are substantially similar to the Federal Trade Commission prescription under this paragraph.

(4) Effectiveness. No disclosures shall be required under this subsection until the date on which the Federal Trade Commission prescribes the form and content of such disclosures under paragraph (3).

## § 610. Conditions and form of disclosure to consumers [15 U.S.C. § 1681h]

(a) In general.

(1) Proper identification. A consumer reporting agency shall require, as a condition of making the disclosures required under section 609 [§ 1681g], that the consumer furnish proper identification.

(2) Disclosure in writing. Except as provided in subsection (b), the disclosures required to be made under section 609 [§ 1681g] shall be provided under that section in writing.

(b) Other forms of disclosure.

(1) In general. If authorized by a consumer, a consumer reporting agency may make the disclosures required under 609 [§ 1681g]

(A) other than in writing; and

(B) in such form as may be

(i) specified by the consumer in accordance with paragraph (2); and

(ii) available from the agency.

(2) Form. A consumer may specify pursuant to paragraph (1) that disclosures under section 609 [§ 1681g] shall be made

(A) in person, upon the appearance of the consumer at the place of business of the consumer reporting agency where disclosures are regularly provided, during normal business hours, and on reasonable notice;

(B) by telephone, if the consumer has made a written request for disclosure by telephone;

(C) by electronic means, if available from the agency; or

(D) by any other reasonable means that is available from the agency.

(c) Trained personnel. Any consumer reporting agency shall provide trained personnel to explain to the consumer any information furnished to him pursuant to section 609 [§ 1681g] of this title.

(d) Persons accompanying consumer. The consumer shall be permitted to be accompanied by one other person of his choosing, who shall furnish reasonable identification. A consumer reporting agency may require the consumer to furnish a written statement granting permission to the consumer reporting agency to discuss the consumer's file in such person's presence.

(e) Limitation of liability. Except as provided in sections 616 and 617 [§§ 1681n and 1681o] of this title, no consumer may bring any action or proceeding in the nature of defamation, invasion of privacy, or negligence with respect to the reporting of information against any consumer reporting agency, any user of information, or any person who furnishes information to a consumer reporting agency, based on information disclosed pursuant to section 609, 610, or 615 [§§ 1681g, 1681h, or 1681m] of this title or based on information disclosed by a user of a consumer report to or for a consumer against whom the user has taken adverse action, based in whole or in part on the report, except as to false information furnished with malice or willful intent to injure such consumer.

## § 611. Procedure in case of disputed accuracy [15 U.S.C. § 1681i]

(a) Reinvestigations of disputed information.

(1) Reinvestigation required.

(A) In general. If the completeness or accuracy of any item of information contained in a consumer's file at a consumer reporting agency is disputed by the consumer and the consumer notifies the agency directly of such dispute, the agency shall reinvestigate free of charge and record the current status of the disputed information, or delete the item from the file in accordance with paragraph (5), before the end of the 30-day period beginning on the date on which the agency receives the notice of the dispute from the consumer.

(B) Extension of period to reinvestigate. Except as provided in subparagraph (C), the 30-day period described in subparagraph (A) may be extended for not more than 15 additional days if the consumer reporting agency receives information from the consumer during that 30-day period that is relevant to the reinvestigation.

(C) Limitations on extension of period to reinvestigate. Subparagraph (B) shall not apply to any reinvestigation in which, during the 30-day period described in subparagraph (A), the information that is the subject of the reinvestigation is found to be inaccurate or incomplete or the consumer reporting agency determines that the information cannot be verified.

(2) Prompt notice of dispute to furnisher of information.

(A) In general. Before the expiration of the 5-business-day period beginning on the date on which a consumer reporting agency receives notice of a dispute from any consumer in accordance with paragraph (1), the agency shall provide notification of the dispute to any person who provided any item of information in dispute, at the address and in the manner established with the person. The notice shall include all relevant information regarding the dispute that the agency has received from the consumer.

(B) Provision of other information from consumer. The consumer reporting agency shall promptly provide to the person who provided the information in dispute all relevant information regarding the dispute that is received by the agency from the consumer after the period referred to in subparagraph (A) and before the end of the period referred to in paragraph (1)(A).

(3) Determination that dispute is frivolous or irrelevant.

(A) In general. Notwithstanding paragraph (1), a consumer reporting agency may terminate a reinvestigation of information disputed by a consumer under that paragraph if the agency reasonably determines that the dispute by the consumer is frivolous or irrelevant, including by reason of a failure by a consumer to provide sufficient information to investigate the disputed information.

(B) Notice of determination. Upon making any determination in accordance with subparagraph (A) that a dispute is frivolous or irrelevant, a consumer reporting agency shall notify the consumer of such determination not later than 5 business days after making such determination, by mail or, if authorized by the consumer for that purpose, by any other means available to the agency.

(C) Contents of notice. A notice under subparagraph (B) shall include

(i) the reasons for the determination under subparagraph (A); and

(ii) identification of any information required to investigate the disputed information, which may consist of a standardized form describing the general nature of such information.

(4) Consideration of consumer information. In conducting any reinvestigation under paragraph (1) with respect to disputed information in the file of any consumer, the consumer reporting agency shall review and consider all relevant information submitted by the consumer in the period described in paragraph (1)(A) with respect to such disputed information.

(5) Treatment of inaccurate or unverifiable information.

(A) In general. If, after any reinvestigation under paragraph (1) of any information disputed by a consumer, an item of the information is found to be inaccurate or incomplete or cannot be verified, the consumer reporting agency shall promptly delete that item of information from the consumer's file or modify that item of information, as appropriate, based on the results of the reinvestigation.

(B) Requirements relating to reinsertion of previously deleted material.

(i) Certification of accuracy of information. If any information is deleted from a consumer's file pursuant to subparagraph (A), the information may not be reinserted in the file by the consumer reporting agency unless the person who furnishes the information certifies that the information is complete and accurate.

(ii) Notice to consumer. If any information that has been deleted from a consumer's file pursuant to subparagraph (A) is reinserted in the file, the consumer reporting agency shall notify the consumer of the reinsertion in writing not later than 5 business days after the reinsertion or, if authorized by the consumer for that purpose, by any other means available to the agency.

(iii) Additional information. As part of, or in addition to, the notice under clause (ii), a consumer reporting agency shall provide to a consumer in writing not later than 5 business days after the date of the reinsertion

(I) a statement that the disputed information has been reinserted;

(II) the business name and address of any furnisher of information contacted and the telephone number of such furnisher, if reasonably available, or of any furnisher of information that contacted the consumer reporting agency, in connection with the reinsertion of such information; and

(III) a notice that the consumer has the right to add a statement to the consumer's file disputing the accuracy or completeness of the disputed information.

C) Procedures to prevent reappearance. A consumer reporting agency shall maintain reasonable procedures designed to prevent the reappearance in a consumer's file, and in consumer reports on the consumer, of information that is deleted pursuant to this paragraph (other than information that is reinserted in accordance with subparagraph (B)(i)).

D) Automated reinvestigation system. Any consumer reporting agency that compiles and maintains files on consumers on a nationwide basis shall implement an automated system through which furnishers of information to that consumer reporting agency may report the results of a reinvestigation that finds incomplete or inaccurate information in a consumer's file to other such consumer reporting agencies.

(6) Notice of results of reinvestigation.

(A) In general. A consumer reporting agency shall provide written notice to a consumer of the results of a reinvestigation under this subsection not later than 5 business days after the completion of the reinvestigation, by mail or, if authorized by the consumer for that purpose, by other means available to the agency.

(B) Contents. As part of, or in addition to, the notice under subparagraph (A), a consumer reporting agency shall provide to a consumer in writing before the expiration of the 5-day period referred to in subparagraph (A)

(i) a statement that the reinvestigation is completed;

(ii) a consumer report that is based upon the consumer's file as that file is revised as a result of the reinvestigation;

(iii) a notice that, if requested by the consumer, a description of the procedure used to determine the accuracy and completeness of the information shall be provided to the consumer by the agency, including the business name and address of any furnisher of information contacted in connection with such information and the telephone number of such furnisher, if reasonably available;

(iv) a notice that the consumer has the right to add a statement to the consumer's file disputing the accuracy or completeness of the information; and

(v) a notice that the consumer has the right to request under subsection (d) that the consumer reporting agency furnish notifications under that subsection.

(7) Description of reinvestigation procedure. A consumer reporting agency shall provide to a consumer a description referred to in paragraph (6)(B)(iii) by not later than 15 days after receiving a request from the consumer for that description.

(8) Expedited dispute resolution. If a dispute regarding an item of information in a consumer's file at a consumer reporting agency is resolved in accordance with paragraph (5)(A) by the deletion of the disputed information by not later than 3 business days after the date on which the agency receives notice of the dispute from the consumer in accordance with paragraph (1)(A), then the agency shall not be required to comply with paragraphs (2), (6), and (7) with respect to that dispute if the agency

(A) provides prompt notice of the deletion to the consumer by telephone;

(B) includes in that notice, or in a written notice that accompanies a confirmation and consumer report provided in accordance with subparagraph (C), a statement of the consumer's right to request under subsection (d) that the agency furnish notifications under that subsection; and

(C) provides written confirmation of the deletion and a copy of a consumer report on the consumer that is based on the consumer's file after the deletion, not later than 5 business days after making the deletion.

(b) Statement of dispute. If the reinvestigation does not resolve the dispute, the consumer may file a brief statement setting forth the nature of the dispute. The consumer reporting agency may limit such statements to not more than one hundred words if it provides the consumer with assistance in writing a clear summary of the dispute.

(c) Notification of consumer dispute in subsequent consumer reports. Whenever a statement of a dispute is filed, unless there are reasonable grounds to believe that it is frivolous or irrelevant, the consumer reporting agency shall, in any subsequent consumer report containing the information in question, clearly note that it is disputed by the consumer and provide either the consumer's statement or a clear and accurate codification or summary thereof.

(d) Notification of deletion of disputed information. Following any deletion of information which is found to be inaccurate or whose accuracy can no longer be verified or any notation as to disputed information, the consumer reporting agency shall, at the request of the consumer, furnish notification that the item has been deleted or the statement, codification or summary pursuant to subsection (b) or (c) of this section to any person specifically designated by the consumer who has within two years prior thereto received a consumer report for employment purposes, or within six months prior thereto received a consumer report for any other purpose, which contained the deleted or disputed information.

## § 612. Charges for certain disclosures [15 U.S.C. § 1681j]

(a) Reasonable charges allowed for certain disclosures.

(1) In general. Except as provided in subsections (b), (c), and (d), a consumer reporting agency may impose a reasonable charge on a consumer

(A) for making a disclosure to the consumer pursuant to section 609 [§ 1681g], which charge

(i) shall not exceed $8;[(3)] and

(ii) shall be indicated to the consumer before making the disclosure; and

(B) for furnishing, pursuant to 611(d) [§ 1681i], following a reinvestigation under section 611(a) [§ 1681i], a statement, codification, or summary to a person designated by the consumer under that section after the 30-day period beginning on the date of notification of the consumer under paragraph (6) or (8) of section 611(a) [§ 1681i] with respect to the reinvestigation, which charge

(i) shall not exceed the charge that the agency would impose on each designated recipient for a consumer report; and

(ii) shall be indicated to the consumer before furnishing such information.

(2) Modification of amount. The Federal Trade Commission shall increase the amount referred to in paragraph (1)(A)(I) on January 1 of each year, based proportionally on changes in the Consumer Price Index, with fractional changes rounded to the nearest fifty cents.

(b) Free disclosure after adverse notice to consumer. Each consumer reporting agency that maintains a file on a consumer shall make all disclosures pursuant to section 609 [§ 1681g] without charge to the consumer if, not later than 60 days after receipt by such consumer of a notification pursuant to section 615 [§ 1681m], or of a notification from a debt collection agency affiliated with that consumer reporting agency stating that the consumer's credit rating may be or has been adversely affected, the consumer makes a request under section 609 [§ 1681g].

(c) Free disclosure under certain other circumstances. Upon the request of the consumer, a consumer reporting agency shall make all disclosures pursuant to section 609 [§ 1681g] once during any 12-month period without charge to that consumer if the consumer certifies in writing that the consumer

(1) is unemployed and intends to apply for employment in the 60-day period beginning on the date on which the certification is made;

(2) is a recipient of public welfare assistance; or

(3) has reason to believe that the file on the consumer at the agency contains inaccurate information due to fraud.

(d) Other charges prohibited. A consumer reporting agency shall not impose any charge on a consumer for providing any notification required by this title or making any disclosure required by this title, except as authorized by subsection (a).

### § 613. Public record information for employment purposes [15 U.S.C. § 1681k]

(a) In general. A consumer reporting agency which furnishes a consumer report for employment purposes and which for that purpose compiles and reports items of information on consumers which are matters of public record and are likely to have an adverse effect upon a consumer's ability to obtain employment shall

(1) at the time such public record information is reported to the user of such consumer report, notify the consumer of the fact that public record information is being reported by the consumer reporting agency, together with the name and address of the person to whom such information is being reported; or

(2) maintain strict procedures designed to insure that whenever public record information which is likely to have an adverse effect on a consumer's ability to obtain employment is reported it is complete and up to date. For purposes of this paragraph, items of public record relating to arrests, indictments, convictions, suits, tax liens, and outstanding judgments shall be considered up to date if the current public record status of the item at the time of the report is reported.

(b) Exemption for national security investigations. Subsection (a) does not apply in the case of an agency or department of the United States Government that seeks to obtain and use a consumer report for employment purposes, if the head of the agency or department makes a written finding as prescribed under section 604(b)(4)(A).

## § 614. Restrictions on investigative consumer reports [15 U.S.C. § 1681l]

Whenever a consumer reporting agency prepares an investigative consumer report, no adverse information in the consumer report (other than information which is a matter of public record) may be included in a subsequent consumer report unless such adverse information has been verified in the process of making such subsequent consumer report, or the adverse information was received within the three-month period preceding the date the subsequent report is furnished.

## § 615. Requirements on users of consumer reports [15 U.S.C. § 1681m]

(a) Duties of users taking adverse actions on the basis of information contained in consumer reports. If any person takes any adverse action with respect to any consumer that is based in whole or in part on any information contained in a consumer report, the person shall

(1) provide oral, written, or electronic notice of the adverse action to the consumer;

(2) provide to the consumer orally, in writing, or electronically

(A) the name, address, and telephone number of the consumer reporting agency (including a toll-free telephone number established by the agency if the agency compiles and maintains files on consumers on a nationwide basis) that furnished the report to the person; and

(B) a statement that the consumer reporting agency did not make the decision to take the adverse action and is unable to provide the consumer the specific reasons why the adverse action was taken; and

(3) provide to the consumer an oral, written, or electronic notice of the consumer's right

(A) to obtain, under section 612 [§ 1681j], a free copy of a consumer report on the consumer from the consumer reporting agency referred to in paragraph (2), which notice shall include an indication of the 60-day period under that section for obtaining such a copy; and

(B) to dispute, under section 611 [§ 1681i], with a consumer reporting agency the accuracy or completeness of any information in a consumer report furnished by the agency.

(b) Adverse action based on information obtained from third parties other than consumer reporting agencies.

(1) In general. Whenever credit for personal, family, or household purposes involving a consumer is denied or the charge for such credit is increased either wholly or partly because of information obtained from a person other than a consumer reporting agency bearing upon the consumer's credit worthiness, credit standing, credit capacity, character, general reputation, personal characteristics, or mode of living, the user of such information shall, within a reasonable period of time, upon the consumer's written request for the reasons for such adverse action received within sixty days after learning of such adverse action, disclose the nature of the information to the consumer. The user of such information shall clearly and accurately disclose to the consumer his right to make such written request at the time such adverse action is communicated to the consumer.

(2) Duties of person taking certain actions based on information provided by affiliate.

(A) Duties, generally. If a person takes an action described in subparagraph (B) with respect to a consumer, based in whole or in part on information described in subparagraph (C), the person shall

(i) notify the consumer of the action, including a statement that the consumer may obtain the information in accordance with clause (ii); and

(ii) upon a written request from the consumer received within 60 days after transmittal of the notice required by clause (I), disclose to the consumer the nature of the information upon which the action is based by not later than 30 days after receipt of the request.

(B) Action described. An action referred to in subparagraph (A) is an adverse action described in section 603(k)(1)(A) [§ 1681a], taken in connection with a transaction initiated by the consumer, or any adverse action described in clause (i) or (ii) of section 603(k)(1)(B) [§ 1681a].

(C) Information described. Information referred to in subparagraph (A)

(i) except as provided in clause (ii), is information that

(I) is furnished to the person taking the action by a person related by common ownership or affiliated by common corporate control to the person taking the action; and

(II) bears on the credit worthiness, credit standing, credit capacity, character, general reputation, personal characteristics, or mode of living of the consumer; and

(ii) does not include

(I) information solely as to transactions or experiences between the consumer and the person furnishing the information; or

(II) information in a consumer report.

(c) Reasonable procedures to assure compliance. No person shall be held liable for any violation of this section if he shows by a preponderance of the evidence that at the time of the alleged violation he maintained reasonable procedures to assure compliance with the provisions of this section.

(d) Duties of users making written credit or insurance solicitations on the basis of information contained in consumer files.

(1) In general. Any person who uses a consumer report on any consumer in connection with any credit or insurance transaction that is not initiated by the consumer, that is provided to that person under section 604(c)(1)(B) [§ 1681b], shall provide with each written solicitation made to the consumer regarding the transaction a clear and conspicuous statement that

(A) information contained in the consumer's consumer report was used in connection with the transaction;

(B) the consumer received the offer of credit or insurance because the consumer satisfied the criteria for credit worthiness or insurability under which the consumer was selected for the offer;

(C) if applicable, the credit or insurance may not be extended if, after the consumer responds to the offer, the consumer does not meet the criteria used to select the consumer for the offer or any applicable criteria bearing on credit worthiness or insurability or does not furnish any required collateral;

(D) the consumer has a right to prohibit information contained in the consumer's file with any consumer reporting agency from being used in connection with any credit or insurance transaction that is not initiated by the consumer; and

(E) the consumer may exercise the right referred to in subparagraph (D) by notifying a notification system established under section 604(e) [§ 1681b].

(2) Disclosure of address and telephone number. A statement under paragraph (1) shall include the address and toll-free telephone number of the appropriate notification system established under section 604(e) [§ 1681b].

(3) Maintaining criteria on file. A person who makes an offer of credit or insurance to a consumer under a credit or insurance transaction described in paragraph (1) shall maintain on file the criteria used to select the consumer to receive the offer, all criteria bearing on credit worthiness or insurability, as applicable, that are the basis for determining whether or not to extend credit or insurance pursuant to the offer, and any requirement for the furnishing of collateral as a condition of the extension of credit or insurance, until the expiration of the 3-year period beginning on the date on which the offer is made to the consumer.

(4) Authority of federal agencies regarding unfair or deceptive acts or practices not affected. This section is not intended to affect the authority of any Federal or State agency to enforce a prohibition against unfair or deceptive acts or practices, including the making of false or misleading statements in connection with a credit or insurance transaction that is not initiated by the consumer.

## § 616. Civil liability for willful noncompliance [15 U.S.C. § 1681n]

(a) In general. Any person who willfully fails to comply with any requirement imposed under this title with respect to any consumer is liable to that consumer in an amount equal to the sum of

> (1) (A) any actual damages sustained by the consumer as a result of the failure or damages of not less than $100 and not more than $1,000; or
>
> (B) in the case of liability of a natural person for obtaining a consumer report under false pretenses or knowingly without a permissible purpose, actual damages sustained by the consumer as a result of the failure or $1,000, whichever is greater;
>
> (2) such amount of punitive damages as the court may allow; and
>
> (3) in the case of any successful action to enforce any liability under this section, the costs of the action together with reasonable attorney's fees as determined by the court.

(b) Civil liability for knowing noncompliance. Any person who obtains a consumer report from a consumer reporting agency under false pretenses or knowingly without a permissible purpose shall be liable to the consumer reporting agency for actual damages sustained by the consumer reporting agency or $1,000, whichever is greater.

(c) Attorney's fees. Upon a finding by the court that an unsuccessful pleading, motion, or other paper filed in connection with an action under this section was filed in bad faith or for purposes of harassment, the court shall award to the prevailing party attorney's fees reasonable in relation to the work expended in responding to the pleading, motion, or other paper.

## § 617. Civil liability for negligent noncompliance [15 U.S.C. § 1681o]

(a) In general. Any person who is negligent in failing to comply with any requirement imposed under this title with respect to any consumer is liable to that consumer in an amount equal to the sum of

> (1) any actual damages sustained by the consumer as a result of the failure;
>
> (2) in the case of any successful action to enforce any liability under this section, the costs of the action together with reasonable attorney's fees as determined by the court.

(b) Attorney's fees. On a finding by the court that an unsuccessful pleading, motion, or other paper filed in connection with an action under this section was filed in bad faith or for purposes of harassment, the court shall award to the prevailing party attorney's fees reasonable in relation to the work expended in responding to the pleading, motion, or other paper.

## § 618. Jurisdiction of courts; limitation of actions [15 U.S.C. § 1681p]

An action to enforce any liability created under this title may be brought in any appropriate United States district court without regard to the amount in controversy, or in any other court of competent jurisdiction, within two years from the date on which the liability arises, except that where a defendant has materially and willfully misrepresented any information required under this title to be disclosed to an individual and the information so misrepresented is material to the establishment of the defendant's liability to that individual under this title, the action may be brought at any time within two years after discovery by the individual of the misrepresentation.

## § 619. Obtaining information under false pretenses [15 U.S.C. § 1681q]

Any person who knowingly and willfully obtains information on a consumer from a consumer reporting agency under false pretenses shall be fined under title 18, United States Code, imprisoned for not more than 2 years, or both.

§ 620. Unauthorized disclosures by officers or employees **[15 U.S.C. § 1681r]**

Any officer or employee of a consumer reporting agency who knowingly and willfully provides information concerning an individual from the agency's files to a person not authorized to receive that information shall be fined under title 18, United States Code, imprisoned for not more than 2 years, or both.

## § 621. Administrative enforcement [15 U.S.C. § 1681s]

(a) (1) Enforcement by Federal Trade Commission. Compliance with the requirements imposed under this title shall be enforced under the Federal Trade Commission Act [15 U.S.C. §§ 41 et seq.] by the Federal Trade Commission with respect to consumer reporting agencies and all other persons subject thereto, except to the extent that enforcement of the requirements imposed under this title is specifically committed to some other government agency under subsection (b) hereof. For the purpose of the exercise by the Federal Trade Commission of its functions and powers under the Federal Trade Commission Act, a violation of any requirement or prohibition imposed under this title shall constitute an unfair or deceptive act or practice in commerce in violation of section 5(a) of the Federal Trade Commission Act [15 U.S.C. § 45(a)] and shall be subject to enforcement by the Federal Trade Commission under section 5(b) thereof [15 U.S.C. § 45(b)] with respect to any consumer reporting agency or person subject to enforcement by the Federal Trade Commission pursuant to this subsection, irrespective of whether that person is engaged in commerce or meets any other jurisdictional tests in the Federal Trade Commission Act. The Federal Trade Commission shall have such procedural, investigative, and enforcement powers, including the power to issue procedural rules in enforcing compliance with the requirements imposed under this title and to require the filing of reports, the production of documents, and the appearance of witnesses as though the applicable terms and conditions of the Federal Trade Commission Act were part of this title. Any person violating any of the provisions of this title shall be subject to the penalties and entitled to the privileges and immunities provided in the Federal Trade Commission Act as though the applicable terms and provisions thereof were part of this title.

(2)(A) In the event of a knowing violation, which constitutes a pattern or practice of violations of this title, the Commission may commence a civil action to recover a civil penalty in a district court of the United States against any person that violates this title. In such action, such person shall be liable for a civil penalty of not more than $2,500 per violation.

(B) In determining the amount of a civil penalty under subparagraph (A), the court shall take into account the degree of culpability, any history of prior such conduct, ability to pay, effect on ability to continue to do business, and such other matters as justice may require.

(3) Notwithstanding paragraph (2), a court may not impose any civil penalty on a person for a violation of section 623(a)(1) [§ 1681s-2] unless the person has been enjoined from committing the violation, or ordered not to commit the violation, in an action or proceeding brought by or on behalf of the Federal Trade Commission, and has violated the injunction or order, and the court may not impose any civil penalty for any violation occurring before the date of the violation of the injunction or order.

(b) Enforcement by other agencies. Compliance with the requirements imposed under this title with respect to consumer reporting agencies, persons who use consumer reports from such agencies, persons who furnish information to such agencies, and users of information that are subject to subsection (d) of section 615 [§ 1681m] shall be enforced under

(1) section 8 of the Federal Deposit Insurance Act [12 U.S.C. § 1818], in the case of

(A) national banks, and Federal branches and Federal agencies of foreign banks, by the Office of the Comptroller of the Currency;

(B) member banks of the Federal Reserve System (other than national banks), branches and agencies of foreign banks (other than Federal branches, Federal agencies, and insured State branches of foreign banks), commercial lending companies owned or controlled by foreign banks, and organizations operating under section 25 or 25(a) [25A] of the Federal Reserve Act [12 U.S.C. §§ 601 et seq., §§ 611 et seq], by the Board of Governors of the Federal Reserve System; and

(C) banks insured by the Federal Deposit Insurance Corporation (other than members of the Federal Reserve System) and insured State branches of foreign banks, by the Board of Directors of the Federal Deposit Insurance Corporation;

(2) section 8 of the Federal Deposit Insurance Act [12 U.S.C. § 1818], by the Director of the Office of Thrift Supervision, in the case of a savings association the deposits of which are insured by the Federal Deposit Insurance Corporation;

(3) the Federal Credit Union Act [12 U.S.C. §§ 1751 et seq.], by the Administrator of the National Credit Union Administration [National Credit Union Administration Board] with respect to any Federal credit union;

(4) subtitle IV of title 49 [49 U.S.C. §§ 10101 et seq.], by the Secretary of Transportation, with respect to all carriers subject to the jurisdiction of the Surface Transportation Board;

(5) the Federal Aviation Act of 1958 [49 U.S.C. Appx §§ 1301 et seq.], by the Secretary of Transportation with respect to any air carrier or foreign air carrier subject to that Act [49 U.S.C. Appx §§ 1301 et seq.]; and

(6) the Packers and Stockyards Act, 1921 [7 U.S.C. §§ 181 et seq.] (except as provided in section 406 of that Act [7 U.S.C. §§ 226 and 227]), by the Secretary of Agriculture with respect to any activities subject to that Act.

The terms used in paragraph (1) that are not defined in this title or otherwise defined in section 3(s) of the Federal Deposit Insurance Act (12 U.S.C. §1813(s)) shall have the meaning given to them in section 1(b) of the International Banking Act of 1978 (12 U.S.C. § 3101).

(c) State action for violations.

(1) Authority of states. In addition to such other remedies as are provided under State law, if the chief law enforcement officer of a State, or an official or agency designated by a State, has reason to believe that any person has violated or is violating this title, the State

(A) may bring an action to enjoin such violation in any appropriate United States district court or in any other court of competent jurisdiction;

(B) subject to paragraph (5), may bring an action on behalf of the residents of the State to recover

(i) damages for which the person is liable to such residents under sections 616 and 617 [§§ 1681n and 1681o] as a result of the violation;

(ii) in the case of a violation of section 623(a) [§ 1681s-2], damages for which the person would, but for section 623(c) [§ 1681s-2], be liable to such residents as a result of the violation; or

(iii) damages of not more than $1,000 for each willful or negligent violation; and

(C) in the case of any successful action under subparagraph (A) or (B), shall be awarded the costs of the action and reasonable attorney fees as determined by the court.

(2) Rights of federal regulators. The State shall serve prior written notice of any action under paragraph (1) upon the Federal Trade Commission or the appropriate Federal regulator determined under subsection (b) and provide the Commission or appropriate Federal regulator with a copy of its complaint, except in any case in which such prior notice is not feasible, in which case the State shall serve such notice immediately upon instituting such action. The Federal Trade Commission or appropriate Federal regulator shall have the right

(A) to intervene in the action;

(B) upon so intervening, to be heard on all matters arising therein;

(C) to remove the action to the appropriate United States district court; and

(D) to file petitions for appeal.

(3) Investigatory powers. For purposes of bringing any action under this subsection, nothing in this subsection shall prevent the chief law enforcement officer, or an official or agency designated by a State, from exercising the powers conferred on the chief law enforcement officer or such official by the laws of such State to conduct investigations or to administer oaths or affirmations or to compel the attendance of witnesses or the production of documentary and other evidence.

(4) Limitation on state action while federal action pending. If the Federal Trade Commission or the appropriate Federal regulator has instituted a civil action or an administrative action under section 8 of the Federal Deposit Insurance Act for a violation of this title, no State may, during the pendency of such action, bring an action under this section against any defendant named in the complaint of the Commission or the appropriate Federal regulator for any violation of this title that is alleged in that complaint.

(5) Limitations on state actions for violation of section 623(a)(1) [§ 1681s-2].

(A) Violation of injunction required. A State may not bring an action against a person under paragraph (1)(B) for a violation of section 623(a)(1) [§ 1681s-2], unless

(i) the person has been enjoined from committing the violation, in an action brought by the State under paragraph (1)(A); and

(ii) the person has violated the injunction.

(B) Limitation on damages recoverable. In an action against a person under paragraph (1)(B) for a violation of section 623(a)(1) [§ 1681s-2], a State may not recover any damages incurred before the date of the violation of an injunction on which the action is based.

(d) Enforcement under other authority. For the purpose of the exercise by any agency referred to in subsection (b) of this section of its powers under any Act referred to in that subsection, a violation of any requirement imposed under this title shall be deemed to be a violation of a requirement imposed under that Act. In addition to its powers under any provision of law specifically referred to in subsection (b) of this section, each of the agencies referred to in that subsection may exercise, for the purpose of enforcing compliance with any requirement imposed under this title any other authority conferred on it by law.

(e) Regulatory authority

(1) The Federal banking agencies referred to in paragraphs (1) and (2) of subsection (b) shall jointly prescribe such regulations as necessary to carry out the purposes of this Act with respect to any persons identified under paragraphs (1) and (2) of subsection (b), and the Board of Governors of the Federal Reserve System shall have authority to prescribe regulations consistent with such joint regulations with respect to bank holding companies and affiliates (other than depository institutions and consumer reporting agencies) of such holding companies.

(2) The Board of the National Credit Union Administration shall prescribe such regulations as necessary to carry out the purposes of this Act with respect to any persons identified under paragraph (3) of subsection (b).

## § 622. Information on overdue child support obligations [15 U.S.C. § 1681s-1]

Notwithstanding any other provision of this title, a consumer reporting agency shall include in any consumer report furnished by the agency in accordance with section 604 [§ 1681b] of this title, any information on the failure of the consumer to pay overdue support which

(1) is provided

(A) to the consumer reporting agency by a State or local child support enforcement agency; or

(B) to the consumer reporting agency and verified by any local, State, or Federal government agency; and

(2) antedates the report by 7 years or less.

## § 623. Responsibilities of furnishers of information to consumer reporting agencies [15 U.S.C. § 1681s-2]

(a) Duty of furnishers of information to provide accurate information.

(1) Prohibition.

(A) Reporting information with actual knowledge of errors. A person shall not furnish any information relating to a consumer to any consumer reporting agency if the person knows or consciously avoids knowing that the information is inaccurate.

(B) Reporting information after notice and confirmation of errors. A person shall not furnish information relating to a consumer to any consumer reporting agency if

(i) the person has been notified by the consumer, at the address specified by the person for such notices, that specific information is inaccurate; and

(ii) the information is, in fact, inaccurate.

(C) No address requirement. A person who clearly and conspicuously specifies to the consumer an address for notices referred to in subparagraph (B) shall not be subject to subparagraph (A); however, nothing in subparagraph (B) shall require a person to specify such an address.

(2) Duty to correct and update information. A person who

(A) regularly and in the ordinary course of business furnishes information to one or more consumer reporting agencies about the person's transactions or experiences with any consumer; and

(B) has furnished to a consumer reporting agency information that the person determines is not complete or accurate, shall promptly notify the consumer reporting agency of that determination and provide to the agency any corrections to that information, or any additional information, that is necessary to make the information provided by the person to the agency complete and accurate, and shall not thereafter furnish to the agency any of the information that remains not complete or accurate.

(3) Duty to provide notice of dispute. If the completeness or accuracy of any information furnished by any person to any consumer reporting agency is disputed to such person by a consumer, the person may not furnish the information to any consumer reporting agency

without notice that such information is disputed by the consumer.

(4) Duty to provide notice of closed accounts. A person who regularly and in the ordinary course of business furnishes information to a consumer reporting agency regarding a consumer who has a credit account with that person shall notify the agency of the voluntary closure of the account by the consumer, in information regularly furnished for the period in which the account is closed.

(5) Duty to provide notice of delinquency of accounts. A person who furnishes information to a consumer reporting agency regarding a delinquent account being placed for collection, charged to profit or loss, or subjected to any similar action shall, not later than 90 days after furnishing the information, notify the agency of the month and year of the commencement of the delinquency that immediately preceded the action.

(b) Duties of furnishers of information upon notice of dispute.

(1) In general. After receiving notice pursuant to section 611(a)(2) [§ 1681i] of a dispute with regard to the completeness or accuracy of any information provided by a person to a consumer reporting agency, the person shall

(A) conduct an investigation with respect to the disputed information;

(B) review all relevant information provided by the consumer reporting agency pursuant to section 611(a)(2) [§ 1681i];

(C) report the results of the investigation to the consumer reporting agency; and

(D) if the investigation finds that the information is incomplete or inaccurate, report those results to all other consumer reporting agencies to which the person furnished the information and that compile and maintain files on consumers on a nationwide basis.

(2) Deadline. A person shall complete all investigations, reviews, and reports required under paragraph (1) regarding information provided by the person to a consumer reporting agency, before the expiration of the period under section 611(a)(1) [§ 1681i] within which the consumer reporting agency is required to complete actions required by that section regarding that information.

(c) Limitation on liability. Sections 616 and 617 [§§ 1681n and 1681o] do not apply to any failure to comply with subsection (a), except as provided in section 621(c)(1)(B) [§ 1681s].

(d) Limitation on enforcement. Subsection (a) shall be enforced exclusively under section 621 [§ 1681s] by the Federal agencies and officials and the State officials identified in that section.

## § 624. Relation to State laws [15 U.S.C. § 1681t]

(a) In general. Except as provided in subsections (b) and (c), this title does not annul, alter, affect, or exempt any person subject to the provisions of this title from complying with the laws of any State with respect to the collection, distribution, or use of any information on consumers, except to the extent that those laws are inconsistent with any provision of this title, and then only to the extent of the inconsistency.

(b) General exceptions. No requirement or prohibition may be imposed under the laws of any State

(1) with respect to any subject matter regulated under

(A) subsection (c) or (e) of section 604 [§ 1681b], relating to the prescreening of consumer reports;

(B) section 611 [§ 1681i], relating to the time by which a consumer reporting agency must take any action, including the provision of notification to a consumer or other person, in any procedure related to the disputed accuracy of information in a consumer's file, except that this subparagraph shall not apply to any State law in effect on the date of enactment of the Consumer Credit Reporting Reform Act of 1996;

(C) subsections (a) and (b) of section 615 [§ 1681m], relating to the duties of a person who takes any adverse action with respect to a consumer;

(D) section 615(d) [§ 1681m], relating to the duties of persons who use a consumer report of a consumer in connection with any credit or insurance transaction that is not initiated by the consumer and that consists of a firm offer of credit or insurance;

(E) section 605 [§ 1681c], relating to information contained in consumer reports, except that this subparagraph shall not apply to any State law in effect on the date of enactment of the Consumer Credit Reporting Reform Act of 1996; or

(F) section 623 [§ 1681s-2], relating to the responsibilities of persons who furnish information to consumer reporting agencies, except that this paragraph shall not apply

(i) with respect to section 54A(a) of chapter 93 of the Massachusetts Annotated Laws (as in effect on the date of enactment of the Consumer Credit Reporting Reform Act of 1996); or

(ii) with respect to section 1785.25(a) of the California Civil Code (as in effect on the date of enactment of the Consumer Credit Reporting Reform Act of 1996);

(2) with respect to the exchange of information among persons affiliated by common ownership or common corporate control, except that this paragraph shall not apply with respect to subsection (a) or (c)(1) of section 2480e of title 9, Vermont Statutes Annotated (as in effect on the date of enactment of the Consumer Credit Reporting Reform Act of 1996); or

(3) with respect to the form and content of any disclosure required to be made under section 609(c) [§ 1681g].

(c) Definition of firm offer of credit or insurance. Notwithstanding any definition of the term "firm offer of credit or insurance" (or any equivalent term) under the laws of any State, the definition of that term contained in section 603(*l*) [§ 1681a] shall be construed to apply in the enforcement and interpretation of the laws of any State governing consumer reports.

(d) Limitations. Subsections (b) and (c)

(1) do not affect any settlement, agreement, or consent judgment between any State Attorney General and any consumer reporting agency in effect on the date of enactment of the Consumer Credit Reporting Reform Act of 1996; and

(2) do not apply to any provision of State law (including any provision of a State constitution) that

(A) is enacted after January 1, 2004;

(B) states explicitly that the provision is intended to supplement this title; and

(C) gives greater protection to consumers than is provided under this title.

## § 625. Disclosures to FBI for counterintelligence purposes [15 U.S.C. § 1681u]

(a) Identity of financial institutions. Notwithstanding section 604 [§ 1681b] or any other provision of this title, a consumer reporting agency shall furnish to the Federal Bureau of Investigation the names and addresses of all financial institutions (as that term is defined in section 1101 of the Right to Financial Privacy Act of 1978 [12 U.S.C. § 3401]) at which a consumer maintains or has maintained an account, to the extent that information is in the files of the agency, when presented with a written request for that information, signed by the Director of the Federal Bureau of Investigation, or the Director's designee in a position not lower than Deputy Assistant Director at Bureau headquarters or a Special Agent in Charge of a Bureau field office designated by the Director, which certifies compliance with this section. The Director or the Director's designee may make such a certification only if the Director or the Director's designee has determined in writing, that such information is sought for the conduct of an authorized investigation to protect against international terrorism or clandestine intelligence activities, provided that such an investigation of a United States person is not conducted solely upon the basis of activities protected by the first amendment to the Constitution of the United States.

(b) Identifying information. Notwithstanding the provisions of section 604 [§ 1681b] or any other provision of this title, a consumer reporting agency shall furnish identifying information respecting a consumer, limited to name, address, former addresses, places of employment, or former places of employment, to the Federal Bureau of Investigation when presented with a written request, signed by the Director or the Director's designee, which certifies compliance with this subsection. The Director or the Director's designee in a position not lower than Deputy Assistant Director at Bureau headquarters or a Special Agent in Charge of a Bureau field office designated by the Director may make such a certification only if the Director or the Director's designee has determined in writing that such information is sought for the conduct of an authorized investigation to protect against international terrorism or clandestine intelligence activities, provided that such an investigation of a United States person is not conducted solely upon the basis of activities protected by the first amendment to the Constitution of the United States.

(c) Court order for disclosure of consumer reports. Notwithstanding section 604 [§ 1681b] or any other provision of this title, if requested in writing by the Director of the Federal Bureau of Investigation, or a designee of the Director in a position not lower than Deputy Assistant Director at Bureau headquarters or a Special Agent in Charge of a Bureau field office designated by the

Director, a court may issue an order ex parte directing a consumer reporting agency to furnish a consumer report to the Federal Bureau of Investigation, upon a showing in camera that the consumer report is sought for the conduct of an authorized investigation to protect against international terrorism or clandestine intelligence activities, provided that such an investigation of a United States person is not conducted solely upon the basis of activities protected by the first amendment to the Constitution of the United States.

The terms of an order issued under this subsection shall not disclose that the order is issued for purposes of a counterintelligence investigation.

(d) Confidentiality. No consumer reporting agency or officer, employee, or agent of a consumer reporting agency shall disclose to any person, other than those officers, employees, or agents of a consumer reporting agency necessary to fulfill the requirement to disclose information to the Federal Bureau of Investigation under this section, that the Federal Bureau of Investigation has sought or obtained the identity of financial institutions or a consumer report respecting any consumer under subsection (a), (b), or (c), and no consumer reporting agency or officer, employee, or agent of a consumer reporting agency shall include in any consumer report any information that would indicate that the Federal Bureau of Investigation has sought or obtained such information or a consumer report.

(e) Payment of fees. The Federal Bureau of Investigation shall, subject to the availability of appropriations, pay to the consumer reporting agency assembling or providing report or information in accordance with procedures established under this section a fee for reimbursement for such costs as are reasonably necessary and which have been directly incurred in searching, reproducing, or transporting books, papers, records, or other data required or requested to be produced under this section.

(f) Limit on dissemination. The Federal Bureau of Investigation may not disseminate information obtained pursuant to this section outside of the Federal Bureau of Investigation, except to other Federal agencies as may be necessary for the approval or conduct of a foreign counterintelligence investigation, or, where the information concerns a person subject to the Uniform Code of Military Justice, to appropriate investigative authorities within the military department concerned as may be necessary for the conduct of a joint foreign counterintelligence investigation.

(g) Rules of construction. Nothing in this section shall be construed to prohibit information from being furnished by the Federal Bureau of Investigation pursuant to a subpoena or court order, in connection with a judicial or administrative proceeding to enforce the provisions of this Act. Nothing in this section shall be construed to authorize or permit the withholding of information from the Congress.

(h) Reports to Congress. On a semiannual basis, the Attorney General shall fully inform the Permanent Select Committee on Intelligence and the Committee on Banking, Finance and Urban Affairs of the House of Representatives, and the Select Committee on Intelligence and the Committee on Banking, Housing, and Urban Affairs of the Senate concerning all requests made pursuant to subsections (a), (b), and (c).

(i) Damages. Any agency or department of the United States obtaining or disclosing any consumer reports, records, or information contained therein in violation of this section is liable to the consumer to whom such consumer reports, records, or information relate in an amount equal to the sum of

(1) $100, without regard to the volume of consumer reports, records, or information involved;

(2) any actual damages sustained by the consumer as a result of the disclosure;

(3) if the violation is found to have been willful or intentional, such punitive damages as a court may allow; and

(4) in the case of any successful action to enforce liability under this subsection, the costs of the action, together with reasonable attorney fees, as determined by the court.

(j) Disciplinary actions for violations. If a court determines that any agency or department of the United States has violated any provision of this section and the court finds that the circumstances surrounding the violation raise questions of whether or not an officer or employee of the agency or department acted willfully or intentionally with respect to the violation, the agency or department shall promptly initiate a proceeding to determine whether or not disciplinary action is warranted against the officer or employee who was responsible for the violation.

(k) Good-faith exception. Notwithstanding any other provision of this title, any consumer reporting agency or agent or employee thereof making disclosure of consumer reports or identifying information pursuant to this subsection in good-faith reliance upon a certification of the Federal Bureau of Investigation pursuant to provisions of this section shall not be liable to any person for such disclosure under this title, the constitution of any State, or any law or regulation of any State or any political subdivision of any State.

(l) Limitation of remedies. Notwithstanding any other provision of this title, the remedies and sanctions set forth in this section shall be the only judicial remedies and sanctions for violation of this section.

(m) Injunctive relief. In addition to any other remedy contained in this section, injunctive relief shall be available to require compliance with the procedures of this section. In the event of any successful action under this subsection, costs together with reasonable attorney fees, as determined by the court, may be recovered.

## § 626. Disclosures to governmental agencies for counterterrorism purposes [15 U.S.C. §1681v]

(a) Disclosure. Notwithstanding section 604 or any other provision of this title, a consumer reporting agency shall furnish a consumer report of a consumer and all other information in a consumer's file to a government agency authorized to conduct investigations of, or intelligence or counterintelligence activities or analysis related to, international terrorism when presented with a written certification by such government agency that such information is necessary for the agency's conduct or such investigation, activity or analysis.

(b) Form of certification. The certification described in subsection (a) shall be signed by a supervisory official designated by the head of a Federal agency or an officer of a Federal agency whose appointment to office is required to be made by the President, by and with the advice and consent of the Senate.

(c) Confidentiality. No consumer reporting agency, or officer, employee, or agent of such consumer reporting agency, shall disclose to any person, or specify in any consumer report, that a government agency has sought or obtained access to information under subsection (a).

(d) Rule of construction. Nothing in section 625 shall be construed to limit the authority of the Director of the Federal Bureau of Investigation under this section.

(e) Safe harbor. Notwithstanding any other provision of this title, any consumer reporting agency or agent or employee thereof making disclosure of consumer reports or other information pursuant to this section in good-faith reliance upon a certification of a governmental agency pursuant to the provisions of this section shall not be liable to any person for such disclosure under this subchapter, the constitution of any State, or any law or regulation of any State or any political subdivision of any State.

# C. Fair Credit Reporting Act

## Reporting to Credit Bureaus and what you need to know

If you decide to report to the credit bureaus you will need to be familiar with the FCRA (Fair Credit Reporting Act). If you do any credit reporting of debts, you are considered a furnisher of information. All information submitted to the credit bureaus is used to help businesses evaluate consumers. You can find more information at *www.ftc.gov/* or by calling 1-877-FTC-HELP.

### § 601. Short title

This title may be cited as the Fair Credit Reporting Act.

### § 602. Congressional findings and statement of purpose [15 U.S.C. § 1681]

(a) Accuracy and fairness of credit reporting. The Congress makes the following findings:

(1) The banking system is dependent upon fair and accurate credit reporting. Inaccurate credit reports directly impair the efficiency of the banking system, and unfair credit reporting methods undermine the public confidence which is essential to the continued functioning of the banking system.

(2) An elaborate mechanism has been developed for investigating and evaluating the credit worthiness, credit standing, credit capacity, character, and general reputation of consumers.

(3) Consumer reporting agencies have assumed a vital role in assembling and evaluating consumer credit and other information on consumers.

(4) There is a need to insure that consumer reporting agencies exercise their grave responsibilities with fairness, impartiality, and a respect for the consumer's right to privacy.

(b) Reasonable procedures. It is the purpose of this title to require that consumer reporting agencies adopt reasonable procedures for meeting the needs of commerce for consumer credit, personnel, insurance, and other information in a manner which is fair and equitable to the consumer, with regard to the confidentiality, accuracy, relevancy, and proper utilization of such information in accordance with the requirements of this title.

### § 603. Definitions; rules of construction [15 U.S.C. § 1681a]

(a) Definitions and rules of construction set forth in this section are applicable for the purposes of this title.

(b) The term "person" means any individual, partnership, corporation, trust, estate, cooperative, association, government or governmental subdivision or agency, or other entity.

(c) The term "consumer" means an individual.

(d) Consumer report.

(1) In general. The term "consumer report" means any written, oral, or other communication of any information by a consumer reporting agency bearing on a consumer's credit worthiness, credit standing, credit capacity, character, general reputation, personal characteristics, or mode of living which is used or expected to be used or collected in whole or in part for the purpose of serving as a factor in establishing the consumer's eligibility for

(A) credit or insurance to be used primarily for personal, family, or household purposes;

(B) employment purposes; or

(C) any other purpose authorized under section 604 [§ 1681b].

(2) Exclusions. The term "consumer report" does not include

(A) any

(i) report containing information solely as to transactions or experiences between the consumer and the person making the report;

(ii) communication of that information among persons related by common ownership or affiliated by corporate control; or

(iii) communication of other information among persons related by common ownership or affiliated by corporate control, if it is clearly and conspicuously disclosed to the consumer that the information may be communicated among such persons and the consumer is given the opportunity, before the time that the information is initially communicated, to direct that such information not be communicated among such persons;

(B) any authorization or approval of a specific extension of credit directly or indirectly by the issuer of a credit card or similar device;

(C) any report in which a person who has been requested by a third party to make a specific extension of credit directly or indirectly to a consumer conveys his or her decision with respect to such request, if the third party advises the consumer of the name and address of the person to whom the request was made, and such person makes the disclosures to the consumer required under section 615 [§ 1681m]; or

(D) a communication described in subsection (o).

(e) The term "investigative consumer report" means a consumer report or portion thereof in which information on a consumer's character, general reputation, personal characteristics, or mode of living is obtained through personal interviews with neighbors, friends, or associates of the consumer reported on or with others with whom he is acquainted or who may have knowledge concerning any such items of information. However, such information shall not include specific factual information on a consumer's credit record obtained directly from a creditor of the consumer or from a consumer reporting agency when such information was obtained directly from a creditor of the consumer or from the consumer.

(f) The term "consumer reporting agency" means any person which, for monetary fees, dues, or on a cooperative nonprofit basis, regularly engages in whole or in part in the practice of assembling or evaluating consumer credit information or other information on consumers for the purpose of furnishing consumer reports to third parties, and which uses any means or facility of interstate commerce for the purpose of preparing or furnishing consumer reports.

(g) The term "file," when used in connection with information on any consumer, means all of the information on that consumer recorded and retained by a consumer reporting agency regardless of how the information is stored.

(h) The term "employment purposes" when used in connection with a consumer report means a report used for the purpose of evaluating a consumer for employment, promotion, reassignment or retention as an employee.

(i) The term "medical information" means information or records obtained, with the consent of the individual to whom it relates, from licensed physicians or medical practitioners, hospitals, clinics, or other medical or medically related facilities.

(j) Definitions relating to child support obligations.

> (1) Overdue support. The term "overdue support" has the meaning given to such term in section 666(e) of title 42 [Social Security Act, 42 U.S.C. § 666(e)].

> (2) State or local child support enforcement agency. The term "State or local child support enforcement agency" means a State or local agency which administers a State or local program for establishing and enforcing child support obligations.

(k) Adverse action.

> (1) Actions included. The term "adverse action"

> > (A) has the same meaning as in section 701(d)(6) of the Equal Credit Opportunity Act; and

> > (B) means

> > > (i) a denial or cancellation of, an increase in any charge for, or a reduction or other adverse or unfavorable change in the terms of coverage or amount of, any insurance, existing or applied for, in connection with the underwriting of insurance;

> > > (ii) a denial of employment or any other decision for employment purposes that adversely affects any current or prospective employee;

> > > (iii) a denial or cancellation of, an increase in any charge for, or any other adverse or unfavorable change in the terms of, any license or benefit described in section 604(a)(3)(D) [§ 1681b]; and

> > > (iv) an action taken or determination that is

> > > > (I) made in connection with an application that was made by, or a transaction

that was initiated by, any consumer, or in connection with a review of an account under section 604(a)(3)(F)(ii)[§ 1681b]; and

(II) adverse to the interests of the consumer.

(2) Applicable findings, decisions, commentary, and orders. For purposes of any determination of whether an action is an adverse action under paragraph (1)(A), all appropriate final findings, decisions, commentary, and orders issued under section 701(d)(6) of the Equal Credit Opportunity Act by the Board of Governors of the Federal Reserve System or any court shall apply.

(l) Firm offer of credit or insurance. The term "firm offer of credit or insurance" means any offer of credit or insurance to a consumer that will be honored if the consumer is determined, based on information in a consumer report on the consumer, to meet the specific criteria used to select the consumer for the offer, except that the offer may be further conditioned on one or more of the following:

(1) The consumer being determined, based on information in the consumer's application for the credit or insurance, to meet specific criteria bearing on credit worthiness or insurability, as applicable, that are established

(A) before selection of the consumer for the offer; and

(B) for the purpose of determining whether to extend credit or insurance pursuant to the offer.

(2) Verification

(A) that the consumer continues to meet the specific criteria used to select the consumer for the offer, by using information in a consumer report on the consumer, information in the consumer's application for the credit or insurance, or other information bearing on the credit worthiness or insurability of the consumer; or

(B) of the information in the consumer's application for the credit or insurance, to determine that the consumer meets the specific criteria bearing on credit worthiness or insurability.

(3) The consumer furnishing any collateral that is a requirement for the extension of the credit or insurance that was

(A) established before selection of the consumer for the offer of credit or insurance; and

(B) disclosed to the consumer in the offer of credit or insurance.

(m) Credit or insurance transaction that is not initiated by the consumer. The term"credit or insurance transaction that is not initiated by the consumer" does not include the use of a consumer report by a person with which the consumer has an account or insurance policy, for purposes of

(1) reviewing the account or insurance policy; or

(2) collecting the account.

(n) State. The term "State" means any State, the Commonwealth of Puerto Rico, the District of Columbia, and any territory or possession of the United States.

(o) Excluded communications. A communication is described in this subsection if it is a communication

(1) that, but for subsection (d)(2)(D), would be an investigative consumer report;

(2) that is made to a prospective employer for the purpose of

(A) procuring an employee for the employer; or

(B) procuring an opportunity for a natural person to work for the employer;

(3) that is made by a person who regularly performs such procurement;

(4) that is not used by any person for any purpose other than a purpose described in subparagraph (A) or (B) of paragraph (2); and

(5) with respect to which

(A) the consumer who is the subject of the communication

(i) consents orally or in writing to the nature and scope of the communication, before the collection of any information for the purpose of making the communication;

(ii) consents orally or in writing to the making of the communication to a prospective employer, before the making of the communication; and

(iii) in the case of consent under clause (i) or (ii) given orally, is provided written confirmation of that consent by the person making the communication, not later than 3 business days after the receipt of the consent by that person;

(B) the person who makes the communication does not, for the purpose of making the communication, make any inquiry that if made by a prospective employer of the consumer who is the subject of the communication would violate any applicable Federal or State equal employment opportunity law or regulation; and

(C) the person who makes the communication

(i) discloses in writing to the consumer who is the subject of the communication, not later than 5 business days after receiving any request from the consumer for such disclosure, the nature and substance of all information in the consumer's file at the time of the request, except that the sources of any information that is acquired solely for use in making the communication and is actually used for no other purpose, need not be disclosed other than under appropriate discovery procedures in any court of competent jurisdiction in which an action is brought; and

(ii) notifies the consumer who is the subject of the communication, in writing, of the consumer's right to request the information described in clause (i).

(p) Consumer reporting agency that compiles and maintains files on consumers on a nationwide basis. The term "consumer reporting agency that compiles and maintains files on consumers on a nationwide basis" means a consumer reporting agency that regularly engages in the practice of assembling or evaluating, and maintaining, for the purpose of furnishing consumer reports to third parties bearing on a consumer's credit worthiness, credit standing, or credit capacity, each of the following regarding consumers residing nationwide:

(1) Public record information.

(2) Credit account information from persons who furnish that information regularly and in the ordinary course of business.

## § 604. Permissible purposes of consumer reports [15 U.S.C. § 1681b]

(a) In general. Subject to subsection (c), any consumer reporting agency may furnish a consumer report under the following circumstances and no other:

(1) In response to the order of a court having jurisdiction to issue such an order, or a subpoena issued in connection with proceedings before a Federal grand jury.

(2) In accordance with the written instructions of the consumer to whom it relates.

(3) To a person which it has reason to believe

(A) intends to use the information in connection with a credit transaction involving the consumer on whom the information is to be furnished and involving the extension of credit to, or review or collection of an account of, the consumer; or

(B) intends to use the information for employment purposes; or

(C) intends to use the information in connection with the underwriting of insurance involving the consumer; or

(D) intends to use the information in connection with a determination of the consumer's eligibility for a license or other benefit granted by a governmental instrumentality required by law to consider an applicant's financial responsibility or status; or

(E) intends to use the information, as a potential investor or servicer, or current insurer, in connection with a valuation of, or an assessment of the credit or prepayment risks associated with, an existing credit obligation; or

(F) otherwise has a legitimate business need for the information

(i) in connection with a business transaction that is initiated by the consumer; or

(ii) to review an account to determine whether the consumer continues to meet the terms of the account.

(4) In response to a request by the head of a State or local child support enforcement agency (or a State or local government official authorized by the head of such an agency), if the person making the request certifies to the consumer reporting agency that

(A) the consumer report is needed for the purpose of establishing an individual's capacity to make child support payments or determining the appropriate level of such payments;

(B) the paternity of the consumer for the child to which the obligation relates has been established or acknowledged by the consumer in accordance with State laws under which the obligation arises (if required by those laws);

(C) the person has provided at least 10 days' prior notice to the consumer whose report is requested, by certified or registered mail to the last known address of the consumer, that the report will be requested; and

(D) the consumer report will be kept confidential, will be used solely for a purpose described in subparagraph (A), and will not be used in connection with any other civil, administrative, or criminal proceeding, or for any other purpose.

(5) To an agency administering a State plan under Section 454 of the Social Security Act (42 U.S.C. § 654) for use to set an initial or modified child support award.

(b) Conditions for furnishing and using consumer reports for employment purposes.

(1) Certification from user. A consumer reporting agency may furnish a consumer report for employment purposes only if

(A) the person who obtains such report from the agency certifies to the agency that

(i) the person has complied with paragraph (2) with respect to the consumer report, and the person will comply with paragraph (3) with respect to the consumer report if paragraph (3) becomes applicable; and

(ii) information from the consumer report will not be used in violation of any applicable Federal or State equal employment opportunity law or regulation; and

(B) the consumer reporting agency provides with the report, or has previously provided, a summary of the consumer's rights under this title, as prescribed by the Federal Trade Commission under section 609(c)(3) [§ 1681g].

(2) Disclosure to consumer.

(A) In general. Except as provided in subparagraph (B), a person may not procure a consumer report, or cause a consumer report to be procured, for employment purposes with respect to any consumer, unless—

(i) a clear and conspicuous disclosure has been made in writing to the consumer at any time before the report is procured or caused to be procured, in a document that consists solely of the disclosure, that a consumer report may be obtained for employment purposes; and

(ii) the consumer has authorized in writing (which authorization may be made on the document referred to in clause (i)) the procurement of the report by that person.

(B) Application by mail, telephone, computer, or other similar means. If a consumer described in subparagraph (C) applies for employment by mail, telephone, computer, or other similar means, at any time before a consumer report is procured or caused to be procured in connection with that application—

(i) the person who procures the consumer report on the consumer for employment purposes shall provide to the consumer, by oral, written, or electronic means, notice that a consumer report may be obtained for employment purposes, and a summary of the consumer's rights under section 615(a)(3); and

(ii) the consumer shall have consented, orally, in writing, or electronically to the procurement of the report by that person.

(C) Scope. Subparagraph (B) shall apply to a person procuring a consumer report on a consumer in connection with the consumer's application for employment only if-

(i) the consumer is applying for a position over which the Secretary of Transportation has the power to establish qualifications and maximum hours of service pursuant to the provisions of section 31502 of title 49, or a position subject to safety regulation by a State transportation agency; and

(ii) as of the time at which the person procures the report or causes the report to be procured the only interaction between the consumer and the person in connection with that employment application has been by mail, telephone, computer, or other similar means.

(3) Conditions on use for adverse actions.

(A) In general. Except as provided in subparagraph (B), in using a consumer report for employment purposes, before taking any adverse action based in whole or in part on the report, the person intending to take such adverse action shall provide to the consumer to whom the report relates—

(i) a copy of the report; and

(ii) a description in writing of the rights of the consumer under this title, as prescribed by the Federal Trade Commission under section 609(c)(3).

(B) Application by mail, telephone, computer, or other similar means.

(i) If a consumer described in subparagraph (C) applies for employment by mail, telephone, computer, or other similar means, and if a person who has procured a consumer report on the consumer for employment purposes takes adverse action on the employment application based in whole or in part on the report, then the person must provide to the consumer to whom the report relates, in lieu of the notices required under subparagraph (A) of this section and under section 615(a), within 3 business days of taking such action, an oral, written or electronic notification—

(I) that adverse action has been taken based in whole or in part on a consumer report received from a consumer reporting agency;

(II) of the name, address and telephone number of the consumer reporting agency that furnished the consumer report (including a toll-free telephone number established by the agency if the agency compiles and maintains files on consumers on a nationwide basis);

(III) that the consumer reporting agency did not make the decision to take the adverse action and is unable to provide to the consumer the specific reasons why the adverse action was taken; and

(IV) that the consumer may, upon providing proper identification, request a free copy of a report and may dispute with the consumer reporting agency the accuracy or completeness of any information in a report.

(ii) If, under clause (B)(i)(IV), the consumer requests a copy of a consumer report from the person who procured the report, then, within 3 business days of receiving the consumer's request, together with proper identification, the person must send or provide to the consumer a copy of a report and a copy of the consumer's rights as prescribed by the Federal Trade Commission under section 609(c)(3).

(C) Scope. Subparagraph (B) shall apply to a person procuring a consumer report on a consumer in connection with the consumer's application for employment only if—

(i) the consumer is applying for a position over which the Secretary of Transportation has the power to establish qualifications and maximum hours of service pursuant to the provisions of section 31502 of title 49, or a position subject to safety regulation by a State transportation agency; and

(ii) as of the time at which the person procures the report or causes the report to be procured the only interaction between the consumer and the person in connection with that employment application has been by mail, telephone, computer, or other similar means.

(4) Exception for national security investigations.

(A) In general. In the case of an agency or department of the United States Government which seeks to obtain and use a consumer report for employment purposes, paragraph (3) shall not apply to any adverse action by such agency or department which is based in part on such consumer report, if the head of such agency or department makes a written finding that—

(i) the consumer report is relevant to a national security investigation of such agency or department;

(ii) the investigation is within the jurisdiction of such agency or department;

(iii) there is reason to believe that compliance with paragraph (3) will—

(I) endanger the life or physical safety of any person;

(II) result in flight from prosecution;

(III) result in the destruction of, or tampering with, evidence relevant to the investigation;

(IV) result in the intimidation of a potential witness relevant to the investigation;

(V) result in the compromise of classified information; or

(VI) otherwise seriously jeopardize or unduly delay the investigation or another official proceeding.

(B) Notification of consumer upon conclusion of investigation. Upon the conclusion of a national security investigation described in subparagraph (A), or upon the determination that the exception under subparagraph (A) is no longer required for the reasons set forth in such subparagraph, the official exercising the authority in such subparagraph shall provide to the consumer who is the subject of the consumer report with regard to which such finding was made -

(i) a copy of such consumer report with any classified information redacted as necessary;

(ii) notice of any adverse action which is based, in part, on the consumer report; and

(iii) the identification with reasonable specificity of the nature of the investigation for which the consumer report was sought.

(C) Delegation by head of agency or department. For purposes of subparagraphs (A) and (B), the head of any agency or department of the United States Government may delegate his or her authorities under this paragraph to an official of such agency or department who has personnel security responsibilities and is a member of the Senior Executive Service or equivalent civilian or military rank.

(D) Report to the congress. Not later than January 31 of each year, the head of each agency and department of the United States Government that exercised authority under this paragraph during the preceding year shall submit a report to the Congress on the number of times the department or agency exercised such authority during the year.

(E) Definitions. For purposes of this paragraph, the following definitions shall apply:

(i) Classified information. The term 'classified information' means information that is protected from unauthorized disclosure under Executive Order No. 12958 or successor orders.

(ii) National security investigation. The term 'national security investigation' means any official inquiry by an agency or department of the United States Government to determine the eligibility of a consumer to receive access or continued access to classified information or to determine whether classified information has been lost or compromised.

(c) Furnishing reports in connection with credit or insurance transactions that are not initiated by the consumer.

(1) In general. A consumer reporting agency may furnish a consumer report relating to any consumer pursuant to subparagraph (A) or (C) of subsection (a)(3) in connection with any credit or insurance transaction that is not initiated by the consumer only if

(A) the consumer authorizes the agency to provide such report to such person; or

(B) (i) the transaction consists of a firm offer of credit or insurance;

(ii) the consumer reporting agency has complied with subsection (e); and

(iii) there is not in effect an election by the consumer, made in accordance with subsection (e), to have the consumer's name and address excluded from lists of names provided by the agency pursuant to this paragraph.

(2) Limits on information received under paragraph (1)(B). A person may receive pursuant to paragraph (1)(B) only

(A) the name and address of a consumer;

(B) an identifier that is not unique to the consumer and that is used by the person solely for the purpose of verifying the identity of the consumer; and

(C) other information pertaining to a consumer that does not identify the relationship or experience of the consumer with respect to a particular creditor or other entity.

(3) Information regarding inquiries. Except as provided in section 609(a)(5) [§ 1681g], a consumer reporting agency shall not furnish to any person a record of inquiries in connection with a credit or insurance transaction that is not initiated by a consumer.

(d) Reserved.

(e) Election of consumer to be excluded from lists.

(1) In general. A consumer may elect to have the consumer's name and address excluded from any list provided by a consumer reporting agency under subsection (c)(1)(B) in connection with a credit or insurance transaction that is not initiated by the consumer, by notifying the agency in accordance with paragraph (2) that the consumer does not consent to any use of a consumer report relating to the consumer in connection with any credit or insurance transaction that is not initiated by the consumer.

(2) Manner of notification. A consumer shall notify a consumer reporting agency under paragraph (1)

(A) through the notification system maintained by the agency under paragraph (5); or

(B) by submitting to the agency a signed notice of election form issued by the agency for purposes of this subparagraph.

(3) Response of agency after notification through system. Upon receipt of notification of the election of a consumer under paragraph (1) through the notification system maintained by the agency under paragraph (5), a consumer reporting agency shall

(A) inform the consumer that the election is effective only for the 2-year period following the election if the consumer does not submit to the agency a signed notice of election form issued by the agency for purposes of paragraph (2)(B); and

(B) provide to the consumer a notice of election form, if requested by the consumer, not later than 5 business days after receipt of the notification of the election through the system established under paragraph (5), in the case of a request made at the time the consumer provides notification through the system.

(4) Effectiveness of election. An election of a consumer under paragraph (1)

(A) shall be effective with respect to a consumer reporting agency beginning 5 business days after the date on which the consumer notifies the agency in accordance with paragraph (2);

(B) shall be effective with respect to a consumer reporting agency

(i) subject to subparagraph (C), during the 2-year period beginning 5 business days after the date on which the consumer notifies the agency of the election, in the case of an election for which a consumer notifies the agency only in accordance with paragraph (2)(A); or

(ii) until the consumer notifies the agency under subparagraph (C), in the case of an election for which a consumer notifies the agency in accordance with paragraph (2)(B);

(C) shall not be effective after the date on which the consumer notifies the agency, through the notification system established by the agency under paragraph (5), that the election is no longer effective; and

(D) shall be effective with respect to each affiliate of the agency.

(5) Notification system.

(A) In general. Each consumer reporting agency that, under subsection (c)(1)(B), furnishes a consumer report in connection with a credit or insurance transaction that is not initiated by a consumer, shall

(i) establish and maintain a notification system, including a toll-free telephone number, which permits any consumer whose consumer report is maintained by the agency to notify the agency, with appropriate identification, of the consumer's election to have the consumer's name and address excluded from any such list of names and addresses provided by the agency for such a transaction; and

(ii) publish by not later than 365 days after the date of enactment of the Consumer Credit Reporting Reform Act of 1996, and not less than annually thereafter, in a publication of general circulation in the area served by the agency

(I) a notification that information in consumer files maintained by the agency may be used in connection with such transactions; and

(II) the address and toll-free telephone number for consumers to use to notify the agency of the consumer's election under clause (I).

(B) Establishment and maintenance as compliance. Establishment and maintenance of a notification system (including a toll-free telephone number) and publication by a consumer reporting agency on the agency's own behalf and on behalf of any of its affiliates in accordance with this paragraph is deemed to be compliance with this paragraph by each of those affiliates.

(6) Notification system by agencies that operate nationwide. Each consumer reporting agency that compiles and maintains files on consumers on a nationwide basis shall establish and maintain a notification system for purposes of paragraph (5) jointly with other such consumer reporting agencies.

(f) Certain use or obtaining of information prohibited. A person shall not use or obtain a consumer report for any purpose unless

(1) the consumer report is obtained for a purpose for which the consumer report is authorized to be furnished under this section; and

(2) the purpose is certified in accordance with section 607 [§ 1681e] by a prospective user of the report through a general or specific certification.

(g) Furnishing reports containing medical information. A consumer reporting agency shall not furnish for employment purposes, or in connection with a credit or insurance transaction, a consumer report that contains medical information about a consumer, unless the consumer consents to the furnishing of the report.

## § 605. Requirements relating to information contained in consumer reports [15 U.S.C. § 1681c]

(a) Information excluded from consumer reports. Except as authorized under subsection (b) of this section, no consumer reporting agency may make any consumer report containing any of the following items of information:

(1) Cases under title 11 [United States Code] or under the Bankruptcy Act that, from the date of entry of the order for relief or the date of adjudication, as the case may be, antedate the report by more than 10 years.

(2) Civil suits, civil judgments, and records of arrest that from date of entry, antedate the

report by more than seven years or until the governing statute of limitations has expired, whichever is the longer period.

(3) Paid tax liens which, from date of payment, antedate the report by more than seven years.

(4) Accounts placed for collection or charged to profit and loss which antedate the report by more than seven years.[(1)]

(5) Any other adverse item of information, other than records of convictions of crimes which antedates the report by more than seven years.[1]

(b) Exempted cases. The provisions of subsection (a) of this section are not applicable in the case of any consumer credit report to be used in connection with

(1) a credit transaction involving, or which may reasonably be expected to involve, a principal amount of $150,000 or more;

(2) the underwriting of life insurance involving, or which may reasonably be expected to involve, a face amount of $150,000 or more; or

(3) the employment of any individual at an annual salary which equals, or which may reasonably be expected to equal $75,000, or more.

(c) Running of reporting period.

(1) In general. The 7-year period referred to in paragraphs (4) and (6)[(2)] of subsection (a) shall begin, with respect to any delinquent account that is placed for collection (internally or by referral to a third party, whichever is earlier), charged to profit and loss, or subjected to any similar action, upon the expiration of the 180-day period beginning on the date of the commencement of the delinquency which immediately preceded the collection activity, charge to profit and loss, or similar action.

(2) Effective date. Paragraph (1) shall apply only to items of information added to the file of a consumer on or after the date that is 455 days after the date of enactment of the Consumer Credit Reporting Reform Act of 1996.

(d) Information required to be disclosed. Any consumer reporting agency that furnishes a consumer report that contains information regarding any case involving the consumer that arises under title 11, United States Code, shall include in the report an identification of the chapter of such title 11 under which such case arises if provided by the source of the information. If any case arising or filed under title 11, United States Code, is withdrawn by the consumer before a final judgment, the consumer reporting agency shall include in the report that such case or filing was withdrawn upon receipt of documentation certifying such withdrawal.

(e) Indication of closure of account by consumer. If a consumer reporting agency is notified pursuant to section 623(a)(4) [§ 1681s-2] that a credit account of a consumer was voluntarily closed by the consumer, the agency shall indicate that fact in any consumer report that includes information related to the account.

(f) Indication of dispute by consumer. If a consumer reporting agency is notified pursuant to section 623(a)(3) [§ 1681s-2] that information regarding a consumer who was furnished to the agency is disputed by the consumer, the agency shall indicate that fact in each consumer report that includes the disputed information.

## § 606. Disclosure of investigative consumer reports [15 U.S.C. § 1681d]

(a) Disclosure of fact of preparation. A person may not procure or cause to be prepared an investigative consumer report on any consumer unless

(1) it is clearly and accurately disclosed to the consumer that an investigative consumer report including information as to his character, general reputation, personal characteristics and mode of living, whichever are applicable, may be made, and such disclosure

(A) is made in a writing mailed, or otherwise delivered, to the consumer, not later than three days after the date on which the report was first requested, and

(B) includes a statement informing the consumer of his right to request the additional disclosures provided for under subsection (b) of this section and the written summary of the rights of the consumer prepared pursuant to section 609(c) [§ 1681g]; and

(2) the person certifies or has certified to the consumer reporting agency that

(A) the person has made the disclosures to the consumer required by paragraph (1); and

(B) the person will comply with subsection (b).

(b) Disclosure on request of nature and scope of investigation. Any person who procures or causes to be prepared an investigative consumer report on any consumer shall, upon written request made by the consumer within a reasonable period of time after the receipt by him of the disclosure required by subsection (a)(1) of this section, make a complete and accurate disclosure of the nature and scope of the investigation requested. This disclosure shall be made in a writing mailed, or otherwise delivered, to the consumer not later than five days after the date on which the request for such disclosure was received from the consumer or such report was first requested, whichever is the later.

(c) Limitation on liability upon showing of reasonable procedures for compliance with provisions. No person may be held liable for any violation of subsection (a) or (b) of this section if he shows by a preponderance of the evidence that at the time of the violation he maintained reasonable procedures to assure compliance with subsection (a) or (b) of this section.

(d) Prohibitions.

(1) Certification. A consumer reporting agency shall not prepare or furnish investigative consumer report unless the agency has received a certification under subsection (a)(2) from the person who requested the report.

(2) Inquiries. A consumer reporting agency shall not make an inquiry for the purpose of preparing an investigative consumer report on a consumer for employment purposes if the

making of the inquiry by an employer or prospective employer of the consumer would violate any applicable Federal or State equal employment opportunity law or regulation

(3) Certain public record information. Except as otherwise provided in section 613 [§ 1681k], a consumer reporting agency shall not furnish an investigative consumer report that includes information that is a matter of public record and that relates to an arrest, indictment, conviction, civil judicial action, tax lien, or outstanding judgment, unless the agency has verified the accuracy of the information during the 30-day period ending on the date on which the report is furnished.

(4) Certain adverse information. A consumer reporting agency shall not prepare or furnish an investigative consumer report on a consumer that contains information that is adverse to the interest of the consumer and that is obtained through a personal interview with a neighbor, friend, or associate of the consumer or with another person with whom the consumer is acquainted or who has knowledge of such item of information, unless

(A) the agency has followed reasonable procedures to obtain confirmation of the information, from an additional source that has independent and direct knowledge of the information; or

(B) the person interviewed is the best possible source of the information.

## § 607. Compliance procedures [15 U.S.C. § 1681e]

(a) Identity and purposes of credit users. Every consumer reporting agency shall maintain reasonable procedures designed to avoid violations of section 605 [§ 1681c] and to limit the furnishing of consumer reports to the purposes listed under section 604 [§ 1681b] of this title. These procedures shall require that prospective users of the information identify themselves, certify the purposes for which the information is sought, and certify that the information will be used for no other purpose. Every consumer reporting agency shall make a reasonable effort to verify the identity of a new prospective user and the uses certified by such prospective user prior to furnishing such user a consumer report. No consumer reporting agency may furnish a consumer report to any person if it has reasonable grounds for believing that the consumer report will not be used for a purpose listed in section 604 [§ 1681b] of this title.

(b) Accuracy of report. Whenever a consumer reporting agency prepares a consumer report it shall follow reasonable procedures to assure maximum possible accuracy of the information concerning the individual about whom the report relates.

(c) Disclosure of consumer reports by users allowed. A consumer reporting agency may not prohibit a user of a consumer report furnished by the agency on a consumer from disclosing the contents of the report to the consumer, if adverse action against the consumer has been taken by the user based in whole or in part on the report.

(d) Notice to users and furnishers of information.

(1) Notice requirement. A consumer reporting agency shall provide to any person

(A) who regularly and in the ordinary course of business furnishes information to the agency with respect to any consumer; or

(B) to whom a consumer report is provided by the agency; a notice of such person's responsibilities under this title.

(2) Content of notice. The Federal Trade Commission shall prescribe the content of notices under paragraph (1), and a consumer reporting agency shall be in compliance with this subsection if it provides a notice under paragraph (1) that is substantially similar to the Federal Trade Commission prescription under this paragraph.

(e) Procurement of consumer report for resale.

(1) Disclosure. A person may not procure a consumer report for purposes of reselling the report (or any information in the report) unless the person discloses to the consumer reporting agency that originally furnishes the report

(A) the identity of the end-user of the report (or information); and

(B) each permissible purpose under section 604 [§ 1681b] for which the report is furnished to the end-user of the report (or information).

(2) Responsibilities of procurers for resale. A person who procures a consumer report for purposes of reselling the report (or any information in the report) shall

(A) establish and comply with reasonable procedures designed to ensure that the report (or information) is resold by the person only for a purpose for which the report may be furnished under section 604 [§ 1681b], including by requiring that each person to which the report (or information) is resold and that resells or provides the report (or information) to any other person

(i) identifies each end user of the resold report (or information);

(ii) certifies each purpose for which the report (or information) will be used; and

(iii) certifies that the report (or information) will be used for no other purpose; and
(B) before reselling the report, make reasonable efforts to verify the identifications and certifications made under subparagraph (A).

(3) Resale of consumer report to a federal agency or department. Notwithstanding paragraph (1) or (2), a person who procures a consumer report for purposes of reselling the report (or any information in the report) shall not disclose the identity of the end-user of the report under paragraph (1) or (2) if—

(A) the end user is an agency or department of the United States Government which procures the report from the person for purposes of determining the eligibility of the consumer concerned to receive access or continued access to classified information (as defined in section 604(b)(4)(E)(i)); and

(B) the agency or department certifies in writing to the person reselling the report that nondisclosure is necessary to protect classified information or the safety of persons employed by or contracting with, or undergoing investigation for work or contracting with the agency or department.

## § 608. Disclosures to governmental agencies [15 U.S.C. § 1681f]

Notwithstanding the provisions of section 604 [§ 1681b] of this title, a consumer reporting agency may furnish identifying information respecting any consumer, limited to his name, address, former addresses, places of employment, or former places of employment, to a governmental agency.

## § 609. Disclosures to consumers [15 U.S.C. § 1681g]

(a) Information on file; sources; report recipients. Every consumer reporting agency shall, upon request, and subject to 610(a)(1) [§ 1681h], clearly and accurately disclose to the consumer:

(1) All information in the consumer's file at the time of the request, except that nothing in this paragraph shall be construed to require a consumer reporting agency to disclose to a consumer any information concerning credit scores or any other risk scores or predictors relating to the consumer.

(2) The sources of the information; except that the sources of information acquired solely for use in preparing an investigative consumer report and actually used for no other purpose need not be disclosed: Provided, That in the event an action is brought under this title, such sources shall be available to the plaintiff under appropriate discovery procedures in the court in which the action is brought.

(3) (A) Identification of each person (including each end-user identified under section 607(e)(1) [§ 1681e]) that procured a consumer report

(i) for employment purposes, during the 2-year period preceding the date on which the request is made; or

(ii) for any other purpose, during the 1-year period preceding the date on which the request is made.

(B) An identification of a person under subparagraph (A) shall include

(i) the name of the person or, if applicable, the trade name (written in full) under which such person conducts business; and

(ii) upon request of the consumer, the address and telephone number of the person.

(C) Subparagraph (A) does not apply if—

(i) the end user is an agency or department of the United States Government that procures the report from the person for purposes of determining the eligibility of the consumer to whom the report relates to receive access or continued access to classified information (as defined in section 604(b)(4)(E)(i)); and

(ii) the head of the agency or department makes a written finding as prescribed under section 604(b)(4)(A).

(4) The dates, original payees, and amounts of any checks upon which is based any adverse characterization of the consumer, included in the file at the time of the disclosure.

(5) A record of all inquiries received by the agency during the 1-year period preceding the request that identified the consumer in connection with a credit or insurance transaction that was not initiated by the consumer.

(b) Exempt information. The requirements of subsection (a) of this section respecting the disclosure of sources of information and the recipients of consumer reports do not apply to information received or consumer reports furnished prior to the effective date of this title except to the extent that the matter involved is contained in the files of the consumer reporting agency on that date.

(c) Summary of rights required to be included with disclosure.

(1) Summary of rights. A consumer reporting agency shall provide to a consumer, with each written disclosure by the agency to the consumer under this section

(A) a written summary of all of the rights that the consumer has under this title; and

(B) in the case of a consumer reporting agency that compiles and maintains files on consumers on a nationwide basis, a toll-free telephone number established by the agency, at which personnel are accessible to consumers during normal business hours.

(2) Specific items required to be included. The summary of rights required under paragraph (1) shall include

(A) a brief description of this title and all rights of consumers under this title;

(B) an explanation of how the consumer may exercise the rights of the consumer under this title;

(C) a list of all Federal agencies responsible for enforcing any provision of this title and the address and any appropriate phone number of each such agency, in a form that will assist the consumer in selecting the appropriate agency;

(D) a statement that the consumer may have additional rights under State law and that the consumer may wish to contact a State or local consumer protection agency or a State attorney general to learn of those rights; and

(E) a statement that a consumer reporting agency is not required to remove accurate derogatory information from a consumer's file, unless the information is outdated under section 605 [§ 1681c] or cannot be verified.

(3) Form of summary of rights. For purposes of this subsection and any disclosure by a consumer reporting agency required under this title with respect to consumers' rights, the Federal Trade Commission (after consultation with each Federal agency referred to in section 621(b) [§ 1681s]) shall prescribe the form and content of any such disclosure of the rights of consumers required under this title. A consumer reporting agency shall be in compliance

with this subsection if it provides disclosures under paragraph (1) that are substantially similar to the Federal Trade Commission prescription under this paragraph.

(4) Effectiveness. No disclosures shall be required under this subsection until the date on which the Federal Trade Commission prescribes the form and content of such disclosures under paragraph (3).

## § 610. Conditions and form of disclosure to consumers [15 U.S.C. § 1681h]

(a) In general.

(1) Proper identification. A consumer reporting agency shall require, as a condition of making the disclosures required under section 609 [§ 1681g], that the consumer furnish proper identification.

(2) Disclosure in writing. Except as provided in subsection (b), the disclosures required to be made under section 609 [§ 1681g] shall be provided under that section in writing.

(b) Other forms of disclosure.

(1) In general. If authorized by a consumer, a consumer reporting agency may make the disclosures required under 609 [§ 1681g]

(A) other than in writing; and

(B) in such form as may be

(i) specified by the consumer in accordance with paragraph (2); and

(ii) available from the agency.

(2) Form. A consumer may specify pursuant to paragraph (1) that disclosures under section 609 [§ 1681g] shall be made

(A) in person, upon the appearance of the consumer at the place of business of the consumer reporting agency where disclosures are regularly provided, during normal business hours, and on reasonable notice;

(B) by telephone, if the consumer has made a written request for disclosure by telephone;

(C) by electronic means, if available from the agency; or

(D) by any other reasonable means that is available from the agency.

(c) Trained personnel. Any consumer reporting agency shall provide trained personnel to explain to the consumer any information furnished to him pursuant to section 609 [§ 1681g] of this title.

(d) Persons accompanying consumer. The consumer shall be permitted to be accompanied by one other person of his choosing, who shall furnish reasonable identification. A consumer reporting agency may require the consumer to furnish a written statement granting permission to the consumer reporting agency to discuss the consumer's file in such person's presence.

(e) Limitation of liability. Except as provided in sections 616 and 617 [§§ 1681n and 1681o] of this title, no consumer may bring any action or proceeding in the nature of defamation, invasion of privacy, or negligence with respect to the reporting of information against any consumer reporting agency, any user of information, or any person who furnishes information to a consumer reporting agency, based on information disclosed pursuant to section 609, 610, or 615 [§§ 1681g, 1681h, or 1681m] of this title or based on information disclosed by a user of a consumer report to or for a consumer against whom the user has taken adverse action, based in whole or in part on the report, except as to false information furnished with malice or willful intent to injure such consumer.

## § 611. Procedure in case of disputed accuracy [15 U.S.C. § 1681i]

(a) Reinvestigations of disputed information.

(1) Reinvestigation required.

(A) In general. If the completeness or accuracy of any item of information contained in a consumer's file at a consumer reporting agency is disputed by the consumer and the consumer notifies the agency directly of such dispute, the agency shall reinvestigate free of charge and record the current status of the disputed information, or delete the item from the file in accordance with paragraph (5), before the end of the 30-day period beginning on the date on which the agency receives the notice of the dispute from the consumer.

(B) Extension of period to reinvestigate. Except as provided in subparagraph (C), the 30-day period described in subparagraph (A) may be extended for not more than 15 additional days if the consumer reporting agency receives information from the consumer during that 30-day period that is relevant to the reinvestigation.

(C) Limitations on extension of period to reinvestigate. Subparagraph (B) shall not apply to any reinvestigation in which, during the 30-day period described in subparagraph (A), the information that is the subject of the reinvestigation is found to be inaccurate or incomplete or the consumer reporting agency determines that the information cannot be verified.

(2) Prompt notice of dispute to furnisher of information.

(A) In general. Before the expiration of the 5-business-day period beginning on the date on which a consumer reporting agency receives notice of a dispute from any consumer in accordance with paragraph (1), the agency shall provide notification of the dispute to any person who provided any item of information in dispute, at the address and in the manner established with the person. The notice shall include all relevant information regarding the dispute that the agency has received from the consumer.

(B) Provision of other information from consumer. The consumer reporting agency shall promptly provide to the person who provided the information in dispute all relevant information regarding the dispute that is received by the agency from the consumer after the period referred to in subparagraph (A) and before the end of the period referred to in paragraph (1)(A).

(3) Determination that dispute is frivolous or irrelevant.

(A) In general. Notwithstanding paragraph (1), a consumer reporting agency may terminate a reinvestigation of information disputed by a consumer under that paragraph if the agency reasonably determines that the dispute by the consumer is frivolous or irrelevant, including by reason of a failure by a consumer to provide sufficient information to investigate the disputed information.

(B) Notice of determination. Upon making any determination in accordance with subparagraph (A) that a dispute is frivolous or irrelevant, a consumer reporting agency shall notify the consumer of such determination not later than 5 business days after making such determination, by mail or, if authorized by the consumer for that purpose, by any other means available to the agency.

(C) Contents of notice. A notice under subparagraph (B) shall include

(i) the reasons for the determination under subparagraph (A); and

(ii) identification of any information required to investigate the disputed information, which may consist of a standardized form describing the general nature of such information.

(4) Consideration of consumer information. In conducting any reinvestigation under paragraph (1) with respect to disputed information in the file of any consumer, the consumer reporting agency shall review and consider all relevant information submitted by the consumer in the period described in paragraph (1)(A) with respect to such disputed information.

(5) Treatment of inaccurate or unverifiable information.

(A) In general. If, after any reinvestigation under paragraph (1) of any information disputed by a consumer, an item of the information is found to be inaccurate or incomplete or cannot be verified, the consumer reporting agency shall promptly delete that item of information from the consumer's file or modify that item of information, as appropriate, based on the results of the reinvestigation.

(B) Requirements relating to reinsertion of previously deleted material.

(i) Certification of accuracy of information. If any information is deleted from a consumer's file pursuant to subparagraph (A), the information may not be reinserted in the file by the consumer reporting agency unless the person who furnishes the information certifies that the information is complete and accurate.

(ii) Notice to consumer. If any information that has been deleted from a consumer's file pursuant to subparagraph (A) is reinserted in the file, the consumer reporting agency shall notify the consumer of the reinsertion in writing not later than 5 business days after the reinsertion or, if authorized by the consumer for that purpose, by any other means available to the agency.

(iii) Additional information. As part of, or in addition to, the notice under clause (ii), a consumer reporting agency shall provide to a consumer in writing not later than 5 business days after the date of the reinsertion

(I) a statement that the disputed information has been reinserted;

(II) the business name and address of any furnisher of information contacted and the telephone number of such furnisher, if reasonably available, or of any furnisher of information that contacted the consumer reporting agency, in connection with the reinsertion of such information; and

(III) a notice that the consumer has the right to add a statement to the consumer's file disputing the accuracy or completeness of the disputed information.

C) Procedures to prevent reappearance. A consumer reporting agency shall maintain reasonable procedures designed to prevent the reappearance in a consumer's file, and in consumer reports on the consumer, of information that is deleted pursuant to this paragraph (other than information that is reinserted in accordance with subparagraph (B)(i)).

D) Automated reinvestigation system. Any consumer reporting agency that compiles and maintains files on consumers on a nationwide basis shall implement an automated system through which furnishers of information to that consumer reporting agency may report the results of a reinvestigation that finds incomplete or inaccurate information in a consumer's file to other such consumer reporting agencies.

(6) Notice of results of reinvestigation.

(A) In general. A consumer reporting agency shall provide written notice to a consumer of the results of a reinvestigation under this subsection not later than 5 business days after the completion of the reinvestigation, by mail or, if authorized by the consumer for that purpose, by other means available to the agency.

(B) Contents. As part of, or in addition to, the notice under subparagraph (A), a consumer reporting agency shall provide to a consumer in writing before the expiration of the 5-day period referred to in subparagraph (A)

(i) a statement that the reinvestigation is completed;

(ii) a consumer report that is based upon the consumer's file as that file is revised as a result of the reinvestigation;

(iii) a notice that, if requested by the consumer, a description of the procedure used to determine the accuracy and completeness of the information shall be provided to the consumer by the agency, including the business name and address of any furnisher of information contacted in connection with such information and the telephone number of such furnisher, if reasonably available;

(iv) a notice that the consumer has the right to add a statement to the consumer's file disputing the accuracy or completeness of the information; and

(v) a notice that the consumer has the right to request under subsection (d) that the consumer reporting agency furnish notifications under that subsection.

(7) Description of reinvestigation procedure. A consumer reporting agency shall provide to a consumer a description referred to in paragraph (6)(B)(iii) by not later than 15 days after receiving a request from the consumer for that description.

(8) Expedited dispute resolution. If a dispute regarding an item of information in a consumer's file at a consumer reporting agency is resolved in accordance with paragraph (5)(A) by the deletion of the disputed information by not later than 3 business days after the date on which the agency receives notice of the dispute from the consumer in accordance with paragraph (1)(A), then the agency shall not be required to comply with paragraphs (2), (6), and (7) with respect to that dispute if the agency

(A) provides prompt notice of the deletion to the consumer by telephone;

(B) includes in that notice, or in a written notice that accompanies a confirmation and consumer report provided in accordance with subparagraph (C), a statement of the consumer's right to request under subsection (d) that the agency furnish notifications under that subsection; and

(C) provides written confirmation of the deletion and a copy of a consumer report on the consumer that is based on the consumer's file after the deletion, not later than 5 business days after making the deletion.

(b) Statement of dispute. If the reinvestigation does not resolve the dispute, the consumer may file a brief statement setting forth the nature of the dispute. The consumer reporting agency may limit such statements to not more than one hundred words if it provides the consumer with assistance in writing a clear summary of the dispute.

(c) Notification of consumer dispute in subsequent consumer reports. Whenever a statement of a dispute is filed, unless there is reasonable grounds to believe that it is frivolous or irrelevant, the consumer reporting agency shall, in any subsequent consumer report containing the information in question, clearly note that it is disputed by the consumer and provide either the consumer's statement or a clear and accurate codification or summary thereof.

(d) Notification of deletion of disputed information. Following any deletion of information which is found to be inaccurate or whose accuracy can no longer be verified or any notation as to disputed information, the consumer reporting agency shall, at the request of the consumer, furnish notification that the item has been deleted or the statement, codification or summary pursuant to subsection (b) or (c) of this section to any person specifically designated by the consumer who has within two years prior thereto received a consumer report for employment purposes, or within six months prior thereto received a consumer report for any other purpose, which contained the deleted or disputed information.

## § 612. Charges for certain disclosures [15 U.S.C. § 1681j]

(a) Reasonable charges allowed for certain disclosures.

> (1) In general. Except as provided in subsections (b), (c), and (d), a consumer reporting agency may impose a reasonable charge on a consumer

>> (A) for making a disclosure to the consumer pursuant to section 609 [§ 1681g], which charge

>>> (i) shall not exceed $8;[3] and

>>> (ii) shall be indicated to the consumer before making the disclosure; and

>> (B) for furnishing, pursuant to 611(d) [§ 1681i], following a reinvestigation under section 611(a) [§ 1681i], a statement, codification, or summary to a person designated by the consumer under that section after the 30-day period beginning on the date of notification of the consumer under paragraph (6) or (8) of section 611(a) [§ 1681i] with respect to the reinvestigation, which charge

>>> (i) shall not exceed the charge that the agency would impose on each designated recipient for a consumer report; and

>>> (ii) shall be indicated to the consumer before furnishing such information.

> (2) Modification of amount. The Federal Trade Commission shall increase the amount referred to in paragraph (1)(A)(I) on January 1 of each year, based proportionally on changes in the Consumer Price Index, with fractional changes rounded to the nearest fifty cents.

(b) Free disclosure after adverse notice to consumer. Each consumer reporting agency that maintains a file on a consumer shall make all disclosures pursuant to section 609 [§ 1681g] without charge to the consumer if, not later than 60 days after receipt by such consumer of a notification pursuant to section 615 [§ 1681m], or of a notification from a debt collection agency affiliated with that consumer reporting agency stating that the consumer's credit rating may be or has been adversely affected, the consumer makes a request under section 609 [§ 1681g].

(c) Free disclosure under certain other circumstances. Upon the request of the consumer, a consumer reporting agency shall make all disclosures pursuant to section 609 [§ 1681g] once during any 12-month period without charge to that consumer if the consumer certifies in writing that the consumer

> (1) is unemployed and intends to apply for employment in the 60-day period beginning on the date on which the certification is made;

> (2) is a recipient of public welfare assistance; or

> (3) has reason to believe that the file on the consumer at the agency contains inaccurate information due to fraud.

(d) Other charges prohibited. A consumer reporting agency shall not impose any charge on a consumer for providing any notification required by this title or making any disclosure required by this title, except as authorized by subsection (a).

## § 613. Public record information for employment purposes [15 U.S.C. § 1681k]

(a) In general. A consumer reporting agency which furnishes a consumer report for employment purposes and which for that purpose compiles and reports items of information on consumers which are matters of public record and are likely to have an adverse effect upon a consumer's ability to obtain employment shall

(1) at the time such public record information is reported to the user of such consumer report, notify the consumer of the fact that public record information is being reported by the consumer reporting agency, together with the name and address of the person to whom such information is being reported; or

(2) maintain strict procedures designed to insure that whenever public record information which is likely to have an adverse effect on a consumer's ability to obtain employment is reported it is complete and up to date. For purposes of this paragraph, items of public record relating to arrests, indictments, convictions, suits, tax liens, and outstanding judgments shall be considered up to date if the current public record status of the item at the time of the report is reported.

(b) Exemption for national security investigations. Subsection (a) does not apply in the case of an agency or department of the United States Government that seeks to obtain and use a consumer report for employment purposes, if the head of the agency or department makes a written finding as prescribed under section 604(b)(4)(A).

## § 614. Restrictions on investigative consumer reports [15 U.S.C. § 1681l]

Whenever a consumer reporting agency prepares an investigative consumer report, no adverse information in the consumer report (other than information which is a matter of public record) may be included in a subsequent consumer report unless such adverse information has been verified in the process of making such subsequent consumer report, or the adverse information was received within the three-month period preceding the date the subsequent report is furnished.

## § 615. Requirements on users of consumer reports [15 U.S.C. § 1681m]

(a) Duties of users taking adverse actions on the basis of information contained in consumer reports. If any person takes any adverse action with respect to any consumer that is based in whole or in part on any information contained in a consumer report, the person shall

(1) provide oral, written, or electronic notice of the adverse action to the consumer;

(2) provide to the consumer orally, in writing, or electronically

(A) the name, address, and telephone number of the consumer reporting agency (including a toll-free telephone number established by the agency if the agency compiles and maintains files on consumers on a nationwide basis) that furnished the report to the person; and

(B) a statement that the consumer reporting agency did not make the decision to take the adverse action and is unable to provide the consumer the specific reasons why the adverse action was taken; and

(3) provide to the consumer an oral, written, or electronic notice of the consumer's right

    (A) to obtain, under section 612 [§ 1681j], a free copy of a consumer report on the consumer from the consumer reporting agency referred to in paragraph (2), which notice shall include an indication of the 60-day period under that section for obtaining such a copy; and

    (B) to dispute, under section 611 [§ 1681i], with a consumer reporting agency the accuracy or completeness of any information in a consumer report furnished by the agency.

(b) Adverse action based on information obtained from third parties other than consumer reporting agencies.

    (1) In general. Whenever credit for personal, family, or household purposes involving a consumer is denied or the charge for such credit is increased either wholly or partly because of information obtained from a person other than a consumer reporting agency bearing upon the consumer's credit worthiness, credit standing, credit capacity, character, general reputation, personal characteristics, or mode of living, the user of such information shall, within a reasonable period of time, upon the consumer's written request for the reasons for such adverse action received within sixty days after learning of such adverse action, disclose the nature of the information to the consumer. The user of such information shall clearly and accurately disclose to the consumer his right to make such written request at the time such adverse action is communicated to the consumer.

    (2) Duties of person taking certain actions based on information provided by affiliate.

        (A) Duties, generally. If a person takes an action described in subparagraph (B) with respect to a consumer, based in whole or in part on information described in subparagraph (C), the person shall

            (i) notify the consumer of the action, including a statement that the consumer may obtain the information in accordance with clause (ii); and

            (ii) upon a written request from the consumer received within 60 days after transmittal of the notice required by clause (I), disclose to the consumer the nature of the information upon which the action is based by not later than 30 days after receipt of the request.

        (B) Action described. An action referred to in subparagraph (A) is an adverse action described in section 603(k)(1)(A) [§ 1681a], taken in connection with a transaction initiated by the consumer, or any adverse action described in clause (i) or (ii) of section 603(k)(1)(B) [§ 1681a].

        (C) Information described. Information referred to in subparagraph (A)

            (i) except as provided in clause (ii), is information that

(I) is furnished to the person taking the action by a person related by common ownership or affiliated by common corporate control to the person taking the action; and

(II) bears on the credit worthiness, credit standing, credit capacity, character, general reputation, personal characteristics, or mode of living of the consumer; and

(ii) does not include

(I) information solely as to transactions or experiences between the consumer and the person furnishing the information; or

(II) information in a consumer report.

(c) Reasonable procedures to assure compliance. No person shall be held liable for any violation of this section if he shows by a preponderance of the evidence that at the time of the alleged violation he maintained reasonable procedures to assure compliance with the provisions of this section.

(d) Duties of users making written credit or insurance solicitations on the basis of information contained in consumer files.

(1) In general. Any person who uses a consumer report on any consumer in connection with any credit or insurance transaction that is not initiated by the consumer, that is provided to that person under section 604(c)(1)(B) [§ 1681b], shall provide with each written solicitation made to the consumer regarding the transaction a clear and conspicuous statement that

(A) information contained in the consumer's consumer report was used in connection with the transaction;

(B) the consumer received the offer of credit or insurance because the consumer satisfied the criteria for credit worthiness or insurability under which the consumer was selected for the offer;

(C) if applicable, the credit or insurance may not be extended if, after the consumer responds to the offer, the consumer does not meet the criteria used to select the consumer for the offer or any applicable criteria bearing on credit worthiness or insurability or does not furnish any required collateral;

(D) the consumer has a right to prohibit information contained in the consumer's file with any consumer reporting agency from being used in connection with any credit or insurance transaction that is not initiated by the consumer; and

(E) the consumer may exercise the right referred to in subparagraph (D) by notifying a notification system established under section 604(e) [§ 1681b].

(2) Disclosure of address and telephone number. A statement under paragraph (1) shall

include the address and toll-free telephone number of the appropriate notification system established under section 604(e) [§ 1681b].

(3) Maintaining criteria on file. A person who makes an offer of credit or insurance to a consumer under a credit or insurance transaction described in paragraph (1) shall maintain on file the criteria used to select the consumer to receive the offer, all criteria bearing on credit worthiness or insurability, as applicable, that are the basis for determining whether or not to extend credit or insurance pursuant to the offer, and any requirement for the furnishing of collateral as a condition of the extension of credit or insurance, until the expiration of the 3-year period beginning on the date on which the offer is made to the consumer.

(4) Authority of federal agencies regarding unfair or deceptive acts or practices not affected. This section is not intended to affect the authority of any Federal or State agency to enforce a prohibition against unfair or deceptive acts or practices, including the making of false or misleading statements in connection with a credit or insurance transaction that is not initiated by the consumer.

## § 616. Civil liability for willful noncompliance [15 U.S.C. § 1681n]

(a) In general. Any person who willfully fails to comply with any requirement imposed under this title with respect to any consumer is liable to that consumer in an amount equal to the sum of

(1)(A) any actual damages sustained by the consumer as a result of the failure or damages of not less than $100 and not more than $1,000; or

(B) in the case of liability of a natural person for obtaining a consumer report under false pretenses or knowingly without a permissible purpose, actual damages sustained by the consumer as a result of the failure or $1,000, whichever is greater;

(2) such amount of punitive damages as the court may allow; and

(3) in the case of any successful action to enforce any liability under this section, the costs of the action together with reasonable attorney's fees as determined by the court.

(b) Civil liability for knowing noncompliance. Any person who obtains a consumer report from a consumer reporting agency under false pretenses or knowingly without a permissible purpose shall be liable to the consumer reporting agency for actual damages sustained by the consumer reporting agency or $1,000, whichever is greater.

(c) Attorney's fees. Upon a finding by the court that an unsuccessful pleading, motion, or other paper filed in connection with an action under this section was filed in bad faith or for purposes of harassment, the court shall award to the prevailing party attorney's fees reasonable in relation to the work expended in responding to the pleading, motion, or other paper.

## § 617. Civil liability for negligent noncompliance [15 U.S.C. § 1681o]

(a) In general. Any person who is negligent in failing to comply with any requirement imposed under this title with respect to any consumer is liable to that consumer in an amount equal to the sum of

(1) any actual damages sustained by the consumer as a result of the failure;

(2) in the case of any successful action to enforce any liability under this section, the costs of the action together with reasonable attorney's fees as determined by the court.

(b) Attorney's fees. On a finding by the court that an unsuccessful pleading, motion, or other paper filed in connection with an action under this section was filed in bad faith or for purposes of harassment, the court shall award to the prevailing party attorney's fees reasonable in relation to the work expended in responding to the pleading, motion, or other paper.

## § 618. Jurisdiction of courts; limitation of actions [15 U.S.C. § 1681p]

An action to enforce any liability created under this title may be brought in any appropriate United States district court without regard to the amount in controversy, or in any other court of competent jurisdiction, within two years from the date on which the liability arises, except that where a defendant has materially and willfully misrepresented any information required under this title to be disclosed to an individual and the information so misrepresented is material to the establishment of the defendant's liability to that individual under this title, the action may be brought at any time within two years after discovery by the individual of the misrepresentation.

§ 619. Obtaining information under false pretenses [15 U.S.C. § 1681q]

Any person who knowingly and willfully obtains information on a consumer from a consumer reporting agency under false pretenses shall be fined under title 18, United States Code, imprisoned for not more than 2 years, or both.

## § 620. Unauthorized disclosures by officers or employees [15 U.S.C. § 1681r]

Any officer or employee of a consumer reporting agency who knowingly and willfully provides information concerning an individual from the agency's files to a person not authorized to receive that information shall be fined under title 18, United States Code, imprisoned for not more than 2 years, or both.

## § 621. Administrative enforcement [15 U.S.C. § 1681s]

(a) (1) Enforcement by Federal Trade Commission. Compliance with the requirements imposed under this title shall be enforced under the Federal Trade Commission Act [15 U.S.C. §§ 41 et seq.] by the Federal Trade Commission with respect to consumer reporting agencies and all other persons subject thereto, except to the extent that enforcement of the requirements imposed under this title is specifically committed to some other government agency under subsection (b) hereof. For the purpose of the exercise by the Federal Trade Commission of its functions and powers under the Federal Trade Commission Act, a violation of any requirement or prohibition imposed under this title shall constitute an unfair or deceptive act or practice in commerce in violation of section 5(a) of the Federal Trade Commission Act [15 U.S.C. § 45(a)] and shall be subject to enforcement by the Federal Trade Commission under section 5(b) thereof [15 U.S.C. § 45(b)] with respect to any consumer reporting agency or person subject to enforcement by the Federal Trade Commission pursuant to this subsection, irrespective of whether that person is engaged in commerce or meets any other jurisdictional tests in the Federal Trade Commission

Act. The Federal Trade Commission shall have such procedural, investigative, and enforcement powers, including the power to issue procedural rules in enforcing compliance with the requirements imposed under this title and to require the filing of reports, the production of documents, and the appearance of witnesses as though the applicable terms and conditions of the Federal Trade Commission Act were part of this title. Any person violating any of the provisions of this title shall be subject to the penalties and entitled to the privileges and immunities provided in the Federal Trade Commission Act as though the applicable terms and provisions thereof were part of this title.

(2)(A) In the event of a knowing violation, which constitutes a pattern or practice of violations of this title, the Commission may commence a civil action to recover a civil penalty in a district court of the United States against any person that violates this title. In such action, such person shall be liable for a civil penalty of not more than $2,500 per violation.

(B) In determining the amount of a civil penalty under subparagraph (A), the court shall take into account the degree of culpability, any history of prior such conduct, ability to pay, effect on ability to continue to do business, and such other matters as justice may require.

(3) Notwithstanding paragraph (2), a court may not impose any civil penalty on a person for a violation of section 623(a)(1) [§ 1681s-2] unless the person has been enjoined from committing the violation, or ordered not to commit the violation, in an action or proceeding brought by or on behalf of the Federal Trade Commission, and has violated the injunction or order, and the court may not impose any civil penalty for any violation occurring before the date of the violation of the injunction or order.

(b) Enforcement by other agencies. Compliance with the requirements imposed under this title with respect to consumer reporting agencies, persons who use consumer reports from such agencies, persons who furnish information to such agencies, and users of information that are subject to subsection (d) of section 615 [§ 1681m] shall be enforced under

(1) section 8 of the Federal Deposit Insurance Act [12 U.S.C. § 1818], in the case of

(A) national banks, and Federal branches and Federal agencies of foreign banks, by the Office of the Comptroller of the Currency;

(B) member banks of the Federal Reserve System (other than national banks), branches and agencies of foreign banks (other than Federal branches, Federal agencies, and insured State branches of foreign banks), commercial lending companies owned or controlled by foreign banks, and organizations operating under section 25 or 25(a) [25A] of the Federal Reserve Act [12 U.S.C. §§ 601 et seq., §§ 611 et seq], by the Board of Governors of the Federal Reserve System; and

(C) banks insured by the Federal Deposit Insurance Corporation (other than members of the Federal Reserve System) and insured State branches of foreign banks, by the Board of Directors of the Federal Deposit Insurance Corporation;

(2) section 8 of the Federal Deposit Insurance Act [12 U.S.C. § 1818], by the Director of the

Office of Thrift Supervision, in the case of a savings association the deposits of which are insured by the Federal Deposit Insurance Corporation;

(3) the Federal Credit Union Act [12 U.S.C. §§ 1751 et seq.], by the Administrator of the National Credit Union Administration [National Credit Union Administration Board] with respect to any Federal credit union;

(4) subtitle IV of title 49 [49 U.S.C. §§ 10101 et seq.], by the Secretary of Transportation, with respect to all carriers subject to the jurisdiction of the Surface Transportation Board;

(5) the Federal Aviation Act of 1958 [49 U.S.C. Appx §§ 1301 et seq.], by the Secretary of Transportation with respect to any air carrier or foreign air carrier subject to that Act [49 U.S.C. Appx §§ 1301 et seq.]; and

(6) the Packers and Stockyards Act, 1921 [7 U.S.C. §§ 181 et seq.] (except as provided in section 406 of that Act [7 U.S.C. §§ 226 and 227]), by the Secretary of Agriculture with respect to any activities subject to that Act.

The terms used in paragraph (1) that are not defined in this title or otherwise defined in section 3(s) of the Federal Deposit Insurance Act (12 U.S.C. §1813(s)) shall have the meaning given to them in section 1(b) of the International Banking Act of 1978 (12 U.S.C. § 3101).

(c) State action for violations.

(1) Authority of states. In addition to such other remedies as are provided under State law, if the chief law enforcement officer of a State, or an official or agency designated by a State, has reason to believe that any person has violated or is violating this title, the State

(A) may bring an action to enjoin such violation in any appropriate United States district court or in any other court of competent jurisdiction;

(B) subject to paragraph (5), may bring an action on behalf of the residents of the State to recover

(i) damages for which the person is liable to such residents under sections 616 and 617 [§§ 1681n and 1681o] as a result of the violation;

(ii) in the case of a violation of section 623(a) [§ 1681s-2], damages for which the person would, but for section 623(c) [§ 1681s-2], be liable to such residents as a result of the violation; or

(iii) damages of not more than $1,000 for each willful or negligent violation; and

(C) in the case of any successful action under subparagraph (A) or (B), shall be awarded the costs of the action and reasonable attorney fees as determined by the court.

(2) Rights of federal regulators. The State shall serve prior written notice of any action under paragraph (1) upon the Federal Trade Commission or the appropriate Federal regulator determined under subsection (b) and provide the Commission or appropriate Federal regulator with a copy of its complaint, except in any case in which such prior notice is not feasible, in

which case the State shall serve such notice immediately upon instituting such action. The Federal Trade Commission or appropriate Federal regulator shall have the right

(A) to intervene in the action;

(B) upon so intervening, to be heard on all matters arising therein;

(C) to remove the action to the appropriate United States district court; and

(D) to file petitions for appeal.

(3) Investigatory powers. For purposes of bringing any action under this subsection, nothing in this subsection shall prevent the chief law enforcement officer, or an official or agency designated by a State, from exercising the powers conferred on the chief law enforcement officer or such official by the laws of such State to conduct investigations or to administer oaths or affirmations or to compel the attendance of witnesses or the production of documentary and other evidence.

(4) Limitation on state action while federal action pending. If the Federal Trade Commission or the appropriate Federal regulator has instituted a civil action or an administrative action under section 8 of the Federal Deposit Insurance Act for a violation of this title, no State may, during the pendency of such action, bring an action under this section against any defendant named in the complaint of the Commission or the appropriate Federal regulator for any violation of this title that is alleged in that complaint.

(5) Limitations on state actions for violation of section 623(a)(1) [§ 1681s-2].

(A) Violation of injunction required. A State may not bring an action against a person under paragraph (1)(B) for a violation of section 623(a)(1) [§ 1681s-2], unless

(i) the person has been enjoined from committing the violation, in an action brought by the State under paragraph (1)(A); and

(ii) the person has violated the injunction.

(B) Limitation on damages recoverable. In an action against a person under paragraph (1)(B) for a violation of section 623(a)(1) [§ 1681s-2], a State may not recover any damages incurred before the date of the violation of an injunction on which the action is based.

(d) Enforcement under other authority. For the purpose of the exercise by any agency referred to in subsection (b) of this section of its powers under any Act referred to in that subsection, a violation of any requirement imposed under this title shall be deemed to be a violation of a requirement imposed under that Act. In addition to its powers under any provision of law specifically referred to in subsection (b) of this section, each of the agencies referred to in that subsection may exercise, for the purpose of enforcing compliance with any requirement imposed under this title any other authority conferred on it by law.

(e) Regulatory authority

(1) The Federal banking agencies referred to in paragraphs (1) and (2) of subsection (b) shall jointly prescribe such regulations as necessary to carry out the purposes of this Act with respect to any persons identified under paragraphs (1) and (2) of subsection (b), and the Board of Governors of the Federal Reserve System shall have authority to prescribe regulations consistent with such joint regulations with respect to bank holding companies and affiliates (other than depository institutions and consumer reporting agencies) of such holding companies.

(2) The Board of the National Credit Union Administration shall prescribe such regulations as necessary to carry out the purposes of this Act with respect to any persons identified under paragraph (3) of subsection (b).

## § 622. Information on overdue child support obligations [15 U.S.C. § 1681s-1]

Notwithstanding any other provision of this title, a consumer reporting agency shall include in any consumer report furnished by the agency in accordance with section 604 [§ 1681b] of this title, any information on the failure of the consumer to pay overdue support which

(1) is provided

(A) to the consumer reporting agency by a State or local child support enforcement agency; or

(B) to the consumer reporting agency and verified by any local, State, or Federal government agency; and

(2) antedates the report by 7 years or less.

## § 623. Responsibilities of furnishers of information to consumer reporting agencies [15 U.S.C. § 1681s-2]

(a) Duty of furnishers of information to provide accurate information.

(1) Prohibition.

(A) Reporting information with actual knowledge of errors. A person shall not furnish any information relating to a consumer to any consumer reporting agency if the person knows or consciously avoids knowing that the information is inaccurate.

(B) Reporting information after notice and confirmation of errors. A person shall not furnish information relating to a consumer to any consumer reporting agency if

(i) the person has been notified by the consumer, at the address specified by the person for such notices, that specific information is inaccurate; and

(ii) the information is, in fact, inaccurate.

(C) No address requirement. A person who clearly and conspicuously specifies to the consumer an address for notices referred to in subparagraph (B) shall not be subject to subparagraph (A); however, nothing in subparagraph (B) shall require a person to specify such an address.

(2) Duty to correct and update information. A person who

(A) regularly and in the ordinary course of business furnishes information to one or more consumer reporting agencies about the person's transactions or experiences with any consumer; and

(B) has furnished to a consumer reporting agency information that the person determines is not complete or accurate, shall promptly notify the consumer reporting agency of that determination and provide to the agency any corrections to that information, or any additional information, that is necessary to make the information provided by the person to the agency complete and accurate, and shall not thereafter furnish to the agency any of the information that remains not complete or accurate.

(3) Duty to provide notice of dispute. If the completeness or accuracy of any information furnished by any person to any consumer reporting agency is disputed to such person by a consumer, the person may not furnish the information to any consumer reporting agency without notice that such information is disputed by the consumer.

(4) Duty to provide notice of closed accounts. A person who regularly and in the ordinary course of business furnishes information to a consumer reporting agency regarding a consumer who has a credit account with that person shall notify the agency of the voluntary closure of the account by the consumer, in information regularly furnished for the period in which the account is closed.

(5) Duty to provide notice of delinquency of accounts. A person who furnishes information to a consumer reporting agency regarding a delinquent account being placed for collection, charged to profit or loss, or subjected to any similar action shall, not later than 90 days after furnishing the information, notify the agency of the month and year of the commencement of the delinquency that immediately preceded the action.

(b) Duties of furnishers of information upon notice of dispute.

(1) In general. After receiving notice pursuant to section 611(a)(2) [§ 1681i] of a dispute with regard to the completeness or accuracy of any information provided by a person to a consumer reporting agency, the person shall

(A) conduct an investigation with respect to the disputed information;

(B) review all relevant information provided by the consumer reporting agency pursuant to section 611(a)(2) [§ 1681i];

(C) report the results of the investigation to the consumer reporting agency; and

(D) if the investigation finds that the information is incomplete or inaccurate, report those results to all other consumer reporting agencies to which the person furnished the information and that compile and maintain files on consumers on a nationwide basis.

(2) Deadline. A person shall complete all investigations, reviews, and reports required under paragraph (1) regarding information provided by the person to a consumer reporting agency, before the expiration of the period under section 611(a)(1) [§ 1681i] within which the consumer reporting agency is required to complete actions required by that section regarding that information.

(c) Limitation on liability. Sections 616 and 617 [§§ 1681n and 1681o] do not apply to any failure to comply with subsection (a), except as provided in section 621(c)(1)(B) [§ 1681s].

(d) Limitation on enforcement. Subsection (a) shall be enforced exclusively under section 621 [§ 1681s] by the Federal agencies and officials and the State officials identified in that section.

## § 624. Relation to State laws [15 U.S.C. § 1681t]

(a) In general. Except as provided in subsections (b) and (c), this title does not annul, alter, affect, or exempt any person subject to the provisions of this title from complying with the laws of any State with respect to the collection, distribution, or use of any information on consumers, except to the extent that those laws are inconsistent with any provision of this title, and then only to the extent of the inconsistency.

(b) General exceptions. No requirement or prohibition may be imposed under the laws of any State

(1) with respect to any subject matter regulated under

(A) subsection (c) or (e) of section 604 [§ 1681b], relating to the prescreening of consumer reports;

(B) section 611 [§ 1681i], relating to the time by which a consumer reporting agency must take any action, including the provision of notification to a consumer or other person, in any procedure related to the disputed accuracy of information in a consumer's file, except that this subparagraph shall not apply to any State law in effect on the date of enactment of the Consumer Credit Reporting Reform Act of 1996;

(C) subsections (a) and (b) of section 615 [§ 1681m], relating to the duties of a person who takes any adverse action with respect to a consumer;

(D) section 615(d) [§ 1681m], relating to the duties of persons who use a consumer report of a consumer in connection with any credit or insurance transaction that is not initiated by the consumer and that consists of a firm offer of credit or insurance;

(E) section 605 [§ 1681c], relating to information contained in consumer reports, except that this subparagraph shall not apply to any State law in effect on the date of enactment of the Consumer Credit Reporting Reform Act of 1996; or

(F) section 623 [§ 1681s-2], relating to the responsibilities of persons who furnish information to consumer reporting agencies, except that this paragraph shall not apply

(i) with respect to section 54A(a) of chapter 93 of the Massachusetts Annotated Laws (as in effect on the date of enactment of the Consumer Credit Reporting

Reform Act of 1996); or

(ii) with respect to section 1785.25(a) of the California Civil Code (as in effect on the date of enactment of the Consumer Credit Reporting Reform Act of 1996);

(2) with respect to the exchange of information among persons affiliated by common ownership or common corporate control, except that this paragraph shall not apply with respect to subsection (a) or (c)(1) of section 2480e of title 9, Vermont Statutes Annotated (as in effect on the date of enactment of the Consumer Credit Reporting Reform Act of 1996); or

(3) with respect to the form and content of any disclosure required to be made under section 609(c) [§ 1681g].

(c) Definition of firm offer of credit or insurance. Notwithstanding any definition of the term "firm offer of credit or insurance" (or any equivalent term) under the laws of any State, the definition of that term contained in section 603(*l*) [§ 1681a] shall be construed to apply in the enforcement and interpretation of the laws of any State governing consumer reports.

(d) Limitations. Subsections (b) and (c)

(1) do not affect any settlement, agreement, or consent judgment between any State Attorney General and any consumer reporting agency in effect on the date of enactment of the Consumer Credit Reporting Reform Act of 1996; and

(2) do not apply to any provision of State law (including any provision of a State constitution) that

(A) is enacted after January 1, 2004;

(B) states explicitly that the provision is intended to supplement this title; and

(C) gives greater protection to consumers than is provided under this title.

## § 625. Disclosures to FBI for counterintelligence purposes [15 U.S.C. § 1681u]

(a) Identity of financial institutions. Notwithstanding section 604 [§ 1681b] or any other provision of this title, a consumer reporting agency shall furnish to the Federal Bureau of Investigation the names and addresses of all financial institutions (as that term is defined in section 1101 of the Right to Financial Privacy Act of 1978 [12 U.S.C. § 3401]) at which a consumer maintains or has maintained an account, to the extent that information is in the files of the agency, when presented with a written request for that information, signed by the Director of the Federal Bureau of Investigation, or the Director's designee in a position not lower than Deputy Assistant Director at Bureau headquarters or a Special Agent in Charge of a Bureau field office designated by the Director, which certifies compliance with this section. The Director or the Director's designee may make such a certification only if the Director or the Director's designee has determined in writing, that such information is sought for the conduct of an authorized investigation to protect against international terrorism or clandestine intelligence activities, provided that such an investigation of a United States person is not conducted solely upon the basis of activities protected by the first amendment to the Constitution of the United States.

(b) Identifying information. Notwithstanding the provisions of section 604 [§ 1681b] or any other provision of this title, a consumer reporting agency shall furnish identifying information respecting a consumer, limited to name, address, former addresses, places of employment, or former places of employment, to the Federal Bureau of Investigation when presented with a written request, signed by the Director or the Director's designee, which certifies compliance with this subsection. The Director or the Director's designee in a position not lower than Deputy Assistant Director at Bureau headquarters or a Special Agent in Charge of a Bureau field office designated by the Director may make such a certification only if the Director or the Director's designee has determined in writing that such information is sought for the conduct of an authorized investigation to protect against international terrorism or clandestine intelligence activities, provided that such an investigation of a United States person is not conducted solely upon the basis of activities protected by the first amendment to the Constitution of the United States.

(c) Court order for disclosure of consumer reports. Notwithstanding section 604 [§ 1681b] or any other provision of this title, if requested in writing by the Director of the Federal Bureau of Investigation, or a designee of the Director in a position not lower than Deputy Assistant Director at Bureau headquarters or a Special Agent in Charge of a Bureau field office designated by the Director, a court may issue an order ex parte directing a consumer reporting agency to furnish a consumer report to the Federal Bureau of Investigation, upon a showing in camera that the consumer report is sought for the conduct of an authorized investigation to protect against international terrorism or clandestine intelligence activities, provided that such an investigation of a United States person is not conducted solely upon the basis of activities protected by the first amendment to the Constitution of the United States.

The terms of an order issued under this subsection shall not disclose that the order is issued for purposes of a counterintelligence investigation.

(d) Confidentiality. No consumer reporting agency or officer, employee, or agent of a consumer reporting agency shall disclose to any person, other than those officers, employees, or agents of a consumer reporting agency necessary to fulfill the requirement to disclose information to the Federal Bureau of Investigation under this section, that the Federal Bureau of Investigation has sought or obtained the identity of financial institutions or a consumer report respecting any consumer under subsection (a), (b), or (c), and no consumer reporting agency or officer, employee, or agent of a consumer reporting agency shall include in any consumer report any information that would indicate that the Federal Bureau of Investigation has sought or obtained such information or a consumer report.

(e) Payment of fees. The Federal Bureau of Investigation shall, subject to the availability of appropriations, pay to the consumer reporting agency assembling or providing report or information in accordance with procedures established under this section a fee for reimbursement for such costs as are reasonably necessary and which have been directly incurred in searching, reproducing, or transporting books, papers, records, or other data required or requested to be produced under this section.

(f) Limit on dissemination. The Federal Bureau of Investigation may not disseminate information obtained pursuant to this section outside of the Federal Bureau of Investigation, except to other Federal agencies as may be necessary for the approval or conduct of a foreign counterintelligence investigation, or, where the information concerns a person subject to the Uniform Code of Military Justice, to appropriate investigative authorities within the military department concerned as may be necessary for the conduct of a joint foreign counterintelligence investigation.

(g) Rules of construction. Nothing in this section shall be construed to prohibit information from being furnished by the Federal Bureau of Investigation pursuant to a subpoena or court order, in connection with a judicial or administrative proceeding to enforce the provisions of this Act. Nothing in this section shall be construed to authorize or permit the withholding of information from the Congress.

(h) Reports to Congress. On a semiannual basis, the Attorney General shall fully inform the Permanent Select Committee on Intelligence and the Committee on Banking, Finance and Urban Affairs of the House of Representatives, and the Select Committee on Intelligence and the Committee on Banking, Housing, and Urban Affairs of the Senate concerning all requests made pursuant to subsections (a), (b), and (c).

(i) Damages. Any agency or department of the United States obtaining or disclosing any consumer reports, records, or information contained therein in violation of this section is liable to the consumer to whom such consumer reports, records, or information relate in an amount equal to the sum of

(1) $100, without regard to the volume of consumer reports, records, or information involved;

(2) any actual damages sustained by the consumer as a result of the disclosure;

(3) if the violation is found to have been willful or intentional, such punitive damages as a court may allow; and

(4) in the case of any successful action to enforce liability under this subsection, the costs of the action, together with reasonable attorney fees, as determined by the court.

(j) Disciplinary actions for violations. If a court determines that any agency or department of the United States has violated any provision of this section and the court finds that the circumstances surrounding the violation raise questions of whether or not an officer or employee of the agency or department acted willfully or intentionally with respect to the violation, the agency or department shall promptly initiate a proceeding to determine whether or not disciplinary action is warranted against the officer or employee who was responsible for the violation.

(k) Good-faith exception. Notwithstanding any other provision of this title, any consumer reporting agency or agent or employee thereof making disclosure of consumer reports or identifying information pursuant to this subsection in good-faith reliance upon a certification of the Federal Bureau of Investigation pursuant to provisions of this section shall not be liable to any person for such disclosure under this title, the constitution of any State, or any law or regulation of any State or any political subdivision of any State.

(l) Limitation of remedies. Notwithstanding any other provision of this title, the remedies and sanctions set forth in this section shall be the only judicial remedies and sanctions for violation of this section.

(m) Injunctive relief. In addition to any other remedy contained in this section, injunctive relief shall be available to require compliance with the procedures of this section. In the event of any successful action under this subsection, costs together with reasonable attorney fees, as determined by the court, may be recovered.

## § 626. Disclosures to governmental agencies for counterterrorism purposes [15 U.S.C. §1681v]

(a) Disclosure. Notwithstanding section 604 or any other provision of this title, a consumer reporting agency shall furnish a consumer report of a consumer and all other information in a consumer's file to a government agency authorized to conduct investigations of, or intelligence or counterintelligence activities or analysis related to, international terrorism when presented with a written certification by such government agency that such information is necessary for the agency's conduct or such investigation, activity or analysis.

(b) Form of certification. The certification described in subsection (a) shall be signed by a supervisory official designated by the head of a Federal agency or an officer of a Federal agency whose appointment to office is required to be made by the President, by and with the advice and consent of the Senate.

(c) Confidentiality. No consumer reporting agency, or officer, employee, or agent of such consumer reporting agency, shall disclose to any person, or specify in any consumer report, that a government agency has sought or obtained access to information under subsection (a).

(d) Rule of construction. Nothing in section 625 shall be construed to limit the authority of the Director of the Federal Bureau of Investigation under this section.

(e) Safe harbor. Notwithstanding any other provision of this title, any consumer reporting agency or agent or employee thereof making disclosure of consumer reports or other information pursuant to this section in good-faith reliance upon a certification of a governmental agency pursuant to the provisions of this section shall not be liable to any person for such disclosure under this subchapter, the constitution of any State, or any law or regulation of any State or any political subdivision of any State.

# D. THE FAIR CREDIT BILLING ACT

### 301. Short Title

This title may be cited as the Fair Credit Billing Act

### 302. Declaration of purpose

The last sentence of section 102 of the Truth in Lending Act (15 U.S.C. 1601) is amended by striking out the period and inserting in lieu thereof a comma and the following: and to protect the consumer against inaccurate and unfair credit billing and credit card practices.

### 303. Definitions of creditor and open end credit plan

The first sentence of section 103(f) of the Truth in Lending Act (15 U.S.C. 1602(f)) is amended to read as follows: The term creditor refers only to creditors who regularly extend, or arrange for the extension of, credit which is payable by agreement in more than four installments or for which the payment of a finance charge is or may be required, whether in connection with loans, sales of property or services, or otherwise. For the purposes of the requirements imposed under Chapter 4 and sections 127(a) (6), 127(a) (7), 127(a) (8), 127(b) (1), 127(b) (2), 127(b) (3), 127(b) (9), and 127(b) (11) of Chapter 2 of this Title, the term creditor shall also include card issuers whether or not the amount due is payable by agreement in more than four installments or the payment of a finance charge is or may be required, and the Board shall, by regulation, apply these requirements to such card issuers, to the extent appropriate, even though the requirements are by their terms applicable only to creditors offering open end credit plans. 1 Post, p. 1512.Infra, 15 USC 1637. PUBLIC LAW 93-495 - October 28, 1974

### 304. Disclosure of fair credit billing rights

(a) Section 127(a) of the Truth in Lending Act (15 U.S.C. 1637(a)) is amended by adding at the end thereof a new paragraph as follows: (8) A statement, in a form prescribed by regulations of the Board of the protection provided by sections 161 and 170 to an obligor and the creditor responsibilities under sections 162 and 170. With respect to each of two billing cycles per year, at semiannual intervals, the creditor shall transmit such statement to each obligor to whom the creditor is required to transmit a statement pursuant to sections 127(b) for such billing cycle.

(b) Section 127(c) of such Act (15 U.S.C. 1637(c)) is amended to read: (c) In the case of any existing account under an open end consumer credit plan having an outstanding balance of more than $1 at or after the close of the creditor first full billing cycle under the plan after the effective date of subsection (a) or any amendments thereto, the items described in subsection (a), to the extent applicable and not previously disclosed, shall be disclosed in a notice mailed or delivered to the obligor not later than the time of mailing the next statement required by subsection (b).

### 305. Disclosure of billing contact

Section 127(b) of the Truth in Lending Act (15 U.S.C. 1637(b)) is amended by adding at the end thereof a new paragraph as follows:

(11) The address to be used by the creditor for the purpose of receiving billing inquiries from the obligor.

### 306. Billing practices

The Truth in Lending Act (15 U.S.C. 1601-1665) is amended by adding at the end thereof a new chapter as follows: 2 Post, pp. 1512, 1515. PUBLIC LAW 93-495 - October 28, 1974

### Chapter 4 CREDIT BILLING

*Sec.*

*161. Correction of billing errors*

*162. Regulation of credit reports.*

*163. Length of billing period.*

*164. Prompt crediting of payments.*

*165. Crediting excess payments.*

*166. Prompt notification of returns.*

*167. Use of cash discounts.*

*168. Prohibition of tie-in services.*

*169. Prohibition of offsets.*

*170. Rights of credit card customers.*

*171. Relation to State laws.*

### 161. Correction of billing errors

(a) If a creditor, within sixty days after having transmitted to an obligor a statement of the obligor account in connection with an extension of consumer credit, receives at the address disclosed under section 127(b) (11) a written notice (other than notice on a payment stub or other payment medium supplied by the creditor if the creditor so stipulates with the disclosure required under section 127(a) (8)) from the obligor in which the obligor

(1) sets forth or otherwise enables the creditor to identify the name and account number (if any) of the obligor,

(2) indicates the obligor belief that the statement contains a billing error and the amount of such billing error, and

(3) sets forth the reasons for the obligor belief (to the extent applicable) that the statement contains a billing error, the creditor shall, unless the obligor has, after giving such written notice and before the expiration of the time limits herein specified, agreed that the statement was correct

(A) not later than thirty days after the receipt of the notice, send a written acknowledgment thereof to the obligor, unless the action required in subparagraph

(B) is taken within such thirty-day period, and (B) not later than two complete billing cycles of the 3 15 USC 1666. Ante, p. 1511. Ante, p. 1511. PUBLIC LAW 93-495 - October 28, 1974 creditor (in no event later than ninety days) after the receipt of the notice and prior to taking any action to collect the amount, or any part thereof, indicated by the obligor under paragraph (2) either (i) make appropriate corrections in the account of the obligor, including the crediting of any finance charges on amounts erroneously billed, and transmit to the obligor a notification of such corrections and the creditor explanation of any cage in the amount indicated by the obligor under paragraph (2) and, if any such change is made and the obligor so requests, copies of documentary evidence of the obligor indebtedness; or (ii) send a written explanation or clarification to the obligor, after having conducted an investigation, setting forth to the extent applicable the reasons why the creditor believes the account of the obligor was correctly shown in the statement and, upon request of the obligor, provide copies of documentary evidence of the obligor indebtedness. In the case of a billing error where the obligor alleges that the creditor billing statement reflects goods not delivered to the obligor or his designee in accordance with the agreement made at the time of the transaction, a creditor may not construe such amount to be correctly shown unless he determines that such goods were actually delivered, mailed, or otherwise sent to the obligor and provides the obligor with a statement of such determination. After complying with the provisions of this subsection with respect to an alleged billing error, a creditor has no further responsibility under this section if the obligor continues to make substantially the same allegation with respect to such error.

(b) For the purpose of this section, a billing error consists of any of the following:

(1) A reflection on a statement of an extension of credit 4 Definitions. PUBLIC LAW 93-495 - October 28, 1974 which was not made to the obligor or, if made, was not in the amount reflected on such statement.

(2) A reflection on a statement of an extension of credit for which the obligor requests additional clarification including documentary evidence thereof.

(3) A reflection on a statement of goods or services not accepted by the obligor or his designee or not delivered to the obligor or his designee in accordance with the agreement made at the time of a transaction.

(4) The creditor's failure to reflect properly on a statement a payment made by the obligor or a credit issued to the obligor.

(5) A computation error or similar error of an accounting nature of the creditor on a statement.

(6) Any other error described in regulations of the Board.

(c) For the purposes of this section, action to collect the amount, or any part thereof, indicated by an obligor under paragraph (2)í does not include the sending of statements of account to the obligor following written notice from the obligor as specified under subsection (a) if

(1) the obligor's account is not restricted or closed because of the failure of the obligor to pay the amount indicated under paragraph (2) of subsection (a) and (2) the creditor indicates the payment of such amount is not required pending the creditor's compliance with this section. Nothing in this section shall be construed to prohibit any action by a creditor to collect any amount which has not been indicated by the obligor to contain a billing error.

(d) Pursuant to regulations of the Board, a creditor operating an open end consumer credit plan may not, prior to the sending of the written explanation or clarification required under paragraph (B) (ii), restrict or close an account with respect to which the obligor has indicated pursuant to subsection (a) that he believes such account to contain a billing error solely because of the obligor's failure to pay the amount indicated to be in error. Nothing in this subsection shall 5 PUBLIC LAW 93-495 - October 28, 1974 be deemed to prohibit a creditor from applying against the credit limit on the obligor's account the amount indicated to be in error.

(e) Any creditor who fails to comply with the requirements of this section or section 162 forfeits any right to collect from the obligor the amount indicated by the obligor under paragraph (2) of subsection (a) of this section, and any finance charges thereon, except that the amount required to be forfeited under this subsection may not exceed $50.

## 162. Regulation of credit reports

(a) After receiving a notice from an obligor as provided in section 161(a), a creditor or his agent may not directly or indirectly threaten to report to any person adversely on the obligor's credit rating or credit standing because of the obligor's failure to pay the amount indicated by the obligor under section 161(a) (2) and such amount may not be reported as delinquent to any third party until the creditor has met the requirements of section 161 and has allowed the obligor the same number of days (not less than ten) thereafter to make payment as is provided under the credit agreement with the obligor for the payment of undisputed amounts.

(b) If a creditor receives a further written notice from an obligor that an amount is still in dispute within the time allowed for payment under subsection (a) of this section, a creditor may not report to any third party that the amount of the obligor is delinquent because the obligor has failed to pay an amount which he has indicated under section 161(a) (2), unless the creditor also reports that the amount is in dispute and, at the same time, notifies the obligor of the name and address of each party to whom the creditor is reporting information concerning the delinquency.

(c) A creditor shall report any subsequent resolution of any delinquencies reported pursuant to subsection (b) to the parties to whom such delinquencies were initially reported. 6 Noncompliance. 15 USC 1666a. PUBLIC LAW 93-495 - October 28, 1974 163. Length of billing period (a) If an open end consumer credit plan provides a time period within which an obligor may repay any portion of the credit extended without incurring an additional finance charge, such additional finance charge may not be imposed with respect to such portion of the credit extended for the billing cycle of which such period is a part unless a statement which includes the amount upon which the finance charge for that period is based was mailed at least fourteen days prior to the date specified in the statement by which payment must be made in order to avoid imposition of that finance charge. (b) Subsection (a) does not apply in any case where a creditor has been prevented, delayed, or hindered in making timely mailing or delivery of such periodic statement within the time period specified in such subsection because of an act of God, war, natural disaster, strike, or other excusable or justifiable cause, as determined under regulations of the Board.

## 164. Prompt crediting of payments

Payments received from an obligor under an open end consumer credit plan by the creditor shall be posted promptly to the obligor's account as specified in regulations of the Board. Such regulations shall prevent a finance charge from being imposed on any obligor if the creditor has received the obligor's payment in readily identifiable form in the amount, manner, location, and time indicated by the creditor to avoid the imposition thereof.

## 165. Crediting excess payments

Whenever an obligor transmits funds to a creditor in excess of the total balance due on an open end consumer credit account, the creditor shall promptly (1) upon request of the obligor refund the amount of the overpayment, or (2) credit such amount to the obligor account. 7 15 USC 1666b. 15 USC 1666c. 15 USC 1666d. PUBLIC LAW 93-495 - October 28, 1974

166. Prompt notification of returns

With respect to any sales transaction where a credit card has been used to obtain credit, where the seller is a person other than the card issuer, and where the seller accepts or allows a return of the goods or forgiveness of a debit for services which were the subject of such sale, the seller shall promptly transmit to the credit card issuer, a credit statement with respect thereto and the credit card issuer shall credit the account of the obligor for the amount of the transaction.

## 167. Use of cash discounts

(a) With respect to credit card which may be used for extensions of credit in sales transactions in which the seller is a person other than the card issuer, the card issuer may not, by contract or otherwise, prohibit any such seller from offering a discount to a cardholder to induce the cardholder to pay by cash, check, or similar means rather than use a credit card.

(b) With respect to any sales transaction, any discount not in excess of 5 per centum offered by the seller for the purpose of inducing payment by cash, check, or other means not involving the use of a credit card shall not constitute a finance charge as determined under section 106, if such discount is offered to all prospective buyers and its availability is disclosed to all prospective buyers clearly and conspicuously in accordance with regulations of the Board.

## 168. Prohibition of tie-in services

Notwithstanding any agreement to the contrary, a card issuer may not require a seller, as a condition to participating in a credit card plan, to open an account with or procure any other service from the card issuer or its subsidiary or agent.

## 169. Prohibition of offsets

(a) A card issuer may not take any action to offset a cardholder's indebtedness arising in connection with a consumer credit transaction under the relevant credit card plan against funds of the cardholder held on deposit with the card 8 15 USC 1666e. 15 USC 1666f. 15 USC 1666g. 15 USC 1666h. PUBLIC LAW 93-495 - October 28, 1974 issuer unless (1) such action was previously authorized in writing by the cardholder in accordance with a credit plan whereby the cardholder agrees periodically to pay debts incurred in his open end credit account by permitting the card issuer periodically to deduct all or a portion of such debt from the cardholder's deposit account, and (2) such action with respect to any outstanding disputed amount not be taken by the card issuer upon request of the cardholder. In the case of any credit card account in existence on the effective date of this section, the previous written authorization referred to in clause (1) shall not be required until the date (after such effective date) when such account is renewed, but in no case later than one year after such effective date. Such written authorization shall be deemed to exist if the card issuer has previously notified the cardholder that the use of his credit card account will subject any funds which the card issuer holds in deposit accounts of such cardholder to offset against any amounts due and payable on his credit card account which have not been paid in accordance with the terms of the agreement between the card issuer and the cardholder.
(b) This section does not alter or affect the right under State law of a card issuer to attach or otherwise levy upon funds of a cardholder held on deposit with the card issuer if that remedy is constitutionally available to creditors generally.

## 170. Rights of credit card customers

(a) Subject to the limitation contained in subsection (b), a card issuer who has issued a credit card to a cardholder pursuant to an open end consumer credit plan shall be subject to all claims (other than tort claims) and defenses arising out of any transaction in which the credit card is used as a method of payment or extension of credit if (1) the obligor has made a good faith attempt to obtain satisfactory resolution of a disagreement or problem relative to the transaction from the person honoring the credit card; (2) the amount of the initial 9 15 USC 1666i. PUBLIC LAW 93-495 - October 28, 1974 transaction exceeds $50; and (3) the place where the initial transaction occurred was in the same State as the mailing address previously provided by the cardholder or was within 100 miles from such address, except that the limitations set forth in clauses (2) and (3) with respect to an obligor's right to assert claims and defenses against a card issuer shall not be applicable to any transaction in which the person honoring the credit card (A) is the same person as the card issuer, (B) is controlled by the card issuer, (C) is under direct or indirect common control with the card issuer, (D) is a franchised dealer in the card issuer's products or services, or (E) has obtained the order for such transaction through a mail solicitation made by or participated in by the card issuer in which the cardholder is solicited to enter into such transaction by using the credit card issued by the card issuer.

(b) The amount of claims or defenses asserted by the cardholder may not exceed the amount of credit outstanding with respect to such transaction at the time the cardholder first notifies the card issuer or the person honoring the credit card of such claim or defense. For the purpose of determining the amount of credit outstanding in the preceding sentence, payments and credits to the cardholder's account are deemed to have been applied, in the order indicated, to the payment of: (1) late charges in the order of their entry to the account; (2) finance charges in order of their entry to the account; and (3) debits to the account other than those set forth above, in the order in which each debit entry to the account was made.

## 171. Relation to State laws

(a) This chapter does not annul, alter, or affect, or exempt any person subject to the provisions of this chapter from complying with, the laws of any State with respect to credit billing practices, except to the extent that those laws are inconsistent with any provision of this chapter, and then only to the extent of the inconsistency. The Board is authorized to determine whether such inconsistencies exist. The Board may not determine that any State law is inconsistent with 10 15 USC 1666j. PUBLIC LAW 93-495 - October 28, 1974 any provision of this chapter if the Board determines that such law gives greater protection to the consumer. (b) The Board shall by regulation exempt from the requirements of this chapter any class of credit transactions within any State if it determines that under the law of that State that class of transactions is subject to requirements substantially similar to those imposed under this chapter or that such law gives greater protection to the consumer, and that there is adequate provision for enforcement.

## 307. Conforming amendments

a) The table of chapter of the Truth in Lending Act is amended by adding immediately under item 3 the following:

## 4. CREDIT BILLING 161

(b) Section 111(d) of such Act (15 U.S.C. 1610(d)) is amended by striking out and 130î and inserting in lieu thereof a comma and the following: 130, and 166

(c) Section 121(a) of such Act (15 U.S.C. 1631(a)) is amended (1) by striking out and upon whom a finance charge is or may be imposed; and (2) by inserting or chapter 4î immediately after this chapter.

(d) Section 121(b) of such Act (15 U.S.C. 1631(b)) is amended by inserting or chapter 4 immediately after this chapter.

(e) Section 122(a) of such Act (15 U.S.C. 1632(a)) is amended by inserting or chapter 4 immediately after this chapter.

(f) Section 122(b) of such Act (15 U.S.C. 1632(b)) is amended by inserting or chapter 4 immediately after this chapter.

## 308. Effective date

This title takes effect upon the expiration of one year after the date of its enactment. 11 15 USC 1666 note. PUBLIC LAW 93-495 - October 28, 1974

# E. The Truth in Lending Act

The Truth In Lending Act requires the disclosure of credit terms prior to entry into a consumer credit contract. These disclosures include the annual percentage rate, amount financed, finance charge, amount and timing of payments, etc., and must be in writing in a form the consumer may keep. Such as a contract, credit application etc. Common violations include:

(1) Hidden finance charges that lenders are required to disclose but conceal in other charges, such as "third party" charges;

(2) Requiring the consumer to sign a blank Truth in Lending disclosure and filling it in later;

(3) Not giving a Truth in Lending disclosure.

The Truth In Lending Act is intended to help consumers understand the credit they are being offered.

**The Annual Percentage Rate or "APR"** This is the interest rate you are really paying after all of the initial financial charges are included. The "APR" is usually higher than the interest rate reflected in the loan documents, which does not include these other charges. Comparing the "APR" is the best way to comparison shop for loans.

**The Amount Financed** The amount financed is the amount of money you are borrowing. It will often include various third party fees that are being financed; that is, when you are using borrowed funds to pay them. Such fees include fees for credit reports, appraisals, warranties and a variety of other things.

**The Finance Charge** This is the total of all of the upfront finance charges, plus all the interest you will pay over the life of the loan. On a long term loan like a mortgage, the finance charge often exceeds the amount financed.

# F. Retail Installment Sales Act

## § 25A-1

This Chapter applies only to consumer credit sales as hereinafter defined, except that G.S. 25A-37, referral sales, applies to all sales of goods or services as provided therein. This Chapter does not apply to a bona fide direct loan transaction in which a lender makes a direct loan to a borrower, and such lender is not regularly engaged, directly or indirectly, in the sale of goods or the furnishing of services as defined in this Chapter.

Except for G.S. 25A-37, referral sales, and those sales defined in G.S. 25A-2(b), this Chapter does not apply to any party or transaction that is not also subject to the provisions of the Consumer Credit Protection Act (Federal Truth-in-Lending Act). (1971, c. 796, s. 1; 1983, c. 686, s. 1.)

## § 25A-2. "Consumer credit sale" defined.

(a) Except as provided in subsection (c) of this section, a "consumer credit sale" is a sale of goods or services in which

(1) The seller is one who in the ordinary course of business regularly extends or arranges for the extension of consumer credit, or offers to extend arrange for the extension of such credit,

(2) The buyer is a natural person,

(3) The goods or services are purchased primarily for a personal, family, household or agricultural purpose,

(4) Either the debt representing the price of the goods or services is payable in installments or a finance charge is imposed, and

(5) The amount financed does not exceed twenty-five thousand dollars ($25,000) or, in the case of a debt secured by real property or a manufactured home as defined in G.S. 143-145(7), regardless of the amount financed.

(b) "Sale" includes but is not limited to any contract in the form of a bailment or lease if the bailee or lessee contracts to pay as compensation for use a sum substantially equivalent to or in excess of the aggregate value of the goods and services involved, and it is agreed that the bailee or lessee will become, or for no other or for a nominal consideration, has the option to become, the owner of the goods and services upon full compliance with his obligations under such contract. The term also includes a contract in the form of a terminable bailment or lease of goods or services in which the bailee or lessee can renew the bailment or lease contract periodically by making the payment or payments specified in the contract if:

(1) The contract obligates the bailor or lessor to transfer ownership of the property to the bailee or lessee for no other or a nominal consideration (no more than ten percent (10%) of the cash price of the property at the time the bailor or lessor initially enters into the contract with the bailee or lessee) upon the making of a specified number of payments by the bailee

or lessee; and

(2) The dollar total of the specified number of payments necessary to exercise the purchase option is more than ten percent (10%) in excess of the aggregate value of the property and services involved. For the purposes of this subsection, the value of goods shall be the average cash retail value of the goods. The value of services shall be the average retail value, if any, of such services, as determined by substantial cash sales of such services. If a contract is found to be a sale under this subsection, these values shall be used to determine the amount financed for purposes of G.S. 25A-15.

(c) A sale in which the seller allows the buyer to purchase goods or services pursuant to a credit card issued by someone other than a seller that is engaged in part or entirely in the business of selling goods or services or similar arrangement is not a consumer credit sale. A sale in which the seller allows the buyer to purchase goods or services pursuant to a credit card issued by the seller, a subsidiary or a parent corporation of the seller, a principal supplier of the seller or any corporation having shareholders in common with the seller holding over twenty-five percent (25%) of the voting stock in each corporation is a consumer credit sale within the terms of this Chapter.

(d) For the purposes of this Chapter, a consumer credit sale shall be deemed to have been made in this State, and therefore subject to the provisions of this Chapter, if the seller offers or agrees in this State to sell to a buyer who is a resident of this State, or if such buyer accepts or makes the offer in this State to buy, regardless of the situs of the contract as specified therein. Any solicitation or communication to sell, oral or written, originating outside of this State, but forwarded to and received in this State by a buyer who is a resident of this State, shall be deemed to be an offer or agreement to sell in this State. Any solicitation or communication to buy, oral or written, originating within this State, from a buyer who is a resident of this State, but forwarded to and received by a retail seller outside of this State, shall be deemed to be an acceptance or offer to buy in this State.

(e) If an advertisement for a terminable bailment or lease defined as a sale in subsection (b) above states the amount of any payment, the advertisement must also clearly and conspicuously state the following items, as applicable:

(1) A statement that the transaction advertised is a lease;

(2) The total amount of periodic payments necessary to acquire ownership or a statement that the consumer has the option to purchase the property and at what time;

(3) That the consumer acquires no ownership rights if either the property is not leased for the term required for ownership to transfer or the terms of purchase are not otherwise satisfied.

If an advertisement for a terminable bailment or lease defined as a sale in subsection (b) above refers to the right to acquire ownership, the advertisement must clearly and conspicuously state whether or not the consumer may terminate the lease at any time without penalty and that the consumer acquires no ownership rights if either the property is not leased for the term required for ownership to transfer or the terms of purchase are not otherwise satisfied. No one shall advertise in connection with any terminable bailment or lease defined as a sale in subsection (b) above the ownership option as a means of deceiving any lessee into believing that he is purchasing the item of personal property. (1971, c. 796, s. 1; 1979, c. 706, s. 1; 1981, c. 970, s. 2; 1983, c. 686, ss. 2, 3; 1987, c. 282, s. 5; 1991, c. 602, s. 1.)

## § 25A-3. "Payable in installments" defined.

A debt is "payable in installments" when the buyer is required or permitted by agreement to make payment in more than four installments, excluding a down payment, and whether or not a finance charge is imposed by the seller. (1971, c. 796, s. 1.)

## § 25A-4. "Goods" defined.

(a)"Goods" means all things which are moveable at the time of the sale or at the time the buyer takes possession, including goods not in existence at the time the transaction is entered into and goods which are furnished or used at the time of sale or subsequently in modernization, rehabilitation, repair, alteration, improvement or construction on real property so as to become a part thereof whether or not they are severable therefrom. "Goods" also includes merchandise certificates.

(b) "Merchandise certificate" means a writing issued by a seller not redeemable in cash and usable in its face amount in lieu of cash in exchange for goods and services. (1971, c. 796, s. 1.)

## § 25A-5. "Services" defined.

(a) "Services" includes:

(1) Work, labor, and other personal services; and

(2) Privileges with respect to transportation, hotel and restaurant accommodations, education, entertainment, recreation, physical culture, hospital accommodations, funerals and other similar services.

(b) "Services" does not include:

(1) Services for which the cost is by law fixed or approved by or filed with or subject to approval or disapproval by the United States or the State of North Carolina or any agency, instrumentality or subdivision thereof;

(2) Insurance premiums financing covered by G.S. 58-35-1 through G.S. 58-35-95 and 58-3-145; or

(3) Insurance provided by an insurer that is licensed to do business in this State. (1971, c. 796, s. 1.)

## § 25A-6. "Seller" defined.

"Seller" means one regularly engaged in the business of selling goods or services. Unless otherwise provided, "seller" also means and includes an assignee of the seller's right to payment but use of the term does not itself impose on an assignee any obligation of the seller with respect to events occurring before the assignment. (1971, c. 796, s. 1.)

## § 25A-7. "Cash price" defined.

"Cash price" of goods and services means the price at which the goods or services are offered for sale by the seller to cash buyers in the ordinary course of business and may include:

(1) Applicable sales, use, and excise and documentary stamp taxes; and

(2) The cash price of accessories or related services such as installation, delivery, servicing, repairs or alterations. (1971, c. 796, s. 1.)

## § 25A-8. "Finance charge" defined.

(a) "Finance charge" means the sum of all charges payable directly or indirectly by the buyer and imposed by the seller as an incident to the extension of credit, including any of the following types of charges which are applicable:

(1) Interest, time price differential, service, carrying or other similar charge however denominated;

(2) Premium or other charges for any guarantee or insurance protecting the seller against the buyer's default or other credit loss;

(3) Loan fee, finder's fee or similar charge; and

(4) Fee for an appraisal, investigation or credit report.

(b) Finance charge does not include transfer of equity fees, substitution of collateral fees, default or deferment charges, or additional charges for insurance as permitted by G.S. 25A-17 or charges for insurance excluded by Section 226.4(a) of Regulation Z promulgated pursuant to section 105 of the Consumer Credit Protection Act.

(c) With respect to a transaction in which the seller acquires a security interest in real property, finance charge does not include charges excluded by section 226.4(e) of Regulation Z promulgated pursuant to section 105 of the Consumer Credit Protection Act. (1971, c. 796, s. 1.)

## § 25A-9. "Amount financed" defined.

(a) "Amount financed" means the total of the following to the extent that payment is deferred by the seller:

(1) The cash price of the goods or services less the amount of any down payment whether made in cash or property traded in,

(2) The amount actually paid or to be paid by the seller pursuant to an agreement with the buyer to discharge a security interest or lien on property traded in,

(3) Additional charges for insurance described in G.S. 25A-8(b) and charges referred to in G.S. 25A-8(c), and

(4) Official fees as described in G.S. 25A-10, to the extent they are itemized and disclosed to the buyer.

(b) If not included in the cash price, the amount financed includes any applicable sales, use or documentary stamp taxes and any amount actually paid or to be paid by the seller for registration, certificate of title or license fees. (1971, c. 796, s. 1.)

## § 25A-10. "Official fees" defined.

"Official fees" means:

(1) Fees and charges prescribed by law which actually are or will be paid to public officials for determining the existence of or for perfecting, releasing, or satisfying a security interest related to a consumer credit sale; or

(2) Premiums payable for insurance in lieu of perfecting a security interest otherwise required by the seller in connection with a consumer credit sale if the premium does not exceed the fees or charges described in subdivision (1) of this section which would otherwise be payable. (1971, c. 796, s. 1.)

## § 25A-11. "Revolving charge account contract" defined.

"Revolving charge account contract" means an agreement or understanding between a seller and a buyer under which consumer credit sales may be made from time to time, under the terms of which a finance charge or service charge is to be computed in relation to the buyer's unpaid balance from time to time, and under which the buyer has the privilege of paying the balance in full or in installments. This definition shall not affect the meaning of the term "revolving charge account" appearing in G.S. 24-11(a). (1971, c. 796, s. 1.)

## § 25A-12. "Consumer credit installment sale contract" defined.

"Consumer credit installment sale contract" means the agreement between a buyer and a seller in a consumer credit sale other than a sale made pursuant to a revolving charge account. (1971, c. 796, s. 1.)

## § 25A-13. "Consumer Credit Protection Act" defined.

"Consumer Credit Protection Act" means the Consumer Credit Protection Act, an act of Congress of May 29, 1968, as amended (Public Law 90-321; 82 Stat. 146; 15 U.S.C. 1601 et seq.), and regulations and rulings promulgated thereunder. (1971, c. 796, s. 1.)

## § 25A-14. Finance charge rates and service charge for revolving charge account contracts.

(a)The finance-charge rate and either the annual charge or the monthly service charge for a consumer credit sale made under a revolving charge account contract may not exceed the rates and charge provided for revolving credit by G.S. 24-11.

(b) In the event the revolving charge account contract is secured in whole or in part by a security interest in real property, then the finance-charge rate shall not exceed the rate set out in G.S. 25A-15(d).

(c) No default or deferral charge shall be imposed by the seller in connection with a revolving charge-account contract, except as specifically provided for in G.S. 24-11(d1). (1971, c. 796, s. 1; 1983, c. 126, s. 7; 1991, c. 506, s. 7.)

## § 25A-15. Finance charge rates for consumer credit installment sale contracts.

(a) With respect to a consumer credit installment sale contract, a seller may contract for and receive a finance charge not exceeding that permitted by this section. For the purposes of this section, the finance charge rates are the rates that are required to be disclosed by the Consumer Credit Protection Act.

(b) Except as hereinafter provided, the finance charge rate for a consumer credit installment sales contract may not exceed:

(1) Twenty-four percent (24%) per annum where the amount financed is less than one thousand five hundred dollars ($1,500);

(2) Twenty-two percent (22%) per annum where the amount financed is one thousand five hundred dollars ($1,500) or greater, but less than two thousand dollars ($2,000);

(3) Twenty percent (20%) where the amount financed is two thousand ($2,000) or greater, but less than three thousand dollars ($3,000);

(4) Eighteen percent (18%) per annum where the amount financed is three thousand dollars ($3,000) or greater, except that a minimum finance charge of five dollars ($5.00) may be imposed.

(c) A finance charge rate not to exceed the higher of the rate established in subsection (b) or the rate set forth below may be imposed in a consumer credit installment sale contract repayable in not less than six installments for a self-propelled motor vehicle:

(1) Eighteen percent (18%) per annum for vehicles one and two model years old;

(2) Twenty percent (20%) per annum for vehicles three model years old;

(3) Twenty-two percent (22%) per annum for vehicles four model years old; and

(4) Twenty-nine percent (29%) per annum for vehicles five model years old and older. A motor vehicle is one model year old on January 1 of the year following the designated year model of the vehicle.

(d) Notwithstanding the provisions of subsections (b) and (c), above, in the event that the amount financed in a consumer credit sale contract is secured in whole or in part by a security interest in real property, the finance charge rate may not exceed sixteen percent (16%) per annum.

(e) A seller may not divide a single credit sale transaction into two or more sales to avoid the limitations as to maximum finance charges imposed by this section.

(f) Notwithstanding the provisions of subsections (b) or (d), the parties to a consumer credit installment sale contract for the sale of a residential manufactured home which is secured by a first lien on that home or on the land on which such home is located may contract in writing for the payment of a finance charge as agreed upon by the parties. Provided, this subsection shall only apply if the parties would have been entitled to so contract by the provisions of section 501 of United States Public Law 96-221, and have complied with the regulations promulgated thereto. For the purposes of this subsection (f), a "residential manufactured home" means a mobile home as defined in G.S. 143-145(7) which is used as a dwelling. (1971, c. 796, s. 1;1979, 2nd Sess., c. 1330, ss. 1, 2; 1981, c. 446, ss. 1-3; 1983, c. 126, s. 2.)

### § 25A-16. Transfer of equity.

If a buyer voluntarily transfers his rights in collateral pursuant to applicable law and the seller agrees, the seller may impose a transfer fee not to exceed ten percent (10%) of the unpaid balance of the debt or thirty-five dollars ($35.00), whichever is less. (1971, c. 796, s. 1; 2000-169, s. 31.)

### § 25A-17. Additional charges for insurance.

(a) As to revolving charge account contracts defined in G.S. 25A-11, in addition to the finance charges permitted in G.S. 24-11(a), a seller in a consumer credit sale may contract for and receive additional charges or premiums

(i) for insurance written in connection with any consumer credit sale, against loss of or damage to property securing the debt pursuant to G.S. 25A-23, provided a clear, conspicuous and specific statement in writing is furnished by the seller to the buyer setting forth the cost of the insurance if obtained from or through the seller and stating that the buyer may choose the insurer through which the insurance is obtained;

(ii) for credit life, credit accident and health, or credit unemployment insurance, written in connection with any consumer credit sale, provided the insurance coverage is not required by the seller and this fact is clearly disclosed to the buyer, and any buyer desiring such insurance coverage gives affirmative indication of such desire after disclosure of the cost of such insurance.

(b) As to revolving charge account contracts defined in G.S. 25A-11, insurance that is required by a seller and is not an additional charge permitted by subsection (a) of this section, shall be included in the finance charge as computed according to G.S. 24-11(a).

(c) As to consumer credit installment sale contracts defined in G.S. 25A-12, in addition to the finance charges permitted in G.S. 25A-15, a seller in a consumer credit sale may contract for and receive additional charges or premiums

(i) for insurance written in connection with any consumer credit sale, for loss of or damage to property or against liability arising out of the ownership or use of property, provided a clear, conspicuous and specific statement in writing is furnished by the seller to the buyer setting forth the cost of the insurance if obtained from or through the seller and stating that the buyer may choose the person through which the insurance is to be obtained;

(ii) for credit life, credit accident and health, or credit unemployment insurance, written in connection with any consumer credit sale, provided the insurance coverage is not required by the seller and this fact is clearly and conspicuously disclosed in writing to the buyer; and any buyer desiring such insurance coverage gives specific dated and separately signed affirmative written indication of such desire after receiving written disclosure to him of the cost of such insurance. (1971, c. 796, s. 1; 1993, c. 226, s. 15.)

## § 25A-18. Confession of judgment.

A buyer may not authorize any person to confess judgment on a claim arising out of a consumer credit sale. An authorization in violation of this section is void. (1971, c. 796, s. 1.)

## § 25A-19. Acceleration.

With respect to a consumer credit sale, the agreement may not provide for repossession of any goods or acceleration of the time when any part or all of the time balance becomes payable other than for breach by the buyer of any promise or condition clearly set forth in the agreement. (1971, c. 796, s. 1.)

## § 25A-20. Disclaimer of warranty.

With respect to any consumer credit sale, the agreement may not contain any provision limiting, excluding, modifying or in any manner altering the terms of any express warranty given by any seller (excluding assignees) to any buyer and made a part of the basis of the bargain between the original parties. (1971, c. 796, s. 1.)

## § 25A-21. Attorneys' fees.

With respect to a consumer credit sale:

(1) In the event that the seller institutes a suit and prevails in the litigation and obtains a money judgment, the presiding judge shall allow a reasonable attorney's fee to the duly licensed attorney representing the seller in such suit, said attorney's fee to be taxed to the buyer as part of the court costs.

(2) In the event that a seller instituting suit does not prevail in the litigation, the presiding judge shall allow a reasonable attorney's fee to the duly licensed attorney representing the buyer in such suit, said attorney's fee to be taxed to the seller as a part of the court costs. (1971, c. 796, s. 1.)

## § 25A-22. Receipts for payments; return of title documents upon full payment.

(a)When any payment is made under any consumer credit sale transaction, the person receiving such payment shall, if the payment is made in cash, give the buyer a written receipt therefor. If the buyer specifies that the payment is made on one of several obligations, the receipt shall so state.

(b) Upon the payment of all sums for which the buyer is obligated under a consumer credit sale, the seller shall promptly release any security interest in accordance with the terms of G.S. 25-9-513 or G.S. 20-58.4, whichever is applicable. In the event a security interest in real property is involved, the seller shall take such action as is necessary to enable the lien to be discharged of record under the provisions of G.S. 45-37. (1971, c. 796, s. 1; 2000-169, s. 32.)

### § 25A-23. Collateral taken by the seller.

(a)The seller in a consumer credit sale may take a security interest only in the following property of the buyer to secure the debt arising from the sale:

(1) The property sold,

(2) Property previously sold by the seller to the buyer and in which the seller has an existing security interest,

(3) Personal property to which the property sold is installed, if the amount financed is more than three hundred dollars ($300.00),

(4) Real property to which the property sold is affixed, if the amount financed is more than one thousand dollars ($1,000), and

(5) A self-propelled motor vehicle to which repairs are made, if the amount financed exceeds one hundred dollars ($100.00).

(6) Any property which is used for agricultural purposes, if the property sold is to be used in the operation of an agricultural business.

(b) A security interest taken in property other than that permitted in subsection (a) of this section shall be void and not enforceable.

(c) Nothing in this section shall affect any right or liens granted by Chapter 44A of the General Statutes.

(d) The provisions of G.S. 24-11(a), limiting the taking of a security interest in property under an open end credit or similar plan, shall not apply to revolving charge account contracts regulated by this Chapter; provided, however, the application of payments rule set out in G.S. 25A-27 shall apply to such contracts; provided further, that in any action initiated by the seller for the possession of such property, a judgment for the possession thereof shall be restricted to commercial units (as defined in G.S. 25-2-105(6)) for which the cash price was one hundred dollars ($100.00) or more. (1971, c. 796, s. 1; 1977, c. 508; c. 789, s. 1.)

### § 25A-24. Identification of instruments of indebtedness.

With respect to consumer credit sales, each instrument of indebtedness shall be identified on the face of the instrument as a consumer credit document, or otherwise clearly indicate on its face that it arises out of a consumer credit sale, provided, that such designation of an instrument of indebtedness regarding as sale which is not by definition a "consumer credit sale," shall not solely because of such designation cause the transaction to be a consumer credit sale. (1971, c. 796, s. 1.)

### § 25A-25. Preservation of consumers' claims and defenses.

(a) In a consumer credit sale, a buyer may assert against the seller, assignee of the seller, or other holder of the instrument or instruments of indebtedness, any claims or defenses available against the original seller, and the buyer may not waive the right to assert these claims or defenses in connection with a consumer credit sales transaction. Affirmative recovery by the buyer on a claim asserted against an assignee of the seller or other holder of the instrument of indebtedness shall not exceed amounts paid by the buyer under the contract.

(b) Every consumer credit sale contract shall contain the following provision in at least ten-point boldface type:

NOTICE

ANY HOLDER OF THIS CONSUMER CREDIT CONTRACT IS SUBJECT TO ALL CLAIMS AND DEFENSES WHICH THE DEBTOR COULD ASSERT AGAINST THE SELLER OF GOODS OR SERVICES OBTAINED PURSUANT HERETO OR WITH THE PROCEEDS HEREOF. RECOVERY HEREUNDER BY THE DEBTOR SHALL NOT EXCEED AMOUNTS PAID BY THE DEBTOR HEREUNDER.

(c) Compliance with the requirements of the Federal Trade Commission rule on preservation of consumer claims and defenses is considered full compliance with this act. (1971, c. 796, s. 1; 1977, c. 921.)

### § 25A-26. Substitution of collateral.

Subject to the provisions of G.S. 25A-23, if all involved parties agree, there may be a substitution of collateral under a security instrument in a consumer credit sale. For such substitution, the seller may impose a fee not to exceed ten percent (10%) of the unpaid balance of the debt or fifteen dollars ($15.00), whichever is less. (1971, c. 796, s. 1.)

### § 25A-27. Application of payments.

(a) Where a seller in a consumer credit sale makes a subsequent sale to a buyer and takes a security interest pursuant to G.S. 25A-23 in goods previously purchased by the buyer from the seller, the seller shall make application of payments received, for the purpose of determining the amount of the debt secured by the various security interests, as follows:

(1) The entire amount of all payments made prior to such subsequent purchase shall be deemed to have been applied to the previous purchases, and

(2) Unless otherwise designated by the buyer, the amount of down payment on such subsequent purchase shall be applied to the subsequent purchase, and

(3) All subsequent payments shall be applied first to finance charges and then to principal. The application of payments to principal shall be applied to the various purchases on the basis that the first sums paid in shall be deemed applied to the oldest purchase or obligation assumed to satisfy the original debt secured by the purchase money security interest until payment is received in full and other payments shall be applied accordingly to all other purchases in the order that each obligation is assumed. At the time any original debt would have been satisfied by subsequent payments, the purchase money security interest in said purchase shall be extinguished.

(b) Where a seller and a buyer agree to consolidate two or more consumer credit installment sale contracts pursuant to G.S. 25A-31, the seller shall apply payments received, for the purpose of determining the amount of the debt secured by the various security interests, as follows:

(1) The entire amount of all payments received prior to the consolidation shall be applied to the respective contracts under which the payments were made, and

(2) All subsequent payments shall be applied first to finance charges and then to principal. The application of payments to principal shall be applied to the various purchases on the basis that the first sums paid in shall be deemed applied to the oldest purchase or obligation assumed to satisfy the original debt secured by the purchase money security interest until payment is received in full and other payments shall be applied accordingly to all other purchases in the order that each obligation is assumed. At the time any original debt would have been satisfied by subsequent payments, the purchase money security interest in said purchase shall be extinguished.

(c) For payments received by a seller on or after October 1, 1988, but before October 1, 1993, a seller may elect to apply the provisions of this section as the section read October 1, 1993, or as the section read September 30, 1993. A seller made this election when the seller determined, and disclosed to the buyer, how payments received on a consumer credit sale would be applied: either on a proportional basis or on a "first in - first out" basis with the payments applied first to finance charges and then to principal in the order that each obligation is assumed.

(d) The exclusive remedy for failure of a seller to apply payments of a buyer as required by subdivision (a)(3) or (b)(2) of this section during the period October 1, 1993, through October 1, 1996, is an order that the seller apply the payments as required by those provisions. (1971, c. 796, s. 1; 1993, c. 370, s. 2; 1993 (Reg. Sess., 1994), c. 745, s. 38.3(a).)

### § 25A-28. Form of consumer credit installment sale contract.

Every consumer credit installment sale contract shall be in writing, dated and signed by the buyer. (1971, c. 796, s. 1.)

### § 25A-29. Default charges.

If any installment is past due for 10 days or more according to the original terms of the consumer credit installment sale contract, a default charge may be made in an amount not to exceed five percent (5%) of the installment past due or six dollars ($6.00), whichever is the lesser. A default charge may be imposed only one time for each default. If a default charge is deducted from a payment made on the contract and such deduction results in a subsequent default on a subsequent payment, no default charge may be imposed for such default. If a default charge has been once imposed with respect to a particular default in payment, no default charge shall be imposed with respect to any future payments which would not have been in default except for the previous default. A default charge for any particular default shall be deemed to have been waived by the seller unless, within 45 days following the default,

(i) the charge is collected or

(ii) written notice of the charge is sent to the buyer. (1971, c. 796, s. 1.)

## § 25A-30. Deferral charges.

(a) A seller may, by agreement with the buyer, defer the due date of all or any part of one or more installments under an existing consumer credit installment sale contract.

(b) Except as provided by subsections (e) and (f) of this section, a deferral agreement must be in writing, dated and signed by the parties.

(c) A deferral agreement may provide for a deferral charge not to exceed the rate of one and one-half percent (1 1/2%) of each installment for each month from the date which such installment or part thereof would otherwise have been payable to the date when such installment or part thereof is made payable under the deferral agreement.

(d) If a deferral charge is made pursuant to a deferral agreement, a default charge provided in G.S. 25A-29 may be imposed only if the installment as deferred is not paid when due and no new deferral agreement is entered into with respect to that installment.

(e) If the deferral agreement extends the due date of only one installment, the agreement need not be in writing.

(f) A deferral agreement for which no charge is made shall not be subject to subsections (b), (c) or (d) of this section. (1971, c. 796, s. 1.)

## § 25A-31. Consolidation and refinancing.

(a) A seller and a buyer may agree at any time to refinance an existing consumer credit installment sale contract or to consolidate into a single debt repayable on a single schedule of payments, two or more consumer credit installment sale contracts.

(b) A refinancing or consolidation agreement must be in writing, dated and signed by the parties.

(c) The refinancing or consolidation agreement may provide for a finance charge which shall not exceed the rates provided in G.S. 25A- 15, with the amount financed being the unpaid time balance of the contract or contracts refinanced or consolidated, less the rebate provided by G.S. 25A-32. In computing the rebate to be credited to the previous time balances for purposes of this section, no prepayment charge shall be imposed. (1971, c. 796, s. 1.)

## § 25A-32. Rebates on prepayment.

Notwithstanding any provision in a consumer credit installment sale contract to the contrary, any buyer may satisfy the debt in full at any time before maturity, and in so satisfying such debt, shall receive a rebate, the amount of which shall be computed under the "rule of 78's," as follows: "The amount of such rebate shall represent as great a proportion of the finance charge (less a prepayment charge of ten percent (10%) of the unpaid balance, not to exceed twenty-five dollars ($25.00)) as the sum of the periodical time balances after the date of prepayment in full bears to the sum of all the periodical time balances under the schedule of payments in the original contract." No rebate is required if the amount thereof is less than one dollar ($1.00). If the prepayment is made otherwise than on the due date of an installment, it shall be deemed to have been made on the installment due date nearest in time to the actual date of payment.

If a seller obtains a judgment on a debt arising out of a consumer credit installment sale or the seller repossesses the collateral securing the debt, the seller shall credit the buyer with a rebate as if the payment in full had been made on the date the judgment was obtained or 15 days after the repossession occurred. If the seller obtains a judgment and repossesses the collateral, the seller shall credit the buyer with a rebate as if payment in full had been made on the date of the judgment or 15 days after the repossession, whichever occurs earlier. (1971, c. 796, s. 1.)

## § 25A-32.1. Unearned finance charge credits on prepayment of loans secured by real property and mobile home loans.

(a)Notwithstanding any statutory or contractual provision to the contrary, in a consumer credit installment sale contract with an amount financed of five thousand dollars ($5000.00) or more secured by real estate or by a residential manufactured home as defined in G.S. 143-145(7), any buyer may satisfy the debt in full at any time before maturity, and in so satisfying the debt, shall be credited with all unearned finance charges as computed on the simple interest or actuarial method.

(b) If a seller obtains a judgment on a debt arising out of a consumer credit installment sale described in subsection (a) of this section, or if the seller forecloses or repossesses the collateral securing the debt, the seller shall credit the buyer with all unearned finance charges as computed on the simple interest or actuarial method as if the payment in full had been made on the date the judgment was obtained or 15 days after the foreclosure or repossession occurred, whichever is earlier. If the seller obtains a judgment and repossesses the collateral, the seller shall credit the buyer with all unearned finance charges as if payment in full had been made on the date of the judgment or 15 days after the repossession, whichever occurs earlier. (1991, c. 602, s. 2.)

## § 25A-33. Terms of payments.

A consumer credit installment sale contract shall provide for complete payment of all charges due under the contract, including the amount financed, the finance charge, and additional insurance charges, if any, within a period from the time of the sale of

(1) Forty-two months, if the amount financed is less than one thousand five hundred dollars ($1,500), or

(2) Sixty-four months, if the amount financed is one thousand five hundred dollars ($1,500) or greater, but less than two thousand five hundred dollars ($2,500), or

(3) One hundred and twenty-two months, if the amount financed is two thousand five hundred dollars ($2,500) or greater, but less than five thousand dollars ($5,000), or

(4) One hundred and eighty-two months, if the amount financed is five thousand dollars ($5,000) or greater, but less than ten thousand dollars ($10,000), or

(5) As the contract provides, if the amount financed is ten thousand dollars ($10,000) or greater. The provisions of this section shall not apply to a consumer credit installment sale contract executed in connection with any financing which is insured under regulations of the Federal Housing Administration or the Veterans Administration. (1971, c. 796, s. 1; 1973, c. 1446, s. 3.)

## § 25A-34. Balloon payments.

With respect to a consumer credit sale, other than one pursuant to a revolving charge account, no scheduled payment may be more than ten percent (10%) (except the final payment may be twenty-five percent (25%)) larger than the average of earlier scheduled payments. This provision does not apply when the payment schedule is adjusted to the seasonal or irregular income of the buyer. (1971, c. 796, s. 1.)

## § 25A-35. Statement of account.

(a) One time during each 12-month period following execution of a consumer credit installment sale contract and when the buyer repays the debt early, the buyer shall be entitled upon request and without charge to a statement of account from the seller. The statement of account shall contain the following information identified as such in the statement:

(1) The itemized amounts paid by or on behalf of the buyer to the date of the statement of account, except that upon early termination of the contract by prepayment or otherwise, the statement shall include itemized charges for expenses of repossession, storage and legal expenses;

(2) The itemized amounts, if any, which have become due but remain unpaid, including any charges for defaults, expenses of repossession and deferral charges;

(3) The number of installment payments and the dollar amount of each installment not due but still to be paid and the remaining period the contract is to run.

(b) The buyer may request and shall be entitled to additional statements of account but for such additional statements the seller may impose a charge of one dollar ($1.00).

(c) If the buyer requests information for income tax purposes as to the amount of the finance charges, the seller shall provide such information within 30 days without charge but only once in each calendar year. (1971, c. 796, s. 1.)

## § 25A-36. Certificates of insurance and rebates.

(a) Within 45 days following the purchase of insurance by the buyer from or through the seller, the seller shall deliver, send or cause to be sent to the buyer a policy or policies of such insurance or a certificate or certificates thereof. If such insurance is cancelled, or the premium adjusted, any rebate received by the seller shall be promptly applied to the purchase of other similar insurance, credited to the buyer's account, or rebated to the buyer. Unless otherwise required by law or the provisions of the policy, rebates of cancelled insurance shall be computed under the rule of 78's, without the deduction of a prepayment charge.

(b) In those cases where the insurance premium is added in the contract, and the buyer did not actually pay the premium, the return premium plus unearned finance charge on the amount of returned premium (at the same rate as used in the contract) shall be credited to the unpaid balance of the contract. If the required insurance premium is adjusted upward by the insurance company or is added in accordance with the contract, the buyer, after 10 days' notice,

(1) May pay the additional premium, or

(2) Have the additional premium plus finance charge (at the same rate as used in the contract) added to the unpaid balance and spread equally over the remaining installments unpaid, provided, the seller may require a buyer who wishes to finance such additional premium to be financed by the seller in accordance with North Carolina insurance regulations. (1971, c. 796, s. 1; 1977, c. 650.)

## § 25A-37. Referral sales.

The advertisement for sale or the actual sale of any goods or services (whether or not a consumer credit sale) at a price or with a rebate or payment or other consideration to the purchaser that is contingent upon the procurement of prospective customers provided by the purchaser, or the procurement of sales to persons suggested by the purchaser, is declared to be unlawful. Any obligation of a buyer arising under such a sale shall be void and a nullity and a buyer shall be entitled to recover from the seller any consideration paid to the seller upon tender to the seller of any tangible consumer goods made the basis of the sale. (1971, c. 796, s. 1.)

## § 25A-38. "Home-solicitation sale" defined.

"Home-solicitation sale" means a consumer credit sale of goods or services in which the seller or a person acting for him engages in a personal solicitation of the sale at a residence of the buyer and the buyer's agreement or offer to purchase is there given to the seller or a person acting for him. It does not include:

(1) A sale made to a buyer who has previously engaged in a similar business transaction with the seller;

(2) A sale made pursuant to a preexisting revolving charge account;

(3) A sale made pursuant to negotiations between the parties on the premises of a business establishment at a fixed location where such goods or services are offered or exhibited for sale;

(4) A sale which is regulated by the provisions of Section 226.9 of Regulation Z promulgated pursuant to Section 105 of the Consumer Credit Protection Act; or

(5) Sales of personal wearing apparel, motor vehicles defined in G.S. 20-286(10), farm equipment and goods and services to be utilized within 10 days in connection with funeral services. (1971, c. 796, s. 1; 1973, c. 672.)

### § 25A-39. Buyer's right to cancel.

(a)Except as provided in subsection (e) of this section, in addition to any right otherwise to revoke an offer, the buyer has the right to cancel a home-solicitation sale until midnight of the third business day after the day on which the buyer signs an agreement or offer to purchase which complies with G.S. 25A-40, or which complies with the requirements of the Federal Trade Commission Trade Regulation Rule Concerning a Cooling-Off Period for Door-to-Door Sales.

(b) Cancellation occurs when the buyer gives written notice of cancellation to the seller at the address stated in the agreement or offer to purchase.

(c) Notice of cancellation, if given by mail, is given when it is deposited in the United States mail properly addressed and postage prepaid.

(d) Unless the seller complies with G.S. 25A-40(b), notice of cancellation given by the buyer need not take a particular form and is sufficient if it indicates by any form of written expression the intention of the buyer not to be bound by the home-solicitation sale.

(e) The buyer may not cancel a home-solicitation sale if the buyer requests the seller in a separate writing to provide goods or services without delay because of an urgency or an emergency, and

(1) The seller in good faith makes a substantial beginning of performance of the contract before the buyer gives notification of cancellation,

(2) In the case of goods, the goods cannot be returned to the seller in substantially as good condition as when received by the buyer, and

(3) Unless the buyer returns the goods, if any, to the seller at his expense.

(f) A buyer, who has not received delivery of the goods and services from the seller in a home-solicitation sale within 30 days following the execution of the contract (and such delay is the fault of the seller), shall have the right at any time thereafter before acceptance of the goods and services to rescind the contract and to receive a refund of all payments made and to a return of all goods traded in to the seller on account of or in contemplation of such contract, or if the goods traded in cannot or are not returned to the buyer within 10 days after cancellation, the buyer may elect to recover an amount equal to the trade-in allowance stated in the contract. By written agreement, the buyer may agree to a later time for the delivery of goods and services. (1971, c. 796, s. 1; 1975, c. 805, s. 1.)

### § 25A-40. Form of agreement or offer; statement of buyer's rights.

(a) In a home-solicitation sale the seller must present to the buyer and obtain his signature to a fully completed written agreement or offer to purchase which is in the same language as that principally used in the oral sales presentation and which designates as the date of the transaction the date on which the buyer actually signs and which contains the name and address of the seller, and which contains in immediate proximity to the space reserved for the signature of the buyer in bold face type of a minimum size of 10 points, a statement in substantially the following form:

"You, the buyer, may cancel this transaction at any time prior to midnight of the third business day after the date of this transaction. See the attached Notice of Cancellation form for an explanation of this right."

(b) The seller must, in addition to furnishing the buyer with a copy of the contract or offer to purchase, furnish to the buyer at the time he signs the home-solicitation sale contract or otherwise agrees to buy consumer goods or services from the seller, a completed form in duplicate, captioned "Notice of Cancellation," which shall be attached to the contract and easily detachable, and which shall contain in 10 point bold face type the following information and statements in the same language as that used in the contract:

"Notice of Cancellation

(enter date of transaction)

(date)

You may cancel this transaction, without any penalty or obligation, within three business days from the above date. If you cancel, any property traded in, and payments made by you under the contract or sale, and any negotiable instrument executed by you will be returned within 10 business days following receipt by the seller of your cancellation notice, and any security interest arising out of the transaction will be cancelled. If you cancel, you must make available to the seller at your residence, in substantially as good condition as when received, any goods delivered to you under this contract or sale; or you may, if you wish, comply with the instructions of the seller regarding the return shipment of the goods at the seller's expense and risk. If you do make the goods available to the seller and the seller does not pick them up within 20 days of the date of your notice of cancellation, you may retain or dispose of the goods without any further obligation. If you fail to make the goods available to the seller, or if you agree to return the goods to the seller and fail to do so, then you remain liable for performance of all obligations under the contract. To cancel this transaction, mail or deliver a signed and dated copy of this cancellation notice or any other written notice, or send a telegram to_____ (name of seller) at _____ ,(address of seller's place of business) not later than midnight of _____ (date)

I hereby cancel this transaction. _____ (date)

_____ (Buyer's Signature)

(1971, c. 796, s. 1; 1975, c. 805, s. 2.)

## § 25A-41. Restoration of down payment; retention of goods.

(a) Except as provided in this section, within 10 business days after a home-solicitation sale has been canceled or an offer to purchase revoked in accordance with G.S. 25A-40, the seller must tender to the buyer any payments made by the buyer and any note or other evidence of indebtedness.

(b) If the down payment includes goods traded in, the goods must be tendered at the buyer's residence in substantially as good condition as when received by the seller. If the seller fails to tender the goods as provided by this section, the buyer may elect to recover an amount equal to the trade-in allowance stated in the agreement.

(c) Repealed by Session Laws 1975, c. 805, s. 3.

(d) Until the seller has complied with the obligations imposed by this section, the buyer may retain possession of goods delivered to him by the seller and has a lien on the goods in his possession or control for any recovery to which he is entitled. (1971, c. 796, s. 1; 1975, c. 805, s. 3.)

### § 25A-42. Duties as to care and return of goods; no compensation for services prior to cancellation.

(a) Except as provided by the provisions on retention of goods by the buyer (G.S. 25A-41(d)), within a reasonable time after a home-solicitation sale has been canceled, the buyer must make available to the seller at the buyer's residence in substantially as good condition as received, any goods delivered under the contract or sale, or in the alternative, the buyer may comply with the instructions of the seller regarding the return shipment of the goods at the seller's expense and risk. The seller shall within 10 business days of receipt of the buyer's notice of cancellation notify the buyer whether the seller intends to repossess or to abandon any shipped or delivered goods. If the buyer makes the goods available to the seller and the seller does not pick them up within 20 days of the date of the notice of cancellation, the buyer may retain or dispose of the goods without any further obligation. If the buyer fails to make the goods available to the seller, or agrees to return the goods to the seller and fails to do so, then the buyer shall remain liable for performance of all obligations under the contract.

(b) The buyer has the duty of a bailee to take reasonable care of the goods in his possession before cancellation or revocation and for a reasonable time thereafter, during which time the goods are otherwise at the seller's risk.

(c) If the seller has performed any services pursuant to a home- solicitation sale prior to its cancellation, the seller is entitled to no compensation therefor.

(d) The seller shall not negotiate, transfer, sell, or assign any note, contract, or other evidence of indebtedness arising out of a home-solicitation sale to a finance company or other third party prior to midnight of the fifth business day following the day the contract was signed or the goods or services were purchased. (1971, c. 796, s. 1; 1975, c. 805, s. 4.)

### § 25A-43. Unconscionability.

(a) With respect to a consumer credit sale, if the court finds the agreement or any clause of the agreement to have been unconscionable at the time it was made, the court may refuse to enforce the agreement, or it may enforce the remainder of the agreement without the unconscionable clause, or it may so limit the application of any unconscionable clause as to avoid any unconscionable result.

(b) If it is claimed or appears to the court that the agreement or any clause thereof may be unconscionable, all parties shall be afforded a reasonable opportunity to present evidence as to its setting, purpose and effect to aid the court in making its determination.

(c) As used in this section, "unconscionable" shall mean totally unreasonable under all of the circumstances. (1971, c. 796, s. 1.)

## § 25A-44. Remedies and penalties.

In addition to remedies hereinbefore provided, the following remedies shall apply to consumer credit sales:

(1) In the event that a consumer credit sale contract requires the payment of a finance charge not more than two times in excess of that permitted by this Chapter, the seller or an assignee of the seller shall not be permitted to recover any finance charge under that contract and, in addition, the seller shall be liable to the buyer in an amount that is two times the amount of any finance charge that has been received by the seller, plus reasonable attorney's fees incurred by the buyer as determined by the court. However, if the requirement of an excess charge results from an accidental or good faith error, the seller shall be liable only for the amount by which the finance charge exceeds the rates permitted by this Chapter.

(2) In the event that a consumer credit sale contract requires the payment of a finance charge more than two times that permitted by this Chapter, the contract shall be void. The buyer may, at his option, retain without any liability any goods delivered under such a contract and the seller or an assignee of the rights shall not be entitled to recover anything under such contract.

(3) In the event the seller or an assignee of the seller (i) shall fail to make any rebate required by G.S. 25A-32 or G.S. 25A-36, (ii) shall charge and receive fees or charges in excess of those specifically authorized by this Chapter, or (iii) shall charge and receive sums not authorized by this Chapter, the buyer shall be entitled to demand and receive the rebate due and excessive or unauthorized charges. Ten days after receiving written request therefor, the seller shall be liable to the buyer for an amount equal to three times the sum of any rebate due and all improper charges which have not been rebated or refunded within the 10-day period.

(4)The knowing and willful violation of any provision of this Chapter shall constitute an unfair trade practice under G.S. 75-1.1.

(5) Any buyer injured by any violation of G.S. 25A-2(e) may bring an action for recovery of damages, including reasonable attorney's fees. (1971, c. 796, s. 1; 1983, c. 686, s. 4.)§ 25A-45. Conflict with Consumer Credit Protection Act.

In all cases of irreconcilable conflict between the provisions of this Chapter and the provisions of the Consumer Credit Protection Act, the provisions of the Consumer Credit Protection Act shall control. (1971, c. 796, s. 3.)

Reprinted with permission from *www.ncga.state.nc.us*

# G. Electronic Signatures in Global and National Commerce Act

**(reprinted with permission *www.whitehouse.gov*)**

## SECTION 1. SHORT TITLE.

This Act may be cited as the 'Electronic Signatures in Global and National Commerce Act'.

## TITLE I—ELECTRONIC RECORDS AND SIGNATURES IN COMMERCE

### SEC. 101. GENERAL RULE OF VALIDITY.

(a) IN GENERAL- Notwithstanding any statute, regulation, or other rule of law (other than this title and title II), with respect to any transaction in or affecting interstate or foreign commerce—

(1) a signature, contract, or other record relating to such transaction may not be denied legal effect, validity, or enforceability solely because it is in electronic form; and

(2) a contract relating to such transaction may not be denied legal effect, validity, or enforceability solely because an electronic signature or electronic record was used in its formation.

(b) PRESERVATION OF RIGHTS AND OBLIGATIONS- This title does not—

(1) limit, alter, or otherwise affect any requirement imposed by a statute, regulation, or rule of law relating to the rights and obligations of persons under such statute, regulation, or rule of law other than a requirement that contracts or other records be written, signed, or in non-electronic form; or

(2) require any person to agree to use or accept electronic records or electronic signatures, other than a governmental agency with respect to a record other than a contract to which it is a party.

(c) CONSUMER DISCLOSURES-

(1) CONSENT TO ELECTRONIC RECORDS- Notwithstanding subsection (a), if a statute, regulation, or other rule of law requires that information relating to a transaction or transactions in or affecting interstate or foreign commerce be provided or made available to a consumer in writing, the use of an electronic record to provide or make available (whichever is required) such information satisfies the requirement that such information be in writing if—

(A) the consumer has affirmatively consented to such use and has not withdrawn such consent;

(B) the consumer, prior to consenting, is provided with a clear and conspicuous statement—

(i) informing the consumer of (I) any right or option of the consumer to have the record provided or made available on paper or in non-electronic form, and (II) the right of the consumer to withdraw the consent to have the record provided or made available in an electronic form and of any conditions, consequences (which may include termination of the parties' relationship), or fees in the event of such withdrawal;

(ii) informing the consumer of whether the consent applies (I) only to the particular transaction which gave rise to the obligation to provide the record, or (II) to identified categories of records that may be provided or made available during the course of the parties' relationship;

(iii) describing the procedures the consumer must use to withdraw consent as provided in clause (i) and to update information needed to contact the consumer electronically; and

(iv) informing the consumer (I) how, after the consent, the consumer may, upon request, obtain a paper copy of an electronic record, and (II) whether any fee will be charged for such copy;

(C) the consumer—

(i) prior to consenting, is provided with a statement of the hardware and software requirements for access to and retention of the electronic records; and

(ii) consents electronically, or confirms his or her consent electronically, in a manner that reasonably demonstrates that the consumer can access information in the electronic form that will be used to provide the information that is the subject of the consent; and

(D) after the consent of a consumer in accordance with subparagraph (A), if a change in the hardware or software requirements needed to access or retain electronic records creates a material risk that the consumer will not be able to access or retain a subsequent electronic record that was the subject of the consent, the person providing the electronic record—

(i) provides the consumer with a statement of (I) the revised hardware and software requirements for access to and retention of the electronic records, and (II) the right to withdraw consent without the imposition of any fees for such withdrawal and without the imposition of any condition or consequence that was not disclosed under subparagraph (B)(i); and

(ii) again complies with subparagraph (C).

(2) OTHER RIGHTS-

(A) PRESERVATION OF CONSUMER PROTECTIONS- Nothing in this title affects the content or timing of any disclosure or other record required to be provided or made available to any consumer under any statute, regulation, or other rule of law.

(B) VERIFICATION OR ACKNOWLEDGMENT- If a law that was enacted prior to this Act expressly requires a record to be provided or made available by a specified method that requires verification or acknowledgment of receipt, the record may be provided or made available electronically only if the method used provides verification or acknowledgment of receipt (whichever is required).

(3) EFFECT OF FAILURE TO OBTAIN ELECTRONIC CONSENT OR CONFIRMATION OF CONSENT- The legal effectiveness, validity, or enforceability of any contract executed by a consumer shall not be denied solely because of the failure to obtain electronic consent or confirmation of consent by that consumer in accordance with paragraph (1)(C)(ii).

(4) PROSPECTIVE EFFECT- Withdrawal of consent by a consumer shall not affect the legal effectiveness, validity, or enforceability of electronic records provided or made available to that consumer in accordance with paragraph (1) prior to implementation of the consumer's withdrawal of consent. A consumer's withdrawal of consent shall be effective within a reasonable period of time after receipt of the withdrawal by the provider of the record. Failure to comply with paragraph (1)(D) may, at the election of the consumer, be treated as a withdrawal of consent for purposes of this paragraph.

(5) PRIOR CONSENT- This subsection does not apply to any records that are provided or made available to a consumer who has consented prior to the effective date of this title to receive such records in electronic form as permitted by any statute, regulation, or other rule of law.

(6) ORAL COMMUNICATIONS- An oral communication or a recording of an oral communication shall not qualify as an electronic record for purposes of this subsection except as otherwise provided under applicable law.

(d) RETENTION OF CONTRACTS AND RECORDS-

(1) ACCURACY AND ACCESSIBILITY- If a statute, regulation, or other rule of law requires that a contract or other record relating to a transaction in or affecting interstate or foreign commerce be retained, that requirement is met by retaining an electronic record of the information in the contract or other record that—

(A) accurately reflects the information set forth in the contract or other record; and

(B) remains accessible to all persons who are entitled to access by statute, regulation, or rule of law, for the period required by such statute, regulation, or rule of law, in a form that is capable of being accurately reproduced for later reference, whether by transmission, printing, or otherwise.

(2) EXCEPTION- A requirement to retain a contract or other record in accordance with paragraph (1) does not apply to any information whose sole purpose is to enable the contract or other record to be sent, communicated, or received.

(3) ORIGINALS- If a statute, regulation, or other rule of law requires a contract or other record relating to a transaction in or affecting interstate or foreign commerce to be provided, available, or retained in its original form, or provides consequences if the contract or other record is not provided, available, or retained in its original form, that statute, regulation, or rule of law is satisfied by an electronic record that complies with paragraph (1).

(4) CHECKS- If a statute, regulation, or other rule of law requires the retention of a check, that requirement is satisfied by retention of an electronic record of the information on the front and back of the check in accordance with paragraph (1).

(e) ACCURACY AND ABILITY TO RETAIN CONTRACTS AND OTHER RECORDS-

Notwithstanding subsection (a), if a statute, regulation, or other rule of law requires that a contract or other record relating to a transaction in or affecting interstate or foreign commerce be in writing, the legal effect, validity, or enforceability of an electronic record of such contract or other record may be denied if such electronic record is not in a form that is capable of being retained and accurately reproduced for later reference by all parties or persons who are entitled to retain the contract or other record.

(f) PROXIMITY- Nothing in this title affects the proximity required by any statute, regulation, or other rule of law with respect to any warning, notice, disclosure, or other record required to be posted, displayed, or publicly affixed.

(g) NOTARIZATION AND ACKNOWLEDGMENT- If a statute, regulation, or other rule of law requires a signature or record relating to a transaction in or affecting interstate or foreign commerce to be notarized, acknowledged, verified, or made under oath, that requirement is satisfied if the electronic signature of the person authorized to perform those acts, together with all other information required to be included by other applicable statute, regulation, or rule of law, is attached to or logically associated with the signature or record.

(h) ELECTRONIC AGENTS- A contract or other record relating to a transaction in or affecting interstate or foreign commerce may not be denied legal effect, validity, or enforceability solely because its formation, creation, or delivery involved the action of one or more electronic agents so long as the action of any such electronic agent is legally attributable to the person to be bound.

(i) INSURANCE- It is the specific intent of the Congress that this title and title II apply to the business of insurance.

(j) INSURANCE AGENTS AND BROKERS- An insurance agent or broker acting under the direction of a party that enters into a contract by means of an electronic record or electronic signature may not be held liable for any deficiency in the electronic procedures agreed to by the parties under that contract if—

(1) the agent or broker has not engaged in negligent, reckless, or intentional tortious conduct;

(2) the agent or broker was not involved in the development or establishment of such electronic procedures; and

(3) the agent or broker did not deviate from such procedures.

# SEC. 102. EXEMPTION TO PREEMPTION.

(a) IN GENERAL- A State statute, regulation, or other rule of law may modify, limit, or supersede the provisions of section 101 with respect to State law only if such statute, regulation, or rule of law—

(1) constitutes an enactment or adoption of the Uniform Electronic Transactions Act as approved and recommended for enactment in all the States by the National Conference of Commissioners on Uniform State Laws in 1999, except that any exception to the scope of such Act enacted by a State under section 3(b)(4) of such Act shall be preempted to the extent such exception is inconsistent with this title or title II, or would not be permitted under paragraph (2)(A)(ii) of this subsection; or

(2)(A) specifies the alternative procedures or requirements for the use or acceptance (or both) of electronic records or electronic signatures to establish the legal effect, validity, or enforceability of contracts or other records, if—

(i) such alternative procedures or requirements are consistent with this title and title II; and

(ii) such alternative procedures or requirements do not require, or accord greater legal status or effect to, the implementation or application of a specific technology or technical specification for performing the functions of creating, storing, generating, receiving, communicating, or authenticating electronic records or electronic signatures; and

(B) if enacted or adopted after the date of the enactment of this Act, makes specific reference to this Act.

(b) EXCEPTIONS FOR ACTIONS BY STATES AS MARKET PARTICIPANTS- Subsection (a)(2)(A)(ii) shall not apply to the statutes, regulations, or other rules of law governing procurement by any State, or any agency or instrumentality thereof.

(c) PREVENTION OF CIRCUMVENTION- Subsection (a) does not permit a State to circumvent this title or title II through the imposition of non-electronic delivery methods under section 8(b)(2) of the Uniform Electronic Transactions Act.

# SEC. 103. SPECIFIC EXCEPTIONS.

(a) EXCEPTED REQUIREMENTS- The provisions of section 101 shall not apply to a contract or other record to the extent it is governed by—

(1) a statute, regulation, or other rule of law governing the creation and execution of wills, codicils, or testamentary trusts;

(2) a State statute, regulation, or other rule of law governing adoption, divorce, or other matters of family law; or

(3) the Uniform Commercial Code, as in effect in any State, other than sections 1-107 and 1-

206 and Articles 2 and 2A.

(b) ADDITIONAL EXCEPTIONS- The provisions of section 101 shall not apply to—

(1) court orders or notices, or official court documents (including briefs, pleadings, and other writings) required to be executed in connection with court proceedings;

(2) any notice of—

(A) the cancellation or termination of utility services (including water, heat, and power);

(B) default, acceleration, repossession, foreclosure, or eviction, or the right to cure, under a credit agreement secured by, or a rental agreement for, a primary residence of an individual;

(C) the cancellation or termination of health insurance or benefits or life insurance benefits (excluding annuities); or

(D) recall of a product, or material failure of a product, that risks endangering health or safety; or

(3) any document required to accompany any transportation or handling of hazardous materials, pesticides, or other toxic or dangerous materials.

(c) REVIEW OF EXCEPTIONS-

(1) EVALUATION REQUIRED- The Secretary of Commerce, acting through the Assistant Secretary for Communications and Information, shall review the operation of the exceptions in subsections (a) and (b) to evaluate, over a period of 3 years, whether such exceptions continue to be necessary for the protection of consumers. Within 3 years after the date of enactment of this Act, the Assistant Secretary shall submit a report to the Congress on the results of such evaluation.

(2) DETERMINATIONS- If a Federal regulatory agency, with respect to matter within its jurisdiction, determines after notice and an opportunity for public comment, and publishes a finding, that one or more such exceptions are no longer necessary for the protection of consumers and eliminating such exceptions will not increase the material risk of harm to consumers, such agency may extend the application of section 101 to the exceptions identified in such finding.

## SEC. 104. APPLICABILITY TO FEDERAL AND STATE GOVERNMENTS.

(a) FILING AND ACCESS REQUIREMENTS- Subject to subsection (c)(2), nothing in this title limits or supersedes any requirement by a Federal regulatory agency, self-regulatory organization, or State regulatory agency that records be filed with such agency or organization in accordance with specified standards or formats.

(b) PRESERVATION OF EXISTING RULEMAKING AUTHORITY-

(1) USE OF AUTHORITY TO INTERPRET- Subject to paragraph (2) and subsection (c), a

Federal regulatory agency or State regulatory agency that is responsible for rulemaking under any other statute may interpret section 101 with respect to such statute through—

(A) the issuance of regulations pursuant to a statute; or

(B) to the extent such agency is authorized by statute to issue orders or guidance, the issuance of orders or guidance of general applicability that are publicly available and published (in the Federal Register in the case of an order or guidance issued by a Federal regulatory agency).

This paragraph does not grant any Federal regulatory agency or State regulatory agency authority to issue regulations, orders, or guidance pursuant to any statute that does not authorize such issuance.

(2) LIMITATIONS ON INTERPRETATION AUTHORITY- Notwithstanding paragraph (1), a Federal regulatory agency shall not adopt any regulation, order, or guidance described in paragraph (1), and a State regulatory agency is preempted by section 101 from adopting any regulation, order, or guidance described in paragraph (1), unless—

(A) such regulation, order, or guidance is consistent with section 101;

(B) such regulation, order, or guidance does not add to the requirements of such section; and

(C) such agency finds, in connection with the issuance of such regulation, order, or guidance, that—

(i) there is a substantial justification for the regulation, order, or guidance;

(ii) the methods selected to carry out that purpose—

(I) are substantially equivalent to the requirements imposed on records that are not electronic records; and

(II) will not impose unreasonable costs on the acceptance and use of electronic records; and

(iii) the methods selected to carry out that purpose do not require, or accord greater legal status or effect to, the implementation or application of a specific technology or technical specification for performing the functions of creating, storing, generating, receiving, communicating, or authenticating electronic records or electronic signatures.

(3) PERFORMANCE STANDARDS-

(A) ACCURACY, RECORD INTEGRITY, ACCESSIBILITY- Notwithstanding paragraph (2)(C)(iii), a Federal regulatory agency or State regulatory agency may interpret section 101(d) to specify performance standards to assure accuracy, record integrity, and accessibility of records that are required to be retained. Such performance standards may be specified in a manner that imposes a requirement in violation of paragraph

(2)(C)(iii) if the requirement (i) serves an important governmental objective; and (ii) is substantially related to the achievement of that objective. Nothing in this paragraph shall be construed to grant any Federal regulatory agency or State regulatory agency authority to require use of a particular type of software or hardware in order to comply with section 101(d).

(B) PAPER OR PRINTED FORM- Notwithstanding subsection (c)(1), a Federal regulatory agency or State regulatory agency may interpret section 101(d) to require retention of a record in a tangible printed or paper form if—

(i) there is a compelling governmental interest relating to law enforcement or national security for imposing such requirement; and

(ii) imposing such requirement is essential to attaining such interest.

(4) EXCEPTIONS FOR ACTIONS BY GOVERNMENT AS MARKET PARTICIPANT- Paragraph (2)(C)(iii) shall not apply to the statutes, regulations, or other rules of law governing procurement by the Federal or any State government, or any agency or instrumentality thereof.

(c) ADDITIONAL LIMITATIONS-

(1) REIMPOSING PAPER PROHIBITED- Nothing in subsection (b) (other than paragraph (3)(B) thereof) shall be construed to grant any Federal regulatory agency or State regulatory agency authority to impose or reimpose any requirement that a record be in a tangible printed or paper form.

(2) CONTINUING OBLIGATION UNDER GOVERNMENT PAPERWORK ELIMINATION ACT- Nothing in subsection (a) or (b) relieves any Federal regulatory agency of its obligations under the Government Paperwork Elimination Act (title XVII of Public Law 105-277).

(d) AUTHORITY TO EXEMPT FROM CONSENT PROVISION-

(1) IN GENERAL- A Federal regulatory agency may, with respect to matter within its jurisdiction, by regulation or order issued after notice and an opportunity for public comment, exempt without condition a specified category or type of record from the requirements relating to consent in section 101(c) if such exemption is necessary to eliminate a substantial burden on electronic commerce and will not increase the material risk of harm to consumers.

(2) PROSPECTUSES- Within 30 days after the date of enactment of this Act, the Securities and Exchange Commission shall issue a regulation or order pursuant to paragraph (1) exempting from section 101(c) any records that are required to be provided in order to allow advertising, sales literature, or other information concerning a security issued by an investment company that is registered under the Investment Company Act of 1940, or concerning the issuer thereof, to be excluded from the definition of a prospectus under section 2(a)(10)(A) of the Securities Act of 1933.

(e) ELECTRONIC LETTERS OF AGENCY- The Federal Communications Commission shall not hold any contract for telecommunications service or letter of agency for a preferred carrier change, that otherwise complies with the Commission's rules, to be legally ineffective, invalid, or unenforceable solely because an electronic record or electronic signature was used in its formation or authorization.

# SEC. 105. STUDIES.

(a) DELIVERY- Within 12 months after the date of the enactment of this Act, the Secretary of Commerce shall conduct an inquiry regarding the effectiveness of the delivery of electronic records to consumers using electronic mail as compared with delivery of written records via the United States Postal Service and private express mail services. The Secretary shall submit a report to the Congress regarding the results of such inquiry by the conclusion of such 12-month period.

(b) STUDY OF ELECTRONIC CONSENT- Within 12 months after the date of the enactment of this Act, the Secretary of Commerce and the Federal Trade Commission shall submit a report to the Congress evaluating any benefits provided to consumers by the procedure required by section 101(c)(1)(C)(ii); any burdens imposed on electronic commerce by that provision; whether the benefits outweigh the burdens; whether the absence of the procedure required by section 101(c)(1)(C)(ii) would increase the incidence of fraud directed against consumers; and suggesting any revisions to the provision deemed appropriate by the Secretary and the Commission. In conducting this evaluation, the Secretary and the Commission shall solicit comment from the general public, consumer representatives, and electronic commerce businesses.

# SEC. 106. DEFINITIONS.

For purposes of this title:

(1) CONSUMER- The term 'consumer' means an individual who obtains, through a transaction, products or services which are used primarily for personal, family, or household purposes, and also means the legal representative of such an individual.

(2) ELECTRONIC- The term 'electronic' means relating to technology having electrical, digital, magnetic, wireless, optical, electromagnetic, or similar capabilities.

(3) ELECTRONIC AGENT- The term 'electronic agent' means a computer program or an electronic or other automated means used independently to initiate an action or respond to electronic records or performances in whole or in part without review or action by an individual at the time of the action or response.

(4) ELECTRONIC RECORD- The term 'electronic record' means a contract or other record created, generated, sent, communicated, received, or stored by electronic means.

(5) ELECTRONIC SIGNATURE- The term 'electronic signature' means an electronic sound, symbol, or process, attached to or logically associated with a contract or other record and executed or adopted by a person with the intent to sign the record.

(6) FEDERAL REGULATORY AGENCY- The term 'Federal regulatory agency' means an agency, as that term is defined in section 552(f) of title 5, United States Code.

(7) INFORMATION- The term 'information' means data, text, images, sounds, codes, computer programs, software, databases, or the like.

(8) PERSON- The term 'person' means an individual, corporation, business trust, estate, trust, partnership, limited liability company, association, joint venture, governmental agency, public corporation, or any other legal or commercial entity.

(9) RECORD- The term 'record' means information that is inscribed on a tangible medium or that is stored in an electronic or other medium and is retrievable in perceivable form.

(10) REQUIREMENT- The term 'requirement' includes a prohibition.

(11) SELF-REGULATORY ORGANIZATION- The term 'self-regulatory organization' means an organization or entity that is not a Federal regulatory agency or a State, but that is under the supervision of a Federal regulatory agency and is authorized under Federal law to adopt and administer rules applicable to its members that are enforced by such organization or entity, by a Federal regulatory agency, or by another self-regulatory organization.

(12) STATE- The term 'State' includes the District of Columbia and the territories and possessions of the United States.

(13) TRANSACTION- The term 'transaction' means an action or set of actions relating to the conduct of business, consumer, or commercial affairs between two or more persons, including any of the following types of conduct—

(A) the sale, lease, exchange, licensing, or other disposition of (i) personal property, including goods and intangibles, (ii) services, and (iii) any combination thereof; and

(B) the sale, lease, exchange, or other disposition of any interest in real property, or any combination thereof.

## SEC. 107. EFFECTIVE DATE.

(a) IN GENERAL- Except as provided in subsection (b), this title shall be effective on October 1, 2000.

(b) EXCEPTIONS-

(1) RECORD RETENTION-

(A) IN GENERAL- Subject to subparagraph (B), this title shall be effective on March 1, 2001, with respect to a requirement that a record be retained imposed by—

(i) a Federal statute, regulation, or other rule of law, or

(ii) a State statute, regulation, or other rule of law administered or promulgated by a State regulatory agency.

(B) DELAYED EFFECT FOR PENDING RULEMAKINGS- If on March 1, 2001, a Federal regulatory agency or State regulatory agency has announced, proposed, or initiated, but not completed, a rulemaking proceeding to prescribe a regulation under section 104(b)(3) with respect to a requirement described in subparagraph (A), this title shall be effective on June 1, 2001, with respect to such requirement.

(2) CERTAIN GUARANTEED AND INSURED LOANS- With regard to any transaction involving a loan guarantee or loan guarantee commitment (as those terms are defined in section 502 of the Federal Credit Reform Act of 1990), or involving a program listed in the Federal Credit Supplement, Budget of the United States, FY 2001, this title applies only to such transactions entered into, and to any loan or mortgage made, insured, or guaranteed by the United States Government thereunder, on and after one year after the date of enactment of this Act.

(3) STUDENT LOANS- With respect to any records that are provided or made available to a consumer pursuant to an application for a loan, or a loan made, pursuant to title IV of the Higher Education Act of 1965, section 101(c) of this Act shall not apply until the earlier of—

(A) such time as the Secretary of Education publishes revised promissory notes under section 432(m) of the Higher Education Act of 1965; or

(B) one year after the date of enactment of this Act.

# TITLE II—TRANSFERABLE RECORDS

## SEC. 201. TRANSFERABLE RECORDS.

(a) DEFINITIONS- For purposes of this section:

(1) TRANSFERABLE RECORD- The term 'transferable record' means an electronic record that—

(A) would be a note under Article 3 of the Uniform Commercial Code if the electronic record were in writing;

(B) the issuer of the electronic record expressly has agreed is a transferable record; and

(C) relates to a loan secured by real property.

A transferable record may be executed using an electronic signature.

(2) OTHER DEFINITIONS- The terms 'electronic record', 'electronic signature', and 'person' have the same meanings provided in section 106 of this Act.

(b) CONTROL- A person has control of a transferable record if a system employed for evidencing the transfer of interests in the transferable record reliably establishes that person as the person to which the transferable record was issued or transferred.

(c) CONDITIONS- A system satisfies subsection (b), and a person is deemed to have control of a transferable record, if the transferable record is created, stored, and assigned in such a manner that—

(1) a single authoritative copy of the transferable record exists which is unique, identifiable, and, except as otherwise provided in paragraphs (4), (5), and (6), unalterable;

(2) the authoritative copy identifies the person asserting control as—

(A) the person to which the transferable record was issued; or

(B) if the authoritative copy indicates that the transferable record has been transferred, the person to which the transferable record was most recently transferred;

(3) the authoritative copy is communicated to and maintained by the person asserting control or its designated custodian;

(4) copies or revisions that add or change an identified assignee of the authoritative copy can be made only with the consent of the person asserting control;

(5) each copy of the authoritative copy and any copy of a copy is readily identifiable as a copy that is not the authoritative copy; and

(6) any revision of the authoritative copy is readily identifiable as authorized or unauthorized.

(d) STATUS AS HOLDER- Except as otherwise agreed, a person having control of a transferable record is the holder, as defined in section 1-201(20) of the Uniform Commercial Code, of the transferable record and has the same rights and defenses as a holder of an equivalent record or writing under the Uniform Commercial Code, including, if the applicable statutory requirements under section 3-302(a), 9-308, or revised section 9-330 of the Uniform Commercial Code are satisfied, the rights and defenses of a holder in due course or a purchaser, respectively. Delivery, possession, and endorsement are not required to obtain or exercise any of the rights under this subsection.

(e) OBLIGOR RIGHTS- Except as otherwise agreed, an obligor under a transferable record has the same rights and defenses as an equivalent obligor under equivalent records or writings under the Uniform Commercial Code.

(f) PROOF OF CONTROL- If requested by a person against which enforcement is sought, the person seeking to enforce the transferable record shall provide reasonable proof that the person is in control of the transferable record. Proof may include access to the authoritative copy of the transferable record and related business records sufficient to review the terms of the transferable record and to establish the identity of the person having control of the transferable record.

(g) UCC REFERENCES- For purposes of this subsection, all references to the Uniform Commercial Code are to the Uniform Commercial Code as in effect in the jurisdiction the law of which governs the transferable record.

## SEC. 202. EFFECTIVE DATE.

This title shall be effective 90 days after the date of enactment of this Act.

# TITLE III—PROMOTION OF INTERNATIONAL ELECTRONIC COMMERCE

## SEC. 301. PRINCIPLES GOVERNING THE USE OF ELECTRONIC SIGNATURES IN INTERNATIONAL TRANSACTIONS.

(a) PROMOTION OF ELECTRONIC SIGNATURES-

(1) REQUIRED ACTIONS- The Secretary of Commerce shall promote the acceptance and use, on an international basis, of electronic signatures in accordance with the principles specified in paragraph (2) and in a manner consistent with section 101 of this Act. The Secretary of Commerce shall take all actions necessary in a manner consistent with such principles to eliminate or reduce, to the maximum extent possible, the impediments to commerce in electronic signatures, for the purpose of facilitating the development of interstate and foreign commerce.

(2) PRINCIPLES- The principles specified in this paragraph are the following:

(A) Remove paper-based obstacles to electronic transactions by adopting relevant principles from the Model Law on Electronic Commerce adopted in 1996 by the United Nations Commission on International Trade Law.

(B) Permit parties to a transaction to determine the appropriate authentication technologies and implementation models for their transactions, with assurance that those technologies and implementation models will be recognized and enforced.

(C) Permit parties to a transaction to have the opportunity to prove in court or other proceedings that their authentication approaches and their transactions are valid.

(D) Take a nondiscriminatory approach to electronic signatures and authentication methods from other jurisdictions.

(b) CONSULTATION- In conducting the activities required by this section, the Secretary shall consult with users and providers of electronic signature products and services and other interested persons.

(c) DEFINITIONS- As used in this section, the terms 'electronic record' and 'electronic signature' have the same meanings provided in section 106 of this Act

# H. EQUAL CREDIT OPPORTUNITY ACT

## Sec. 202.1 Authority, scope and purpose.

(a) Authority and scope. This regulation is issued by the Board of Governors of the Federal Reserve System pursuant to title VII (Equal Credit Opportunity Act) of the Consumer Credit Protection Act, as amended (15 U.S.C. 1601 et seq.). Except as otherwise provided herein, the regulation applies to all persons who are creditors, as defined in Sec. 202.2(1). Information collection requirements contained in this regulation have been approved by the Office of Management and Budget under the provisions of 44 U.S.C. 3501 et seq. and have been assigned OMB control number 7100-0201.

(b) Purpose. The purpose of this regulation is to promote the availability of credit to all creditworthy applicants without regard to race, color, religion, national origin, sex, marital status, or age (provided the applicant has the capacity to contract); to the fact that all or part of the applicant's income derives from a public assistance program; or to the fact that the applicant has in good faith exercised any right under the Consumer Credit Protection Act. The regulation prohibits creditor practices that discriminate on the basis of any of these factors. The regulation also requires creditors to notify applicants of action taken on their applications; to report credit history in the names of both spouses on an account; to retain records of credit applications; to collect information about the applicant's race and other personal characteristics in applications for certain dwelling- related loans; and to provide applicants with copies of appraisal reports used in connection with credit transactions.

## Sec. 202.2 Definitions.

For the purposes of this regulation, unless the context indicates otherwise, the following definitions apply.

(a) Account means an extension of credit. When employed in relation to an account, the word use refers only to open-end credit.

(b) Act means the Equal Credit Opportunity Act (title VII of the Consumer Credit Protection Act).

(c) Adverse action.

    (1) The term means:

        (i) A refusal to grant credit in substantially the amount or on substantially the terms requested in an application unless the creditor makes a counteroffer (to grant credit in a different amount or on other terms) and the applicant uses or expressly accepts the credit offered;

        (ii) A termination of an account or an unfavorable change in the terms of an account that does not affect all or a substantial portion of a class of the creditor's accounts; or

        (iii) A refusal to increase the amount of credit available to an applicant who has made an application for an increase.

(2) The term does not include:

(i) A change in the terms of an account expressly agreed to by an applicant.

(ii) Any action or forbearance relating to an account taken in connection with inactivity, default, or delinquency as to that account;

(iii) A refusal or failure to authorize an account transaction at a point of sale or loan, except when the refusal is a termination or an unfavorable change in the terms of an account that does not affect all or a substantial portion of a class of the creditor's accounts, or when the refusal is a denial of an application for an increase in the amount of credit available under the account;

(iv) A refusal to extend credit because applicable law prohibits the creditor from extending the credit requested; or

(v) A refusal to extend credit because the creditor does not offer the type of credit or credit plan requested. (3) An action that falls within the definition of both paragraphs (c)(1) and (c)(2) of this section is governed by paragraph (c)(2) of this section.

(d) Age refers only to the age of natural persons and means the number of fully elapsed years from the date of an applicant's birth.

(e) Applicant means any person who requests or who has received an extension of credit from a creditor, and includes any person who is or may become contractually liable regarding an extension of credit. For purposes of Sec. 202.7(d), the term includes guarantors, sureties, endorsers and similar parties.

(f) Application means an oral or written request for an extension of credit that is made in accordance with procedures established by a creditor for the type of credit requested. The term does not include the use of an account or line of credit to obtain an amount of credit that is within a previously established credit limit. A completed application means an application in connection with which a creditor has received all the information that the creditor regularly obtains and considers in evaluating applications for the amount and type of credit requested (including, but not limited to, credit reports, any additional information requested from the applicant, and any approvals or reports by governmental agencies or other persons that are necessary to guarantee, insure, or provide security for the credit or collateral). The creditor shall exercise reasonable diligence in obtaining such information.

(g) Business credit refers to extensions of credit primarily for business or commercial (including agricultural) purposes, but excluding extensions of credit of the types described in Sec. 202.3 (a), (b), and (d).

(h) Consumer credit means credit extended to a natural person primarily for personal, family, or household purposes.

(i) Contractually liable means expressly obligated to repay all debts arising on an account by reason of an agreement to that effect.

(j) Credit means the right granted by a creditor to an applicant to defer payment of a debt, incur debt and defer its payment, or purchase property or services and defer payment therefor.

(k) Credit card means any card, plate, coupon book, or other single credit device that may be used from time to time to obtain money, property, or services on credit.

(l) Creditor means a person who, in the ordinary course of business, regularly participates in the decision of whether or not to extend credit. The term includes a creditor's assignee, transferee, or subrogee who so participates. For purposes of Secs. 202.4 and 202.5(a), the term also includes a person who, in the ordinary course of business, regularly refers applicants or prospective applicants to creditors, or selects or offers to select creditors to whom requests for credit may be made. A person is not a creditor regarding any violation of the act or this regulation committed by another creditor unless the person knew or had reasonable notice of the act, policy, or practice that constituted the violation before becoming involved in the credit transaction. The term does not include a person whose only participation in a credit transaction involves honoring a credit card.

(m) Credit transaction means every aspect of an applicant's dealings with a creditor regarding an application for credit or an existing extension of credit (including, but not limited to, information requirements; investigation procedures; standards of creditworthiness; terms of credit; furnishing of credit information; revocation, alteration, or termination of credit; and collection procedures).

(n) Discriminate against an applicant means to treat an applicant less favorably than other applicants.

(o) Elderly means age 62 or older.

(p) Empirically derived and other credit scoring systems—

(1) A credit scoring system is a system that evaluates an applicant's creditworthiness mechanically, based on key attributes of the applicant and aspects of the transaction, and that determines, alone or in conjunction with an evaluation of additional information about the applicant, whether an applicant is deemed creditworthy. To qualify as an empirically derived, demonstrably and statistically sound, credit scoring system, the system must be:

(i) Based on data that are derived from an empirical comparison of sample groups or the population of creditworthy and noncreditworthy applicants who applied for credit within a reasonable preceding period of time;

(ii) Developed for the purpose of evaluating the creditworthiness of applicants with respect to the legitimate business interests of the creditor utilizing the system (including, but not limited to, minimizing bad debt losses and operating expenses in accordance with the creditor's business judgment);

(iii) Developed and validated using accepted statistical principles and methodology; and

(iv) Periodically revalidated by the use of appropriate statistical principles and methodology and adjusted as necessary to maintain predictive ability.

(2) A creditor may use an empirically derived, demonstrably and statistically sound, credit

scoring system obtained from another person or may obtain credit experience from which to develop such a system. Any such system must satisfy the criteria set forth in paragraphs (p)(1) (i) through (iv) of this section; if the creditor is unable during the development process to validate the system based on its own credit experience in accordance with paragraph (p)(1) of this section, the system must be validated when sufficient credit experience becomes available. A system that fails this validity test is no longer an empirically derived, demonstrably and statistically sound, credit scoring system for that creditor.

(q) Extend credit and extension of credit mean the granting of credit in any form (including, but not limited to, credit granted in addition to any existing credit or credit limit; credit granted pursuant to an open-end credit plan; the refinancing or other renewal of credit, including the issuance of a new credit card in place of an expiring credit card or in substitution for an existing credit card; the consolidation of two or more obligations; or the continuance of existing credit without any special effort to collect at or after maturity).

(r) Good faith means honesty in fact in the conduct or transaction.

(s) Inadvertent error means a mechanical, electronic, or clerical error that a creditor demonstrates was not intentional and occurred notwithstanding the maintenance of procedures reasonably adapted to avoid such errors.

(t) Judgmental system of evaluating applicants means any system for evaluating the creditworthiness of an applicant other than an empirically derived, demonstrably and statistically sound, credit scoring system.

(u) Marital status means the state of being unmarried, married, or separated, as defined by applicable state law. The term unmarried includes persons who are single, divorced, or widowed.

(v) Negative factor or value, in relation to the age of elderly applicants, means utilizing a factor, value, or weight that is less favorable regarding elderly applicants than the creditor's experience warrants or is less favorable than the factor, value, or weight assigned to the class of applicants that are not classified as elderly and are most favored by a creditor on the basis of age.

(w) Open-end credit means credit extended under a plan under which a creditor may permit an applicant to make purchases or obtain loans from time to time directly from the creditor or indirectly by use of a credit card, check, or other device.

(x) Person means a natural person, corporation, government or governmental subdivision or agency, trust, estate, partnership, cooperative, or association.

(y) Pertinent element of creditworthiness, in relation to a judgmental system of evaluating applicants, means any information about applicants that a creditor obtains and considers and that has a demonstrable relationship to a determination of creditworthiness.

(z) Prohibited basis means race, color, religion, national origin, sex, marital status, or age (provided that the applicant has the capacity to enter into a binding contract); the fact that all or part of the applicant's income derives from any public assistance program; or the fact that the applicant has in good faith exercised any right under the Consumer Credit Protection Act or any state law upon which an exemption has been granted by the Board.

(aa) State means any State, the District of Columbia, the Commonwealth of Puerto Rico, or any territory or possession of the United States.

## Sec. 202.3 Limited exceptions for certain classes of transactions

(a) Public utilities credit—

(1) Definition. Public utilities credit refers to extensions of credit that involve public utility services provided through pipe, wire, or other connected facilities, or radio or similar transmission (including extensions of such facilities), if the charges for service, delayed payment, and any discount for prompt payment are filed with or regulated by a government unit.

(2) Exceptions. The following provisions of this regulation do not apply to public utilities credit:

(i) Section 202.5(d)(1) concerning information about marital status;

(ii) Section 202.10 relating to furnishing of credit information; and

(iii) Section 202.12(b) relating to record retention.

(b) Securities credit—

(1) Definition. Securities credit refers to extensions of credit subject to regulation under section 7 of the Securities Exchange Act of 1934 or extensions of credit by a broker or dealer subject to regulation as a broker or dealer under the Securities Exchange Act of 1934.

(2) Exceptions. The following provisions of this regulation do not apply to securities credit:

(i) Section 202.5(c) concerning information about a spouse or former spouse;

(ii) Section 202.5(d)(1) concerning information about marital status;

(iii) Section 202.5(d)(3) concerning information about the sex of an applicant;

(iv) Section 202.7(b) relating to designation of name, but only to the extent necessary to prevent violation of rules regarding an account in which a broker or dealer has an interest, or rules necessitating the aggregation of accounts of spouses for the purpose of determining controlling interests, beneficial interests, beneficial ownership, or purchase limitations and restrictions;

(v) Section 202.7(c) relating to action concerning open-end accounts, but only to the extent the action taken is on the basis of a change of name or marital status;

(vi) Section 202.7(d) relating to the signature of a spouse or other person;

(vii) Section 202.10 relating to furnishing of credit information; and

(viii) Section 202.12(b) relating to record retention.

(c) Incidental credit.

(1) Definition. Incidental credit refers to extensions of consumer credit other than credit of the types described in paragraphs (a) and (b) of this section:

(i) That are not made pursuant to the terms of a credit card account;

(ii) That are not subject to a finance charge (as defined in Regulation Z, 12 CFR 226.4); and

(iii) That are not payable by agreement in more than four installments.

(2) Exceptions. The following provisions of this regulation do not apply to incidental credit:

(i) Section 202.5(c) concerning information about a spouse or former spouse;

(ii) Section 202.5(d)(1) concerning information about marital status;

(iii) Section 202.5(d)(2) concerning information about income derived from alimony, child support, or separate maintenance payments;

(iv) Section 202.5(d)(3) concerning information about the sex of an applicant, but only to the extent necessary for medical records or similar purposes;

(v) Section 202.7(d) relating to the signature of a spouse or other person;

(vi) Section 202.9 relating to notifications;

(vii) Section 202.10 relating to furnishing of credit information; and

(viii) Section 202.12(b) relating to record retention.

(d) Government credit—

(1) Definition. Government credit refers to extensions of credit made to governments or governmental subdivisions, agencies, or instrumentalities.

(2) Applicability of regulation. Except for Sec. 202.4, the general rule prohibiting discrimination on a prohibited basis, the requirements of this regulation do not apply to government credit.

## Sec. 202.4 General rule prohibiting discrimination.

A creditor shall not discriminate against an applicant on a prohibited basis regarding any aspect of a credit transaction.

## Sec. 202.5 Rules concerning taking of applications.

(a) Discouraging applications. A creditor shall not make any oral or written statement, in advertising or otherwise, to applicants or prospective applicants that would discourage on a prohibited basis a reasonable person from making or pursuing an application.

(b) General rules concerning requests for information.

(1) Except as provided in paragraphs (c) and (d) of this section, a creditor may request any information in connection with an application. [1]

(2) Required collection of information. Notwithstanding paragraphs (c) and (d) of this section, a creditor shall request information for monitoring purposes as required by Sec. 202.13 for credit secured by the applicant's dwelling. In addition, a creditor may obtain information required by a regulation, order, or agreement issued by, or entered into with, a court or an enforcement agency (including the Attorney General of the United States or a similar state official) to monitor or enforce compliance with the act, this regulation, or other federal or state statute or regulation.

(3) Special purpose credit. A creditor may obtain information that is otherwise restricted to determine eligibility for a special purpose credit program, as provided in Sec. 202.8 (c) and (d).

(c) Information about a spouse or former spouse.

(1) Except as permitted in this paragraph, a creditor may not request any information concerning the spouse or former spouse of an applicant.

(2) Permissible inquiries. A creditor may request any information concerning an applicant's spouse (or former spouse under paragraph (c)(2)(v) of this section that may be requested about the applicant if:

(i) The spouse will be permitted to use the account;

(ii) The spouse will be contractually liable on the account;

(iii) The applicant is relying on the spouse's income as a basis for repayment of the credit requested;

(iv) The applicant resides in a community property state or property on which the applicant is relying as a basis for repayment of the credit requested is located in such a state; or

(v) The applicant is relying on alimony, child support, or separate maintenance payments from a spouse or former spouse as a basis for repayment of the credit requested.

(3) Other accounts of the applicant. A creditor may request an applicant to list any account upon which the applicant is liable and to provide the name and address in which the account is carried. A creditor may also ask the names in which an applicant has previously received credit.

(d) Other limitations on information requests—

(1) Marital status. If an applicant applies for individual unsecured credit, a creditor shall not inquire about the applicant's marital status unless the applicant resides in a community property state or is relying on property located in such a state as a basis for repayment of the credit requested. If an application is for other than individual unsecured credit, a creditor may inquire about the applicant's marital status, but shall use only the terms married, unmarried, and separated. A creditor may explain that the category unmarried includes single, divorced, and widowed persons.

(2) Disclosure about income from alimony, child support, or separate maintenance. A creditor shall not inquire whether income stated in an application is derived from alimony, child support, or separate maintenance payments unless the creditor discloses to the applicant that such income need not be revealed if the applicant does not want the creditor to consider it in determining the applicant's creditworthiness.

(3) Sex. A creditor shall not inquire about the sex of an applicant. An applicant may be requested to designate a title on an application form (such as Ms., Miss, Mr., or Mrs.) if the form discloses that the designation of a title is optional. An application form shall otherwise use only terms that are neutral as to sex.

(4) Childbearing, childrearing. A creditor shall not inquire about birth control practices, intentions concerning the bearing or rearing of children, or capability to bear children. A creditor may inquire about the number and ages of an applicant's dependents or about dependent-related financial obligations or expenditures, provided such information is requested without regard to sex, marital status, or any other prohibited basis.

(5) Race, color, religion, national origin. A creditor shall not inquire about the race, color, religion, or national origin of an applicant or any other person in connection with a credit transaction. A creditor may inquire about an applicant's permanent residence and immigration status.

(e) Written applications. A creditor shall take written applications for the types of credit covered by Sec. 202.13(a), but need not take written applications for other types of credit.

## Sec. 202.5a Rules on providing appraisal reports.

(a) Providing appraisals. A creditor shall provide a copy of the appraisal report used in connection with an application for credit that is to be secured by a lien on a dwelling. A creditor shall comply with either paragraph (a)(1) or (a)(2) of this section.

(1) Routine delivery. A creditor may routinely provide a copy of the appraisal report to an applicant (whether credit is granted or denied or the application is withdrawn).

(2) Upon request. A creditor that does not routinely provide appraisal reports shall provide a copy upon an applicant's written request.

(i) Notice. A creditor that provides appraisal reports only upon request shall notify an applicant in writing of the right to receive a copy of an appraisal report. The notice may be given at any time during the application process but no later than when the creditor provides notice of action taken under Sec. 202.9 of this part. The notice shall specify that the applicant's request must be in writing, give the creditor's mailing address, and state the time for making the request as provided in paragraph (a)(2)(ii) of this section.

(ii) Delivery. A creditor shall mail or deliver a copy of the appraisal report promptly (generally within 30 days) after the creditor receives an applicant's request, receives the report, or receives reimbursement from the applicant for the report, whichever is last to occur. A creditor need not provide a copy when the applicant's request is received more than 90 days after the creditor has provided notice of action taken on the application under Sec. 202.9 of this part or 90 days after the application is withdrawn.

(b) Credit unions. A creditor that is subject to the regulations of the National Credit Union Administration on making copies of appraisals available is not subject to this section.

(c) Definitions. For purposes of paragraph (a) of this section, the term dwelling means a residential structure that contains one to four units whether or not that structure is attached to real property. The term includes, but is not limited to, an individual condominium or cooperative unit, and a mobile or other manufactured home. The term appraisal report means the document(s) relied upon by a creditor in evaluating the value of the dwelling.

## Sec. 202.6 Rules concerning evaluation of applications.

(a) General rule concerning use of information. Except as otherwise provided in the Act and this regulation, a creditor may consider any information obtained, so long as the information is not used to discriminate against an applicant on a prohibited basis. [2]

(b) Specific rules concerning use of information.

(1) Except as provided in the act and this regulation, a creditor shall not take a prohibited basis into account in any system of evaluating the creditworthiness of applicants.

(2) Age, receipt of public assistance.

(i) Except as permitted in this paragraph (b)(2), a creditor shall not take into account an applicant's age (provided that the applicant has the capacity to enter into a binding contract) or whether an applicant's income derives from any public assistance program.

(ii) In an empirically derived, demonstrably and statistically sound, credit scoring system, a creditor may use an applicant's age as a predictive variable, provided that the age of an elderly applicant is not assigned a negative factor or value.

(iii) In a judgmental system of evaluating creditworthiness, a creditor may consider an applicant's age or whether an applicant's income derives from any public assistance program only for the purpose of determining a pertinent element of creditworthiness.

(iv) In any system of evaluating creditworthiness, a creditor may consider the age of an elderly applicant when such age is used to favor the elderly applicant in extending credit.

(3) Childbearing, childrearing. In evaluating creditworthiness, a creditor shall not use assumptions or aggregate statistics relating to the likelihood that any group of persons will

bear or rear children or will, for that reason, receive diminished or interrupted income in the future.

(4) Telephone listing. A creditor shall not take into account whether there is a telephone listing in the name of an applicant for consumer credit, but may take into account whether there is a telephone in the applicant's residence.

(5) Income. A creditor shall not discount or exclude from consideration the income of an applicant or the spouse of an applicant because of a prohibited basis or because the income is derived from part-time employment or is an annuity, pension, or other retirement benefit; a creditor may consider the amount and probable continuance of any income in evaluating an applicant's creditworthiness. When an applicant relies on alimony, child support, or separate maintenance payments in applying for credit, the creditor shall consider such payments as income to the extent that they are likely to be consistently made.

(6) Credit history. To the extent that a creditor considers credit history in evaluating the creditworthiness of similarly qualified applicants for a similar type and amount of credit, in evaluating an applicant's creditworthiness a creditor shall consider:

(i) The credit history, when available, of accounts designated as accounts that the applicant and the applicant's spouse are permitted to use or for which both are contractually liable;

(ii) On the applicant's request, any information the applicant may present that tends to indicate that the credit history being considered by the creditor does not accurately reflect the applicant's creditworthiness; and

(iii) On the applicant's request, the credit history, when available, of any account reported in the name of the applicant's spouse or former spouse that the applicant can demonstrate accurately reflects the applicant's creditworthiness.

(7) Immigration status. A creditor may consider whether an applicant is a permanent resident of the United States, the applicant's immigration status, and any additional information that may be necessary to ascertain the creditor's rights and remedies regarding repayment.

(c) State property laws. A creditor's consideration or application of state property laws directly or indirectly affecting creditworthiness does not constitute unlawful discrimination for the purposes of the Act or this regulation.

## Sec. 202.7 Rules concerning extensions of credit.

(a) Individual accounts. A creditor shall not refuse to grant an individual account to a creditworthy applicant on the basis of sex, marital status, or any other prohibited basis.

(b) Designation of name. A creditor shall not refuse to allow an applicant to open or maintain an account in a birth-given first name and a surname that is the applicant's birth-given surname, the spouse's surname, or a combined surname.

(c) Action concerning existing open-end accounts—

(1) Limitations. In the absence of evidence of the applicant's inability or unwillingness to repay, a creditor shall not take any of the following actions regarding an applicant who is contractually liable on an existing open-end account on the basis of the applicant's reaching a certain age or retiring or on the basis of a change in the applicant's name or marital status:

(i) Require a reapplication, except as provided in paragraph (c)(2) of this section;

(ii) Change the terms of the account; or

(iii) Terminate the account.

(2) Requiring reapplication. A creditor may require a reapplication for an open-end account on the basis of a change in the marital status of an applicant who is contractually liable if the credit granted was based in whole or in part on income of the applicant's spouse and if information available to the creditor indicates that the applicant's income may not support the amount of credit currently available.

(d) Signature of spouse or other person—

(1) Rule for qualified applicant. Except as provided in this paragraph, a creditor shall not require the signature of an applicant's spouse or other person, other than a joint applicant, on any credit instrument if the applicant qualifies under the creditor's standards of creditworthiness for the amount and terms of the credit requested.

(2) Unsecured credit. If an applicant requests unsecured credit and relies in part upon property that the applicant owns jointly with another person to satisfy the creditor's standards of creditworthiness, the creditor may require the signature of the other person only on the instrument(s) necessary, or reasonably believed by the creditor to be necessary, under the law of the state in which the property is located, to enable the creditor to reach the property being relied upon in the event of the death or default of the applicant.

(3) Unsecured credit—community property states. If a married applicant requests unsecured credit and resides in a community property state, or if the property upon which the applicant is relying is located in such a state, a creditor may require the signature of the spouse on any instrument necessary, or reasonably believed by the creditor to be necessary, under applicable state law to make the community property available to satisfy the debt in the event of default if:

(i) Applicable state law denies the applicant power to manage or control sufficient community property to qualify for the amount of credit requested under the creditor's standards of creditworthiness; and

(ii) The applicant does not have sufficient separate property to qualify for the amount of credit requested without regard to community property.

(4) Secured credit. If an applicant requests secured credit, a creditor may require the signature of the applicant's spouse or other person on any instrument necessary, or reasonably believed by the creditor to be necessary, under applicable state law to make the property being offered as security available to satisfy the debt in the event of default, for example, an instrument to create a valid lien, pass clear title, waive inchoate rights or assign earnings.

(5) Additional parties. If, under a creditor's standards of creditworthiness, the personal liability of an additional party is necessary to support the extension of the credit requested, a creditor may request a cosigner, guarantor, or the like. The applicant's spouse may serve as an additional party, but the creditor shall not require that the spouse be the additional party.

(6) Rights of additional parties. A creditor shall not impose requirements upon an additional party that the creditor is prohibited from imposing upon an applicant under this section.

(e) Insurance. A creditor shall not refuse to extend credit and shall not terminate an account because credit life, health, accident, disability, or other credit-related insurance is not available on the basis of the applicant's age.

## Sec. 202.8 Special purpose credit programs.

(a) Standards for programs. Subject to the provisions of paragraph (b) of this section, the act and this regulation permit a creditor to extend special purpose credit to applicants who meet eligibility requirements under the following types of credit programs:

(1) Any credit assistance program expressly authorized by federal or state law for the benefit of an economically disadvantaged class of persons;

(2) Any credit assistance program offered by a not-for-profit organization, as defined under section 501(c) of the Internal Revenue Code of 1954, as amended, for the benefit of its members or for the benefit of an economically disadvantaged class of persons; or

(3) Any special purpose credit program offered by a for-profit organization or in which such an organization participates to meet special social needs, if:

(i) The program is established and administered pursuant to a written plan that identifies the class of persons that the program is designed to benefit and sets forth the procedures and standards for extending credit pursuant to the program; and

(ii) The program is established and administered to extend credit to a class of persons who, under the organization's customary standards of creditworthiness, probably would not receive such credit or would receive it on less favorable terms than are ordinarily available to other applicants applying to the organization for a similar type and amount of credit.

(b) Rules in other sections.

(1) General applicability. All of the provisions of this regulation apply to each of the special purpose credit programs described in paragraph (a) of this section unless modified by this section.

(2) Common characteristics. A program described in paragraph (a)(2) or (a)(3) of this section qualifies as a special purpose credit program only if it was established and is administered so as not to discriminate against an applicant on any prohibited basis; however, all program participants may be required to share one or more common characteristics (for example, race, national origin, or sex) so long as the program was not established and is not administered with the purpose of evading the requirements of the act or this regulation.

(c) Special rule concerning requests and use of information. If participants in a special purpose credit program described in paragraph (a) of this section are required to possess one or more common characteristics (for example, race, national origin, or sex) and if the program otherwise satisfies the requirements of paragraph (a) of this section, a creditor may request and consider information regarding the common characteristic(s) in determining the applicant's eligibility for the program.

(d) Special rule in the case of financial need. If financial need is one of the criteria under a special purpose program described in paragraph (a) of this section, the creditor may request and consider, in determining an applicant's eligibility for the program, information regarding the applicant's martial status; alimony, child support, and separate maintenance income; and the spouse's financial resources. In addition, a creditor may obtain the signature of an applicant's spouse or other person on an application or credit instrument relating to a special purpose program if the signature is required by Federal or State law.

### Sec. 202.9 Notifications.

(a) Notification of action taken, ECOA notice, and statement of specific reasons—

(1) When notification is required. A creditor shall notify an applicant of action taken within:

(i) 30 days after receiving a completed application concerning the creditor's approval of, counteroffer to, or adverse action on the application;

(ii) 30 days after taking adverse action on an incomplete application, unless notice is provided in accordance with paragraph (c) of this section;

(iii) 30 days after taking adverse action on an existing account; or

(iv) 90 days after notifying the applicant of a counteroffer if the applicant does not expressly accept or use the credit offered.

(2) Content of notification when adverse action is taken. A notification given to an applicant when adverse action is taken shall be in writing and shall contain: a statement of the action taken; the name and address of the creditor; a statement of the provisions of section 701(a) of the Act; the name and address of the Federal agency that administers compliance with respect to the creditor; and either:

(i) A statement of specific reasons for the action taken; or

(ii) A disclosure of the applicant's right to a statement of specific reasons within 30 days, if the statement is requested within 60 days of the creditor's notification. The disclosure shall include the name, address, and telephone number of the person or office from which the statement of reasons can be obtained. If the creditor chooses to provide the reasons orally, the creditor shall also disclose the applicant's right to have them confirmed in writing within 30 days of receiving a written request for confirmation from the applicant.

(3) Notification to business credit applicants. For business credit, a creditor shall comply with the requirements of this paragraph in the following manner:

(i) With regard to a business that had gross revenues of $1,000,000 or less in its preceding fiscal year (other than an extension of trade credit, credit incident to a factoring agreement, or other similar types of business credit), a creditor shall comply with paragraphs (a) (1) and (2) of this section, except that:

(A) The statement of the action taken may be given orally or in writing, when adverse action is taken;

(B) Disclosure of an applicant's right to a statement of reasons may be given at the time of application, instead of when adverse action is taken, provided the disclosure is in a form the applicant may retain and contains the information required by paragraph (a)(2)(ii) of this section and the ECOA notice specified in paragraph (b)(1) of this section;

(C) For an application made solely by telephone, a creditor satisfies the requirements of this paragraph by an oral statement of the action taken and of the applicant's right to a statement of reasons for adverse action.

(ii) With regard to a business that had gross revenues in excess of $1,000,000 in its preceding fiscal year or an extension of trade credit, credit incident to a factoring agreement, or other similar types of business credit, a creditor shall:

(A) Notify the applicant, orally or in writing, within a reasonable time of the action taken; and

(B) Provide a written statement of the reasons for adverse action and the ECOA notice specified in paragraph (b)(1) of this section if the applicant makes a written request for the reasons within 60 days of being notified of the adverse action.

(b) Form of ECOA notice and statement of specific reasons—

(1) ECOA notice. To satisfy the disclosure requirements of paragraph (a)(2) of this section regarding section 701(a) of the Act, the creditor shall provide a notice that is substantially similar to the following: The Federal Equal Credit Opportunity Act prohibits creditors from discriminating against credit applicants on the basis of race, color, religion, national origin, sex, marital status, age (provided the applicant has the capacity to enter into a binding contract); because all or part of the applicant's income derives from any public assistance program; or because the applicant has in good faith exercised any right under the Consumer Credit Protection Act. The Federal agency that administers compliance with this law concerning this creditor is (name and address as specified by the appropriate agency listed in appendix A of this regulation).

(2) Statement of specific reasons. The statement of reasons for adverse action required by paragraph (a)(2)(i) of this section must be specific and indicate the principal reason(s) for the adverse action. Statements that the adverse action was based on the creditor's internal standards or policies or that the applicant failed to achieve the qualifying score on the creditor's credit scoring system are insufficient.

(c) Incomplete applications—

(1) Notice alternatives. Within 30 days after receiving application that is incomplete regarding matters that an applicant can complete, the creditor shall notify the applicant either:

(i) Of action taken, in accordance with paragraph (a) of this section; or

(ii) Of the incompleteness, in accordance with paragraph (c)(2) of this section.

(2) Notice of incompleteness. If additional information is needed from an applicant, the creditor shall send a written notice to the applicant specifying the information needed, designating a reasonable period of time for the applicant to provide the information, and informing the applicant that failure to provide the information requested will result in no further consideration being given to the application. The creditor shall have no further obligation under this section if the applicant fails to respond within the designated time period. If the applicant supplies the requested information within the designated time period, the creditor shall take action on the application and notify the applicant in accordance with paragraph (a) of this section.

(3) Oral request for information. At its option, a creditor may inform the applicant orally of the need for additional information; but if the application remains incomplete the creditor shall send a notice in accordance with paragraph (c)(1) of this section.

(d) Oral notifications by small-volume creditors. The requirements of this section (including statements of specific reasons) are satisfied by oral notifications in the case of any creditor that did not receive more than 150 applications during the preceding calendar year.

(e) Withdrawal of approved application. When an applicant submits an application and the parties contemplate that the applicant will inquire about its status, if the creditor approves the application and the applicant has not inquired within 30 days after applying, the creditor may treat the application as withdrawn and need not comply with paragraph (a)(1) of this section.

(f) Multiple applicants. When an application involves more than one applicant, notification need only be given to one of them, but must be given to the primary applicant where one is readily apparent.

(g) Applications submitted through a third party. When an application is made on behalf of an applicant to more than one creditor and the applicant expressly accepts or uses credit offered by one of the creditors, notification of action taken by any of the other creditors is not required. If no credit is offered or if the applicant does not expressly accept or use any credit offered, each creditor taking adverse action must comply with this section, directly or through a third party. A notice given by a third party shall disclose the identify of each creditor on whose behalf the notice is given.

## Sec. 202.10 Furnishing of credit information.

(a) Designation of accounts. A creditor that furnishes credit information shall designate:

(1) Any new account to reflect the participation of both spouses if the applicant's spouse is permitted to use or is contractually liable on the account (other than as a guarantor, surety, endorser, or similar party); and

(2) Any existing account to reflect such participation, within 90 days after receiving a written request to do so from one of the spouses.

(b) Routine reports to consumer reporting agency. If a creditor furnishes credit information to a consumer reporting agency concerning an account designated to reflect the participation of both spouses, the creditor shall furnish the information in a manner that will enable the agency to provide access to the information in the name of each spouse.

(c) Reporting in response to inquiry. If a creditor furnishes credit information in response to an inquiry concerning an account designated to reflect the participation of both spouses, the creditor shall furnish the information in the name of the spouse about whom the information is requested.

## Sec. 202.11 Relation to state law.

(a) Inconsistent state laws. Except as otherwise provided in this section, this regulation alters, affects, or preempts only those state laws that are inconsistent with the act and this regulation and then only to the extent of the inconsistency. A state law is not inconsistent if it is more protective of an applicant.

(b) Preempted provisions of state law.

(1) A state law is deemed to be inconsistent with the requirements of the Act and this regulation and less protective of an applicant within the meaning of section 705(f) of the Act to the extent that the law:

(i) Requires or permits a practice or act prohibited by the Act or this regulation;

(ii) Prohibits the individual extension of consumer credit to both parties to a marriage if each spouse individually and voluntarily applies for such credit;

(iii) Prohibits inquiries or collection of data required to comply with the act or this regulation;

(iv) Prohibits asking or considering age in an empirically derived, demonstrably and statistically sound, credit scoring system to determine a pertinent element of creditworthiness, or to favor an elderly applicant; or

(v) Prohibits inquiries necessary to establish or administer as special purpose credit program as defined by Sec. 202.8.

(2) A creditor, state, or other interested party may request the Board to determine whether a state law is inconsistent with the requirements of the Act and this regulation.

(c) Laws on finance charges, loan ceilings. If married applicants voluntarily apply for and obtained individual accounts with the same creditor, the accounts shall not be aggregated or otherwise combined for purposes of determining permissible finance charges or loan ceilings under any federal or state law. Permissible loan ceiling laws shall be construed to permit each spouse to become individually liable up to the amount of the loan ceilings, less the amount for which the applicant is jointly liable.

(d) State and Federal laws not affected. This section does not alter or annul any provision of state property laws, laws relating to the disposition of decedents' estates, or Federal or state banking regulations directed only toward insuring the solvency of financial institutions.

(e) Exemption for state-regulated transactions—

(1) Applications. A state may apply to the Board for an exemption from the requirements of the Act and this regulation for any class of credit transactions within the state. The Board will grant such an exemption if the Board determines that:

(i) The class of credit transactions is subject to state law requirements substantially similar to the Act and this regulation or that applicants are afforded greater protection under state law; and

(ii) There is adequate provision for state enforcement.

(2) Liability and enforcement. (i) No exemption will extend to the civil liability provisions of section 706 or the administrative enforcement provisions of section 704 of the Act.

(ii) After an exemption has been granted, the requirements of the applicable state law (except for additional requirements not imposed by Federal law) will constitute the requirements of the Act and this regulation.

## Sec. 202.12 Record retention.

(a) Retention of prohibited information. A creditor may retain in its files information that is prohibited by the Act or this regulation in evaluating applications, without violating the Act or this regulation, if the information was obtained:

(1) From any source prior to March 23, 1977;

(2) From consumer reporting agencies, an applicant, or others without the specific request of the creditor; or

(3) As required to monitor compliance with the Act and this regulation or other Federal or state statutes or regulations.

(b) Preservation of records—

(1) Applications. For 25 months (12 months for business credit) after the date that a creditor notifies an applicant of action taken on an application or of incompleteness, the creditor shall retain in original form or a copy thereof:

(i) Any application that it receives, any information required to be obtained concerning characteristics of the applicant to monitor compliance with the Act and this regulation or other similar law, and any other written or recorded information used in evaluating the application and not returned to the applicant at the applicant's request;

(ii) A copy of the following documents if furnished to the applicant in written form (or, if furnished orally, any notation or memorandum made by the creditor):

(A) The notification of action taken; and

(B) The statement of specific reasons for adverse action; and

(iii) Any written statement submitted by the applicant alleging a violation of the Act or this regulation.

(2) Existing accounts. For 25 months (12 months for business credit) after the date that a creditor notifies an applicant of adverse action regarding an existing account, the creditor shall retain as to that account, in original form or a copy thereof:

(i) Any written or recorded information concerning the adverse action; and

(ii) Any written statement submitted by the applicant alleging a violation of the act or this regulation.

(3) Other applications. For 25 months (12 months for business credit) after the date that a creditor receives an application for which the creditor is not required to comply with the notification requirements of Sec. 202.9, the creditor shall retain all written or recorded information in its possession concerning the applicant, including any notation of action taken.

(4) Enforcement proceedings and investigations. A creditor shall retain the information specified in this section beyond 25 months (12 months for business credit) if it has actual notice that it is under investigation or is subject to an enforcement proceeding for an alleged violation of the act or this regulation by the Attorney General of the United States or by an enforcement agency charged with monitoring that creditor's compliance with the act and this regulation, or if it has been served with notice of an action filed pursuant to section 706 of the Act and Sec. 202.14 of this regulation. The creditor shall retain the information until final disposition of the matter, unless an earlier time is allowed by order of the agency or court.

(5) Special rule for certain business credit applications. With regard to a business with gross revenues in excess of $1,000,000 in its preceding fiscal year, or an extension of trade credit, credit incident to a factoring agreement or other similar types of business credit, the creditor shall retain records for at least 60 days after notifying the applicant of the action taken. If within that time period the applicant requests in writing the reasons for adverse action or that records be retained, the creditor shall retain records for 12 months.

(6)Self-tests. For 25 months after a self-test (as defined in § 202.15) has been completed, the creditor shall retain all written or recorded information about the self-test. A creditor shall retain information beyond 25 months if it has actual notice that it is under investigation or is subject to an enforcement proceeding for an alleged violation, or if it has been served with notice of a civil action. In such cases, the creditor shall retain the information until final disposition of the matter, unless an earlier time is allowed by the appropriate agency or court order.

## Sec. 202.13 Information for monitoring purposes.

(a) Information to be requested. A creditor that receives an application for credit primarily for the purchase or refinancing of a dwelling occupied or to be occupied by the applicant as a principal residence, where the extension of credit will be secured by the dwelling, shall request as part of the application the following information regarding the applicant(s):

(1) Race or national origin, using the categories American Indian or Alaskan Native; Asian or Pacific Islander; Black; White; Hispanic; Other (Specify);

(2) Sex;

(3) Marital status, using the categories married, unmarried, and separated; and

(4) Age.

Dwelling means a residential structure that contains one to four units, whether or not that structure is attached to real property. The term includes, but is not limited to, an individual condominium or cooperative unit, and a mobile or other manufactured home.

(b) Obtaining of information. Questions regarding race or national origin, sex, marital status, and age may be listed, at the creditor's option, on the application form or on a separate form that refers to the application. The applicant(s) shall be asked but not required to supply the requested information. If the applicant(s) chooses not to provide the information or any part of it, that fact shall be noted on the form. The creditor shall then also note on the form, to the extent possible, the race or national origin and sex of the applicant(s) on the basis of visual observation or surname.

(c) Disclosure to applicant(s). The creditor shall inform the applicant(s) that the information regarding race or national origin, sex, marital status, and age is being requested by the Federal government for the purpose of monitoring compliance with Federal statutes that prohibit creditors from discriminating against applicants on those bases. The creditor shall also inform the applicant(s) that if the applicant(s) chooses note to provide the information, the creditor is required to note the race or national origin and sex on the basis of visual observation or surname.

(d) Substitute monitoring program. A monitoring program required by an agency charged with administrative enforcement under section 704 of the Act may be substituted for the requirements contained in paragraphs (a), (b), and (c).

### Sec. 202.14 Enforcement, penalties and liabilities.

(a) Administrative enforcement.

(1) As set forth more fully in section 704 of the Act, administrative enforcement of the Act and this regulation regarding certain creditors is assigned to the Comptroller of the Currency, Board of Governors of the Federal Reserve System, Board of Directors of the Federal Deposit Insurance Corporation, Office of Thrift Supervision, National Credit Union Administration, Interstate Commerce Commission, Secretary of Agriculture, Farm Credit Administration, Securities and Exchange Commission, Small Business Administration, and Secretary of Transportation.

(2) Except to the extent that administrative enforcement is specifically assigned to other authorities, compliance with the requirements imposed under the act and this regulation is enforced by the Federal Trade Commission.

(b) Penalties and liabilities.

(1) Sections 706 (a) and (b) and 702(g) of the Act provide that any creditor that fails to comply with a requirement imposed by the Act or this regulation is subject to civil liability for actual and punitive damages in individual or class actions. Pursuant to sections 704 (b), (c), and (d) and

702(g) of the Act, violations of the Act or regulations also constitute violations of other Federal laws. Liability for punitive damages is restricted to nongovernmental entities and is limited to $10,000 in individual actions and the lesser of $500,000 or 1 percent of the creditor's net worth in class actions. Section 706(c) provides for equitable and declaratory relief and section 706(d) authorizes the awarding of costs and reasonable attorney's fees to an aggrieved applicant in a successful action.

(2) As provided in section 706(f), a civil action under the Act or this regulation may be brought in the appropriate United States district court without regard to the amount in controversy or in any other court of competent jurisdiction within two years after the date of the occurrence of the violation, or within one year after the commencement of an administrative enforcement proceeding or of a civil action brought by the Attorney General of the United States within two years after the alleged violation.

(3) If an agency responsible for administrative enforcement is unable to obtain compliance with the act or this part, it may refer the matter to the Attorney General of the United States. In addition, if the Board, the Comptroller of the Currency, the Federal Deposit Insurance Corporation, the Office of Thrift Supervision, or the National Credit Union Administration has reason to believe that one or more creditors engaged in a pattern or practice of discouraging or denying applications in violation of the act or this part, the agency shall refer the matter to the Attorney General. Furthermore, the agency may refer a matter to the Attorney General if the agency has reason to believe that one or more creditors violated section 701(a) of the act.

(4) On referral, or whenever the Attorney General has reason to believe that one or more creditors engaged in a pattern or practice in violation of the act or this regulation, the Attorney General may bring a civil action for such relief as may be appropriate, including actual and punitive damages and injunctive relief.

(5) If the Board, the Comptroller of the Currency, the Federal Deposit Insurance Corporation, the Office of Thrift Supervision, or the National Credit Union Administration has reason to believe (as a result of a consumer complaint, conducting a consumer compliance examination, or otherwise) that a violation of the act or this part has occurred which is also a violation of the Fair Housing Act, and the matter is not referred to the Attorney General, the agency shall notify:

(i) The Secretary of Housing and Urban Development; and

(ii) The applicant that the Secretary of Housing and Urban Development has been notified and that remedies for the violation may be available under the Fair Housing Act.

(c) Failure of compliance. A creditor's failure to comply with Secs. 202.6(b)(6), 202.9, 202.10, 202.12 or 202.13 is not a violation if it results from an inadvertent error. On discovering an error under Secs. 202.9 and 202.10, the creditor shall correct it as soon as possible. If a creditor inadvertently obtains the monitoring information regarding the race or national origin and sex of the applicant in a dwelling-related transaction not covered by Sec. 202.13, the creditor may act on and retain the application without violating the regulation.

### Sec. 202.15 - Incentives for self-testing and self-correction.

(a) General rules-

(1) Voluntary self-testing and correction. The report or results of the self-test that a creditor voluntarily conducts (or authorizes) are privileged as provided in this section. Data collection required by law or by any governmental authority is not a voluntary self-test.

(2) Corrective action required. The privilege in this section applies only if the creditor has taken or is taking appropriate corrective action.

(3) Other privileges. The privilege created by this section does not preclude the assertion of any other privilege that may also apply.

(b) Self-test defined-

(1) Definition. A self-test is any program, practice, or study that:

(i) Is designed and used specifically to determine the extent or effectiveness of a creditor's compliance with the act or this regulation; and

(ii) Creates data or factual information that is not available and cannot be derived from loan or application files or other records related to credit transactions.

(2) Types of information privileged. The privilege under this section applies to the report or results of the self-test, data or factual information created by the self-test, and any analysis, opinions, and conclusions pertaining to the self-test report or results. The privilege covers workpapers or draft documents as well as final documents.

(3) Types of information not privileged. The privilege under this section does not apply to:

(i) Information about whether a creditor conducted a self-test, the methodology used or the scope of the self-test, the time period covered by the self-test, or the dates it was conducted; or

(ii) Loan and application files or other business records related to credit transactions, and information derived from such files and records, even if it has been aggregated, summarized, or reorganized to facilitate analysis.

(c) Appropriate corrective action-

(1) General requirement. For the privilege in this section to apply, appropriate corrective action is required when the self-test shows that it is more likely than not that a violation occurred, even though no violation has been formally adjudicated.

(2) Determining the scope of appropriate corrective action. A creditor must take corrective action that is reasonably likely to remedy the cause and effect of a likely violation by:

(i) Identifying the policies or practices that are the likely cause of the violation; and

(ii) Assessing the extent and scope of any violation.

(3) Types of relief. Appropriate corrective action may include both prospective and remedial relief, except that to establish a privilege under this section:

(i) A creditor is not required to provide remedial relief to a tester used in a self-test;

(ii) A creditor is only required to provide remedial relief to an applicant identified by the self-test as one whose rights were more likely than not violated; and

(iii) A creditor is not required to provide remedial relief to a particular applicant if the statute of limitations applicable to the violation expired before the creditor obtained the results of the self-test or the applicant is otherwise ineligible for such relief.

4) No admission of violation. Taking corrective action is not an admission that a violation occurred.

(d) Scope of privilege.

(1) The report or results of a privileged self-test may not be obtained or used:

(i) By a government agency in any examination or investigation relating to compliance with the act or this regulation; or

(ii) By a government agency or an applicant (including a prospective applicant who alleges a violation of § 202.5(a)) in any proceeding or civil action in which a violation of the act or this regulation is alleged.

(2) Loss of privilege. The report or results of a self-test are not privileged under paragraph (d)(1) of this section if the creditor or a person with lawful access to the report or results):

(i) Voluntarily discloses any part of the report or results, or any other information privileged under this section, to an applicant or government agency or to the public;

(ii) Discloses any part of the report or results, or any other information privileged under this section, as a defense to charges that the creditor has violated the act or regulation; or

(iii) Fails or is unable to produce written or recorded information about the self-test that is required to be retained under § 202.12(b)(6) when the information is needed to determine whether the privilege applies. This paragraph does not limit any other penalty or remedy that may be available for a violation of § 202.12.

(3) Limited use of privileged information. Notwithstanding paragraph (d)(1) of this section, the self-test report or results and any other information privileged under this section may be obtained and used by an applicant or government agency solely to determine a penalty or remedy after a violation of the act or this regulation has been adjudicated or admitted. Disclosures for this limited purpose may be used only for the particular proceeding in which the adjudication or admission was made. Information disclosed under this paragraph (d)(3) remains privileged under paragraph (d)(1) of this section.

**(Footnotes)**

For purposes of this Agreement, "Affiliate" shall mean any person or entity that shall directly or indirectly controls, is controlled by, or is under common control with the Company

# Chapter 33

# Conclusion

Keep this book on your desk to refer back to as you create or update your credit policy. If you have any questions please visit *www.credit-and-collections.com* or email me at michelle@michelledunn.com. Your questions will help me when I update this book.

*5 MUST HAVES for creditors:*
1. Signed credit application
2. Familiarity with Federal & State credit laws
3. Enforced credit procedures DO NOT WAIVER!
4. Effective collection letters & forms
5. A reliable collection agency

**BONUS ITEM: People skills and PATIENCE!**

*Credit sites worth checking out:*
Credit & Collections
*www.credit-and-collections.com*
Collection Industry.com
*www.collectionindustry.com*
Collections World
*www.collectionsworld.com*
The National Association of Credit Management
*www.nacm.com*
Credit Risk Monitor
*www.creditriskmonitor.com*
Business Credit USA.com
*www.businesscreditusa.com*
The Credit Research Foundation
*www.crfonline.org*
Creditworthy
*www.creditworthy.com*

# How to Get Your Customers to Pay

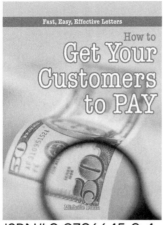

ISBN# 0-9706645-2-4

## From the Author

Why not have more money? Wouldn't you rather spend your time doing what you enjoy?

Writing a clear concise letter that generates a result is an art. When you buy *How to Get Your Customers to Pay, Fast, Easy, Effective Letters,* you will learn how to create and use letters to collect more money with less effort.

Your letter should: Tell the reason for your letter in the first sentence; Explain more about the first sentence in your second sentence; Suggest a solution; and, thank the recipient.

You can use the letters and forms in this book to collect the money that is owed to you. If you use these ready to use letters and forms in this book as part of your credit policy you will:

- Have more money
- Have and keep good customers that pay with minimum effort on your part
- Be successful

A few Tips Michelle shares with you in her book are:

1.  Send a reminder immediately when account is past due
2.  Tell your reason for the letter in the first sentence
3.  Include the balance due amount
4.   Make collection letters short and to the point
5.  Offer a solution
6.  Enclose an envelope for payment
7.  Be firm
8.  Assume the debtor will pay
9.  Be friendly
10.   Make each letter stronger

Order your copy today, read the rest of the tips and collect more money today!

## From the Author

I created this e-book because so many clients and other entrepreneurs who own their own businesses ask me for examples of collection letters. I thought it would be beneficial for everyone if I compiled several examples into an easy-to-use reference. This will allow everyone, including YOU, to possess different collection letters to utilize for different situations as they arise.

The letters can be changed to suit your business or situation, and/or they can be used as is.

This book includes the following types of letters and forms:
- Before Court Action
- Check Returned
- Credit Reporting
- Deductions
- envelope Enclosed
- Legal Action
- NSF checks
- Partial Payments
- Payment Obligations
- Payment Reminder
- Placing for collection
- Request for Payment Letter
- Return Call Letter
- Small Amounts
- The 3-Letter Series
- We Value Fairness

*Bonus Items:*
Credit Application
Request a Letter

# Book Order Form

**Online orders**: www.michelledunn.com
Securely accepting Visa, MasterCard, Discover, Paypal, checks, Debit &
   Credit cards

**Email orders**: michelle@michelledunn.com

**Postal orders**:  Mail to: Never Dunn Publishing LLC, Michelle Dunn, PO
   Box 40, Plymouth, NH 03264 USA.

**Please send the following books**:
❏   *How to Make Money Collecting Money, Starting a Collection Agency*
    ISBN#: 0-9706645-0-8
    $33.99, E-Book $29.99
❏   *Become the Squeaky Wheel, A Credit and Collections Guide for Everyone*
    ISBN#: 0-9706645-1-6
    $33.99, E-Book $29.99
❏   *Credit & Collections Forms & Letters, How to Help You Get Paid*
    $12.95; E-Book Version $9.95
❏   *The First Book of Effective Collection Agency Letters & Forms*  ISBN#:
    0970664540
    (E-Book only) $19.95
❏   ISBN#: 0970664524
    *Fast, Easy, Effective Letters, How to Get Your Customers to Pay*
    $33.99, E-Book Version $29.99

**Shipping:  INCLUDED** in all prices above (to U.S. Addresses)

**Payment**: ❏ Check
        (enclose with form, payable to "Michelle Dunn Writer, LLC")

        ❏ Credit or Debit         ❏ Visa     ❏ MasterCard     ❏
   Discover

Card#:

_____

Name on Card: _____Exp. Date: ____/____

Shipping Address:

_____

_____

For more information on any of Michelle Dunn's other books
please visit www.michelledunn.com
or email at michelle@michelledunn.com
**Thank you for your order!**

**Online orders**: www.michelledunn.com
Securely accepting Visa, MasterCard, Discover, Paypal, checks, Debit & Credit cards

**Email orders**: michelle@michelledunn.com

**Postal orders**:  Mail to: Never Dunn Publishing LLC, Michelle Dunn, PO Box 40, Plymouth, NH 03264 USA.

**Please send the following books**:

❒ *How to Make Money Collecting Money, Starting a Collection Agency*
ISBN#: 0-9706645-0-8
$33.99, E-Book $29.99

❒ *Become the Squeaky Wheel, A Credit and Collections Guide for Everyone*
ISBN#: 0-9706645-1-6
$33.99, E-Book $29.99

❒ *Credit & Collections Forms & Letters, How to Help You Get Paid*
$12.95; E-Book Version $9.95

❒ *The First Book of Effective Collection Agency Letters & Forms*  ISBN#: 0970664540
(E-Book only) $19.95

❒ ISBN#: 0970664524
*Fast, Easy, Effective Letters, How to Get Your Customers to Pay*
$33.99, E-Book Version $29.99

**Shipping:  INCLUDED** in all prices above (to U.S. Addresses)

**Payment**: ❒ Check
(enclose with form, payable to "Michelle Dunn Writer, LLC")

❒ Credit or Debit          ❒ Visa     ❒ MasterCard     ❒ Discover

Card#:

_____

Name on Card: _____Exp. Date: ____/____

Shipping Address:

_____

_____

For more information on any of Michelle Dunn's other books
please visit *www.michelledunn.com*
or email at michelle@michelledunn.com
**Thank you for your order!**

# Testimonials

## Read what others are saying about:

*How to Make Money Collecting Money, Starting a Collection Agency*

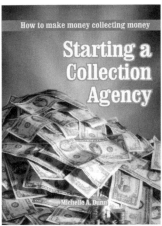

" ...An excellent easy-to-read guide which will definitely take you to a level of success. This self-help guide to success is a must have if you are tired of working your 9-5 and know that you can be powerful working for yourself....JOB WELL DONE!!! "
**Aalim & Heather Elitou**, *Founder, Neshee Publications*

ISBN#: 0-9706645-0-8

" Fifteen years of collection experience lends to this great little book that presents an offer for a great business opportunity. Dunn shares her expertise in the art of collecting money from those who have fallen behind in payments etc. Michelle goes through the whole setup process step by step with resources included to show you how to start your own collection agency. Its power packed with tips, suggestions, do's and don'ts, and wonderful resources to boot. It's like a "business in a box". This is a great addition to the library of those looking to start a business of their own."
**Rebecca Game**, *www.digital-women.com*

" I'd just like to say thanks for all you do for us newbie's. I know I couldn't have possibly gotten my collections department up and running without you and I'm sure I speak for many when I say THANK YOU! You are definitely a rare gem."
**Tina Campbell**, *President, Octagon Professional Business Services, LLC*

" I just finished reading your book today. Thank you for the "ABC's" in starting a collection agency. Lots of good information in a very easy to read format."
*Paula Weiss-Cohen*

" I would like to say that my wife and I thoroughly enjoyed your book. My wife and I have started a collection agency in Denver."
**Len Eskridge**, *TNL Financial*

ISBN#: 0-9706645-0-8

## From the Author

*How to Make Money Collecting Money: Starting a Collection Agency* is full of useful information, tips and ideas for anyone who wants to start their own collection agency

The information in this book is based on my own personal research and experience. The internet changed how people do business, so I have also included links to resources, forms and many other business-related websites.

You will find information on collection laws by state, whom to contact to obtain a collection agency license in your state, information on business plans, marketing, The Fair Debt Collection Practices Act, and many other things you will want to be aware of when starting your agency.

When I started my agency I tried to find books on Amazon.com, Barnes & Noble, Borders and even Ebay about starting a collection agency. I could not find any that were specific to starting your own agency. I just read everything I could find about starting a business in general, and about credit and collections. I did have 15 years experience in the Credit and Collections field and used my knowledge to help me start my agency. I also started a discussion group and website to network and meet other professionals in the credit and collections industry and this was a great help. You can join this list for FREE at *www.credit-and-collections.com*, and once you are a member you can be added to the website for free. This is a great resource for anyone wanting to start their own agency.

*Starting a Collection Agency* has been entered into the 13th Annual Writers Digest International Self-Published Book Awards competition, co-sponsored by Book Marketing Works, LLC–*www.writersdigest.com*. It has also been nominated for a Stevie Award, a national, all-encompassing business award governed by a board of distinguished judges and advisors–*www.stevieawards.com*.

This book, *The First book of Effective Letters & Forms for your Collection Agency* is the perfect companion book to *Starting a Collection Agency*.

I hope that you find the information helpful and enjoy my book! Good luck to you!

ISBN# 0-97066454-0

# From the Author

*Where can I find letters and forms to use for my Collection Agency?* **Right here!**

Finally, a book of letters and forms specific to Collection Agencies! When you buy *The First Book of Effective Collection Agency LETTERS & FORMS*, you will have the tools you need to create and use debt collection letters effectively for your agency. Included in this book are collection agency letters and forms that you can use as is or modify to suit your needs, information on letter compliance for collection agencies, samples of forms, information on FDCPA and more.

This book was created as a companion to *How to Make Money Collecting Money, Starting a Collection Agency.*

I have had so many people ask me where they can find such letters and forms that I had to provide you with this information. There are many books written with letters, forms and contracts but they are for creditors and do not focus on Collection Agencies. I created this book so you could have some examples of letters agencies successfully use. This books is a guide for you to create or modify your debt collection letters to be more effective and help you collect more money. This book was not written or designed to provide legal advice, but as a guide to help you collect more money using letters and forms.

Some exciting information included in this book:
- How to use Debt Collection Letters Effectively
- Letter Compliance for Collection Agencies
- Collection Agency Letters
- Investigation Letters
- Easy Credit Forms
- FDCPA
- Mini-Miranda

and more!

Order your copy today of this great e-book and start collecting more money today!